ARNOLD SCHOENBERG CORRESPONDENCE

a collection of translated and annotated letters exchanged with

GUIDO ADLER
PABLO CASALS
EMANUEL FEUERMANN
and OLIN DOWNES

by

Egbert M. Ennulat

The Scarecrow Press, Inc.
Metuchen, N.J., & London
1991

Frontispiece: Arnold Schoenberg in one of his Berlin homes. Copyright © Alexander Bengsch, Berlin.

British Library Cataloguing-in-Publication data available

Library of Congress Cataloging-in-Publication Data

Schoenberg, Arnold, 1874-1951.
  [Correspondence. English. Selections]
  Arnold Schoenberg correspondence : a collection of translated
and annotated letters exchanged with Guido Adler, Pablo Casals,
Emanuel Feuermann, and Olin Downes / compiled and annotated by
Egbert M. Ennulat.
     p.   cm.
  Includes bibliographical references and index.
  ISBN 0-8108-2452-3 (alk. paper)
  1. Schoenberg, Arnold, 1874-1951--Correspondence.   2. Composers
--Correspondence. I. Ennulat, Egbert M. II. Title.
ML410.S283A4 1991
780'.92--dc20
[B]   91-18955

For Margund and Daniela Ennulat,
Christine and David Wilson, my
granddaughter Anna Ennulat Wilson,
and to the memory of my mother, Martha Ennulat, and
C. Stewart Lare

TABLE OF CONTENTS

TABLE OF FACSIMILES

ACKNOWLEDGMENTS

A great many people have contributed to this book. My special thanks go to Lawrence Schoenberg for the privilege of publishing this collection of his father's letters and documents, and to Marta Casals Istomin for her gracious permission to publish Pablo Casals's unknown letters to Schoenberg and her transcriptions and translations from French into English.

Had it not been for the encouragement and patient help of my friend the late Dr. Almonte Howell, this book would probably never have been written. After Professor Howell's untimely death, David Schiller took on the task of helping me edit the manuscript. I am also greatly indebted to Dr. Diana L. Ransom, who provided a meticulous reading of the French portions of Chapters III and IV. Further thanks are due to Dr. Edward R. Reilly, Elisabeth Gareis, Robin Hensley, and Dell Hitchcock for reading portions of the manuscript.

The research for a project of this magnitude could not have been accomplished without significant support from various sources. Among the more important are an award from the German Exchange Service for an extended period of research at the Deutsche Staatsbibliothek, Preussischer Kulturbesitz in Berlin; a grant from the University of Georgia Research Foundation that enabled me to do research at the Österreichische Nationalbibliothek in Vienna; and generous research grants from the School of Music at the University of Georgia, made possible by the support of its director, Dr. Ralph Verrastro.

The staff at the Library of Congress and likewise at the Arnold Schoenberg Institute in Los Angeles met all requests most expeditiously, and Tom Camden, the director of the Hargrett Rarebook Library at the University of Georgia, gave me unlimited access to both the Adler and Downes collections housed at this institution.

Computers and I do not get along very well. For this reason I wish also to express my appreciation to John T. Scoville for his patience, helpfulness and resourcefulness.

The many contributors to this book deserve credit for its merits; shortcomings are solely my responsibility.

PREFACE

Although an exchange of letters, especially the correspondence with professional colleagues exclusively, can paint only a unidimensional picture of the writer, nevertheless, there emerges a panoramic portrait of Schoenberg. He comes alive in this painstakingly translated and annotated collection as no biography--and I dare say, autobiography--could possibly do. Schoenberg's passion, his integrity which we know from his music and from his teaching, is omnipresent in his written word as well.

The exchange of letters spans the 50 years of the first half of this century. They were written in both the Old and the New world; in his native tongue and in a painfully acquired American-English. They mirror, often poignantly, the fate of the eternal outsider who disrupted the status quo and the complacency of the academicians, musicians and critics of his time. The unending misunderstandings and ambiguities that must inevitably lead to a feeling of helplessness and alienation (the hallmark of art in general in the 20th century!) do not appear to exhaust Schoenberg's spirit. Quite to the contrary. He vitally defends his viewpoint aggressively and steadfastly to the end: in matters of artistic import, with the intuition and intellectual force of the genius; in the arena of commerce--the "music business"--with the fallibility of the mere mortal.

The correspondence with Olin Downes, from 1948 onwards, awakened vivid memories since, as Schoenberg's amanuensis, I was responsible for taking dictation and then typing the letters for the master or, more likely, transcribing them from the Webster Wire Recorder, which he wittily called his "Dick-taphone" (my nickname was frequently the object of numerous puns!). Forty years later, I still hear Schoenberg's voice as he sang--by heart--the Mahler 7th Symphony excerpts which I was asked to copy from the score so that they could be included in the letter of admonishment to Olin Downes. During the summer of 1949 or '50, after Schoenberg had bequeathed his voluminous correspondence to the Library of Congress, I was entrusted by Harold Spivacke, Chief of the Music Division with the task of ordering and filing the collection. Prior to the actual sorting of documents, I constructed large containers (out of corrugated-cardboard boxes, with alphabetized compartments of varying widths) with Schoenberg's enthusiastic approval. The next step was to find the thousands of letters from various locations in his two-room, (separated by a narrow passageway) studio. (Many years later, quite by accident, I came across an additional, large wooden crate in the garage which contained hundreds of letters from the late 1920s and early '30s.) The discussion of how to file the correspondence was the next logical and necessary step. Without hesitation, Schoenberg responded to my suggestion that they be filed alphabetically and chronologically with his customary direct manner: "Yes, but there should be two main categories. Letters from friends and those from enemies." I pleaded that this was impossible for me to do, since I was not aware of who his friends and who his foes were, and would have to consult him personally for every entry. Besides, I pointed out, the case of Thomas Mann (first friend, then enemy and finally, in 1951, once again friend) exceeded the logic of the unique filing scheme which he had spontaneously devised. Schoenberg immediately agreed with me and suggested two other main categories: 1) personal letters and 2) business letters. And this, in alphabetical/chronological order was the way in which the collection was organized and filed for the Library of Congress.

The sheer bulk of the correspondence--a minute portion of the totality appears in this volume--dramatically contradicts, in at least one respect, the widely held belief that Schoenberg identified himself with the tongue-tied Moses in his opera *Moses und Aron* where, at the conclusion, Moses in despair and total abjection utters: "O Wort, du Wort das mir fehlt [O word, thou word, which escapes me!"] The power of Schoenberg's verbal communication will be acknowledged by all who read this exchange of letters: be they friend or be they enemy!

Richard Hoffmann
Oberlin, December 1990

INTRODUCTION

Arnold Schoenberg, the founder and leader of the Second Viennese School, is recognized as one of the greatest composers of this century. Music journalism became very much a part of the activities of many Romantic composers; one need only be reminded of the most famous examples, which include Schumann, Mendelssohn, Wagner, Berlioz and even E.T.A. Hoffmann and various lesser figures. All of these were very literate; they were involved in music criticism, in the publication of professional journals, in the writing of their own libretti, and in the advancement of their personal concepts and views through extensive treatises. But very few took such a keen interest in every aspect of life as did Arnold Schoenberg. Besides his books on harmony and counterpoint there are several hundred essays on every possible aspect of music. Quite frequently Schoenberg resorted to his own inspiration for texts used in his compositions. The text for his oratorio-opera *Moses und Aron* is possibly the most significant of these, for this libretto has the epical proportions of the Old Testament. Moreover, there are countless essays on every imaginable extra-musical concern, especially on religious themes, but also on a wide variety of philosophical, aesthetic, political, economic, moral, and practical issues.

The composer was also a very gifted craftsman, and he took great pride in his accomplishments. Not only did he design the figures for a super chess game that he had invented and expanded to about 100 pieces, he even produced them himself in wood. He delighted in many practical aspects of the crafts, ranging from holders for crayons to furniture in his studio. Bookbinding he had mastered to the point of perfection, and he was especially proud of his work here. Painting was very important to the composer, and quite a number of paintings attest to the fact that he was also very gifted in this medium. To a degree, all of this comes through in the monographs on Schoenberg which have appeared so far. But it seems that for a truly comprehensive and all-inclusive biography of such a complex Renaissance man it will be necessary to research and then incorporate the immense holdings of his literary estate in a definitive biography, a task which may be many years in the making.

Joseph Rufer's article "Hommage à Schoenberg"[1] was inspired by the impact of the literary estate, which he was charged to survey during 1957. Rufer's essay touches on many of the sentiments expressed above. In addition, Rufer captured the essence of Schoenberg's personality as he experienced it early in this century as Schoenberg's student. When surveying Schoenberg's papers in the master's study in Los Angeles, Rufer felt that his mind and soul were transported back to his earlier experiences as Schoenberg's student in Mödling, Austria. There is much new in Rufer's account and, because of this and his special insights, the essay may well be one of the more important ones of the post-Schoenberg period. It therefore seems fitting to open this book with Rufer's "Hommage à Schoenberg," which appears here for the first time in a translation from German into English.

Other sources of special interest include Schoenberg's extensive correspondence. Copies of his letters, until 1922 in longhand with the German cursive script, were carefully preserved by the composer. Before the typewritten letters, of which Schoenberg kept carbon copies, he retained some copies of his handwritten letters in copybooks. Schoenberg willed most of his manuscripts and letters to the Library of Congress, where they have been preserved since 1974. Several of his letters, not kept in the Library of Congress, are in other libraries or private collections, for example in the papers of Guido Adler and Olin Downes, both of which are located at the University of Georgia.

My original intention was to publish only the professional correspondence of Schoenberg-Adler and Schoenberg-Downes. These exchanges, however, led to other correspondence, that tied in with the subject matters under discussion, persuading me to include these letters also in this volume.

Letters by significant personalities frequently have been published in the past without the responses of those to whom they were directed. However, for a thorough understanding of such letters the responses to them are quite indispensable, especially in light of the fact that Schoenberg never raised professional issues with people whose reactions were not of interest to him. In one case the exchange of letters was further expanded, when Olin

Downes published Schoenberg's famous letter on Mahler in the *New York Times*, bringing about responses on both sides of the issue raised. All of the pertinent materials, including the subsequent public responses in the *New York Times*, have been presented in Chapter VI (pp. 214 ff.), enabling the reader to gain insight into how this controversy was perceived at the time.

Schoenberg was quite particular concerning translations of his writings, insisting that they had to be as literal as possible. Often his objections to "improvements" by translators called forth strong reactions:

> I expected that you will have the respect for an artist, to make no changes other than those of grammar and idiom. But you have no right to embellish my style by using different words without necessity, thereby frequently destroying the power of my expression and sometimes even the wit. . . . I must ask you to restore my version, in all cases where grammar and idiom permits. I don't want my style to be beautified. . . .
> I would be sorry if you could not accept these conditions - but it goes against everything that I fought for, if I would allow a foreign hand to interfere with my work. I don't want exquisite terms - my principle is Schopenhauer's "With the most usual words, express the most unusual thoughts."
> Let me have my simple words restored....[2]

Unfortunately the fact still remains that there are limits as to what a literal translation can bear, and opinions may even differ widely on that. It is for this reason that all letters included in this volume are reproduced here in their original languages (German and French), with English translations on facing pages, and, for practical purposes, each exchange of letters is given in a separate chapter with interpretive commentaries. The transcriptions of the letters are completely literal, including misspellings. This approach enabled the translators to avoid the pitfalls of idioms which cannot be reflected in another language; it permits the readers of the present translations to check them against the originals. Necessary editorial clarifications are added in square brackets, but I have avoided cluttering the original letters with sics.

Arnold Schoenberg and Guido Adler exchanged letters between 1903 and 1913 regarding Schoenberg's basso-continuo realizations for the *Denkmäler der Tonkunst in Österreich* (Monuments of Music in Austria) and the cello cadenzas written for Pablo Casals.

The Schoenberg - Casals correspondence of 1933 is concerned with Schoenberg's *Cello Concerto in D Major* (an adaptation of Monn's harpsichord concerto in D Major) dedicated to Pablo Casals. Unfortunately, it was not possible for Casals to play the first performance, and it was not until 1935 that this work was performed for the first time, by Emanuel Feuermann with the BBC orchestra in London.

The last letters between Schoenberg and Feuermann explore the possibilities of transforming some compositions by Johann Sebastian Bach into cello concertos.

Olin Downes' exchanges with Schoenberg, especially the famous controversy about Mahler's music, have been published in part here and there. A publication of the entire correspondence in this context is intended to provide greater insight and understanding of their opposite viewpoints concerning musical taste. At the Schoenberg Institute I also found some drafts of Schoenberg's letters to Downes which were never sent. These rather frank letters will add considerable interest to the argument.

Four basso-continuo realizations by Schoenberg are included in the so-called "Tuma Manuscripts." These realizations have been published (1968) by Rudolf Lück,[3] who also wrote the only article on Schoenberg's continuo realizations.[4]

Schoenberg took great pride in his basso-continuo realizations, which strongly reflect his interest in the music of other composers and in the teaching of all styles. As a result, his basso-continuo realizations were far ahead of their time. They are discussed in the final chapter of this book in the light of today's standards of criticism and performance practices.

Egbert M. Ennulat
School of Music
University of Georgia

Notes

1. Josef Rufer, *Hommage à Schoenberg* in Arnold Schoenberg. Berliner Tagebuch. Ullstein GmbH, Propyläen Verlag, Frankfurt am Main-Berlin-Vienna, 1974, pp. 47-92. The translation (pp. 1-50) is published by permission from the Ullstein Verlag, Berlin.

2. From Schoenberg's letter to Dika Newlin of January 12, 1948. The transcriptions and translations from German to English are by Egbert Ennulat, and from French into English by Marta Casals Istomin.

3. See pp. 278-281.

4. Rudolf Lück, "Die Generalbass-Aussetzungen Arnold Schoenberg's" in *Deutsches Jahrbuch der Musikwissenschaft für 1963,* by Walter Vetter, ed. Peters: Leipzig, 1968, pp. 26-35.

CHAPTER I

Hommage à Schoenberg
Josef Rufer, translated by Egbert M. Ennulat

During the spring of 1957 I went to Arnold Schoenberg's home in Los Angeles on behalf of the Academy of the Arts in Berlin, the successor to the Prussian Academy of the Arts, in order to survey and to catalogue the artistic estate of the master and to publish my findings.

When I entered Schoenberg's study, everything seemed to me to be suddenly turned around in a strange way. I had come to a completely alien country thousands of kilometers away, foreign in its nature and climate, as well as in the education, mentality, and language of its people. Yet all the experiences--moments ago still strong, immediate and fascinating--that absorbed the novice traveler during his entire journey seemed to have been removed suddenly to a distant past as if wiped away. I found myself within the same four walls that I had entered for the first time in Mödling near Vienna in 1919. All about was the same simple, polished, black-stained furniture that Schoenberg himself had designed back then; in the middle of the room was the grand piano; on the walls were cupboards and shelves for books and music; here stood a working table and a writing desk, on which in bowls and flat cigar boxes were pencils of all sizes and crayons, some in holders he had made himself; there were rulers, triangles, and here and there among the rest were gadgets he had made himself and notebooks he had bound. Almost everything that lay about there--as if Schoenberg had just ceased to work--seemed touched by his own hands, and everything was exactly as it had been decades earlier in Vienna and then in Berlin. I saw the volumes of the "Bach-Gesamtausgabe," familiar to me from his teaching, the Mozart scores, the Beethoven symphonies and sonatas, and also Schoenberg's own works, all bound by himself because he was perfectly trained in bookbinding and had occasionally demonstrated to us students how carefully one had to treat and prepare the materials for this. The cello he so loved to play still stood in the corner. In Mödling he once smiled

1

at our somewhat startled faces when we heard him play the cello sonata by Grieg, accompanied on the piano by his daughter, and commented, "Yes, you know, one can 'dig into it' so nicely. It is so important to write well for the instrument. After all, the performer wants to show what he is able to do." That also had happened in this room. Even the view into the green of the garden was reminiscent of the past. All of this was for me like a return home.

An actual return to Vienna during the last years of his life was denied to Schoenberg because of his precarious health. Yet in spirit he had never left his homeland, for he could never really escape it; from his youth onward he had become part of it. He carried it with him wherever he went in his daily life, in his thoughts and his feelings, this homeland of the German spirit, of German music. No political event, no decree, no emigration was able to affect his world or even influence it. I have a letter by Schoenberg dated August 1933, and hence written a few months after he had left Germany. In this letter he refers to a note in a French newspaper in order to separate himself most emphatically from those prominent emigrants who, at that time, condemned Germany altogether. He possessed an unfailing sense for the distinction by means of which he was able to discriminate between chaff and wheat in his art as well as in his life. He had learned his musical language and thinking from German music, from Bach, Beethoven, Mozart and Brahms. When in the summer of 1921--it was in Traunkirchen on the Traun Lake--I picked him up for our customary evening walk and the conversation turned to his work, he remarked: "Today I succeeded in something by which I have assured the dominance of German music for the next century." At that time Schoenberg had finalized and tried out in his compositions his "Method of Composition with Twelve Tones which are Related only to One Another" (Methode der Komposition mit zwölf nur aufeinander bezogenen Tönen). Today, after more than fifty years, the entire musical world knows how right he was with this prediction: this concept of composition with twelve notes has become the central moving force, the unceasing and still operative impulse of twentieth-century music. Its core and point of departure, however, is the music of the German classical and preclassical masters.

My feeling of having returned home was intensified by my

encounter with what Schoenberg had left behind. Thus, for example, I found a little yellowed paper slip with the pencil draft of a contribution to the magazine "Faithful Eckard" (Der getreue Eckard)[1] which opened with the words: "Whenever I think about music, I never visualize--consciously or subconsciously--any other than German music." I came across an article of 1931 with the title "Nationale Musik" in which Schoenberg proceeds to demonstrate precise and comprehensive evidence that the art contained within his music is thoroughly grounded in the traditions of German music. It goes on to say: "My teachers were primarily Bach and Mozart, and secondarily Beethoven, Brahms and Wagner." Schoenberg explains in detail what he had learned from these masters. He does so in such an explicit manner that this listing itself represents a small compendium of compositional techniques. Beyond this, his explanations reveal profound characteristics of the musical style of each of these masters in such a way that entirely new viewpoints are established concerning the essence of their music and the analysis of their works. But Schoenberg's music, too, documents precisely the composer's roots in the essence of the German spirit, which is often quite obvious and recognizable. I mention only the almost unknown masterful arrangements that he made of old German songs of the fifteenth or sixteenth centuries, partly for mixed chorus, and partly for voice and piano. Any connoisseur will find the compositional elegance of these arrangements most enchanting.

When I left Los Angeles after three months of work, I knew that here the thought and work of a mind as original as it was ingenious had found its documented reflection, and that this documentation had been preserved almost complete, at least since approximately 1910, the beginning of the non-tonal epoch. From piles of manuscripts and single sheets, numerous notes of every kind, remarks on the margins of books, scores, and journals there gradually emerged the picture of a fascinating personality whose intellectual scope was of an undreamt-of and at first perplexing universality. There was virtually nothing that did not engage this open, always alert mentality, this sharp and precise thinker, or with which he did not occupy himself in a captivatingly clear and novel manner. If a later period wished to gain insight into the culture and sociological status of the first half of our century, it would be possible to derive a rather revealing picture from Schoenberg's literary estate alone. I shall attempt to give a brief survey of the areas with which Schoenberg occupied himself in over 700 essays; among these his numerous music-theoretical writings are not included. There are essays on morality, his outlook on life, his world view, philosophy and aesthetics, essays about politics, economics, social welfare, and essays which have nature, physics, and animals as their topics. Of a particularly wide scope are the religious topics; these, by the way, like so many others, are linked with his works, which include a great number of religious compositions. Difficulties arose again and again when surveying and cataloguing his writings, since the topics of many essays pointed in two or even more directions. It is the power of thinking in wider contexts that distinguishes him as a human being, an artist, and a teacher. He always saw everything as part of a greater context. In this manner he gained remarkably significant insights that could not have been attained by isolated considerations. "Every good thought has at least two sides," he used to say (and he meant by this also musical ideas). A number of essays and notes concern language. The purity of the German language was for him an indispensable presupposition for the clarity of thought, for the precision of expression in language. How he could mock advertisements such as "seven cheap glove-days" (Sieben billige Handschuhtage)![2] What biting remarks came about because of the slovenly German in the newspapers! How often he showed in concrete examples that vagueness of thinking and writing went hand in hand, in language as well as in composition!

A special folder contained interpretations, explanations, inventions, suggestions, and improvements. From these emerge some curiosities which illustrate especially Schoenberg's mental acuity and versatility: there are patentable drawings for a book-binder's press, and drawings with annotated text for a typewriter table or a music typewriter. The BVG, Berlin Traffic Authority (Berliner Verkehrsgesellschaft) can take pride (provided that they know how to appreciate it) in having an autograph by Schoenberg. In a letter of January 12, 1927, he sent detailed samples and explanations for a transfer ticket to the board of directors of the Berlin Tramway Authority. He never received an answer. The musician Schoenberg came forward with the invention of a twelve-tone music-writing system, which was published during the twenties in a Viennese music journal. From practical experience as a conductor and from rehearsing modern chamber music, he had recognized the deficiencies which had developed in the musical craft as music continued to develop, and which inhibited composers as well as performers. As our present-day notation changed for practical reasons in the course of the centuries, so that the uninformed remain perplexed in the presence of, let us say, a music manuscript of the fourteenth century, so did Schoenberg recognize the need for far-reaching changes which have developed in music notation as a result of the transition from tonality to atonality. Concerning practical simplification, similar considerations motivated him to invent a "simplified full score for study and performance" which, because of its clarity, makes it possible to recognize and realize the structure of modern music much more readily. This happened around 1914, and ever since that time Schoenberg notated his works for orchestra in the form of a "particell," while the printed editions, with few exeptions, retained the old format, which is surprising since our technical thinking adapts to the best solutions quickly and flexibly. I found a striking example of this in the folder mentioned before: a detailed drawing of a highway which originated before 1933. This draft conforms with the turnpike interchanges built later in the USA and meanwhile also in Europe, proving once again Schoenberg's ability to grasp the essence of any problem and to think it through. To find the focus and to derive from it the appropriate assessment of a problem often provides--according to Schoenberg--the key to the solution.

Schoenberg was inducted into the Viennese "Hausregiment der Hoch- und Deutschmeister" as a volunteer in 1915, but discharged after a little over a year because of health reasons (asthma). From World War I on he concerned himself again and again with political, economic and social questions. There are records of 1914 in a journal entitled "Diary of the Clouds of War" (Kriegswolken-Tagebuch). An essay entitled "International Peace Guarantee by the Military" (Internationale militärische Friedenssicherung), viewed today as a prophetic train of thought, dates from 1917, after his second and final discharge from military service. Furthermore, the estate includes some musical works from Schoenberg's period of duty with the military: the beginnings of instrumental arrangements of Austrian military marches and an original composition, a march, "The Iron Brigade" (Die eiserne Brigade), which he wrote for a social evening of the one-year volunteers in the boot camp at Bruck on the Leitha. The title page carries a handwritten note: "Original manuscript, presented to Dr. Kusmitsch, 1916, Oberleutnant in Bruck on the Leitha, court official in Budapest (who did not know how to appreciate it)." "He writes music as fast indeed as we write letters," his comrades exclaimed in amazement on this occasion. From that time an amusing anecdote has circulated which is not without deeper significance. In the years before 1914 Schoenberg's name was mentioned frequently in Viennese newspapers in connection with the concert scandals at performances of his works, and hence the recruit Schoenberg was asked again and again (very much to his displeasure): "Are you this composer who has been so much persecuted?" Schoenberg then explained: "Yes, but this is how it happened: somebody had to do it; nobody wanted to; so I just had to resign myself to it." And when an obviously friendly questioner remarked that it was a great honor for everybody to serve in the same company with a man like Schoenberg, he answered: "It is not that much of an honor, for a company has 400 men, and that doesn't leave very much honor for each of them."

In his political essays of 1932, when the German catastrophe was already foreseeable, concepts like power, majority, and fascism concerned him again and again, and until his death he wrestled with the concept of the state. "The World Economy" (Die Weltwirtschaft) dates from about 1929 and is, according to its subtitle, a recommendation for a solution to the economic crisis, which--as is well known--spread from the USA over the entire world and incited political unrest. Thus the takeover by the Nazis at the end of January 1933 found Schoenberg prepared; yet it still came as a surprise to him. He knew what was to come. With deep sadness, yet without any feelings of hate, he followed the inevitable developments in the country which he had considered his own since his youth. He only could shake his head incredulously for the many who at that time expressed the opinion, "Just let the Nazis come to power, they will fall all the sooner." I shall never forget his words: "German soil will become more and more rocky until it has completely turned into a desert." With disturbing prophecy he predicted the ruin of 1945 as it was not imaginable to most people. When I met Hindemith during those weeks (of the Nazi takeover), he asked me whether or not it was true that Schoenberg intended to leave Germany, and he pleaded with me to try to change his mind. He thought that especially now everybody should stay in

order to join together for resistance. Nevertheless, Schoenberg left
Germany in May of 1933. From the USA he wrote the following
letter to the Preussische Akademie der Künste where in 1925 he
had been appointed successor to Busoni as director of the master
class in composition:

> In the meeting of March 1st at the academy,
> statements were made which made it obvious that
> as of now it appears no longer desirable that I
> remain in a leading position. Pride and the con-
> sciousness of my achievement would have induced
> me long ago to resign voluntarily. For   when I
> gave   in to the   temptation of the academy's
> flattering offer, it was because they appealed to my
> ambition as a teacher, and held up to me my duty
> to disseminate my knowledge, and because I knew
> what I was able to do for the students.   This
> indeed I have done and more. Anyone who was
> my student became aware of the seriousness and
> morality of the mission of the artist; this awareness
> will, under any circumstances of life, bring him
> honor if he is able to remain true to it! I believe
> it appropriate to forgo the reiteration of details in
> order not to diminish my accomplishments. In any
> case, when I was appointed, it was not out of an
> obscure background, nor was an undeserved honor
> bestowed on me. And I always had students, so
> many that I was able to make a very good living as
> a private teacher.
>
> Because of this appointment, however, I
> gave up my former position and moved here with
> all my belongings. An individual, who like myself,
> is politically and morally irreproachable, yet whose
> honor as an artist and a human being is deeply im-
> pinged upon through his forced resignation from
> his sphere of activity, should not, in addition to
> this, see his economic security endangered or
> indeed see himself threatened with total ruin.
>
> For this reason I take the liberty to ask
> you to remit in cash what I am entitled to accord-

ing to my contract (which extends to Sept. 30,
1935), as well as the cost of my return move, and
to permit me at the same time to transfer this
amount to a foreign country. For I will be forced
to use the next years for the establishment of a
new existence. In the hope of a favorable decision
I remain sincerely yours,
Arnold Schoenberg, director of
the master class in composition.

Incidentally, this justifiable request was not granted.

Politics occupied Schoenberg even under the completely
different circumstances of the USA where he lived from the fall of
1933 until his death, first in New York and very soon afterward in
Los Angeles; here he had moved for reasons of health because of
the mild California climate. His own harsh fate was an additional reason for him to keep an eye on the world's political
developments with all their consequences. Thus, for example, there
exists an essay entitled "America and Japan" from 1937, and even in
1950, one year before his death, he reflected on his relationship to
politics. The fate of the State of Israel was especially close to his
heart.

As a young man in Vienna, Schoenberg had become a con-
vert to the Protestant denomination of the Augsburg Confession.
During the following thirty years he concerned himself again and
again with the problems of God, man, and the world, disregarding
all confessional questions of faith and denominational arguments.
This is also reflected in his work, especially the oratorio *Die
Jakobsleiter* (Jacob's Ladder) for which he wrote the text himself
around 1915, after many fruitless attempts to compile it from works
of world literature. Three years earlier, stimulated by a letter from
Richard Dehmel about his string sextet *Verklärte Nacht* which the
latter had heard, he responded to the poet: ". . . for a long time I
wanted to write an oratorio which should have as its contents how
man of today, who has gone through materialism, socialism, anar-
chy, who was an atheist, but who also has preserved for himself a
little of the old faith in the form of superstition--how this modern

man argues with God (see also *Jakob ringt* [Jacob Wrestles] by Strindberg) and finally arrives at the point of finding God and becoming religious. To learn how to pray! ..." This is a revealing confession of the human being Schoenberg, who in struggling with God never gave up the faith at the core of his searching. A mighty arch stretches from the words of the thirty-eight-year-old, "to learn how to pray," to "and I pray nevertheless. . . ." With the latter phrase, his last incomplete work breaks off, the setting of the first in a group of modern psalms that Schoenberg wrote during his last year. "Nevertheless": only a word, but it makes one conscious of the tragedy which, by necessity, belongs to genius.

      Schoenberg's return to the Jewish faith dated back to the 1920s; in this regard, a distinction should be made between what he thought, said, and wrote because of an inner need, and what he considered appropriate for warding off the anti-Semitism which increased constantly with the Hitler movement. As appears from his completely preserved writings, Schoenberg concerned himself with anti-Semitism for the first time in July 1923. He commented on a report entitled "Meetings in Munich" (Münchner Versammlungen) which had appeared in the Berlin "Daily" (Tag). Schoenberg, who after World War I discussed with his friends and students all external events that concerned him, did not mention either this topic or political-religious questions in general until about 1920, not because they may have been taboo, but because they evidently did not exist for him. It is my firm conviction that it was an incident during the summer of 1921 that first brought about a kind of beginning for his increasingly intense preoccupation with the Jewish religion. It was then that we, a group of his students, had gone with the Schoenbergs to the upper-Austrian vacation spot of Mattsee, not knowing that for a long time this place had been notorious for its radical anti-Semitic attitudes. There Schoenberg received a postcard with the following message: "To the famous composer A. Schoenberg, unfortunately at present in Mattsee. Most esteemed Master!? Should you be interested in the Jewish problem in Mattsee, read the article about it in today's "Chronik"; in any case, it is commended to your attention. [signed] An Aryan vacationer." Soon after, we all took our departure. Schoenberg kept this postcard as a document. Given his feeling of being unwanted, rejected, and hated, it becomes understandable that this uncompromising thinker began to seek out the root causes of the matter and to occupy himself thoroughly with the concepts of the Jewish faith. It is little wonder, therefore, that I found in the estate an abundance of essays, documents and studies on Judaism, the Jewish state and other matters, as well as a drama *Der biblische Weg* (The Way of the Bible) which Schoenberg later sent to Franz Werfel with the request that he develop a script from it. In a cover letter which is undated but nevertheless written after 1945, and which includes the significant sentence, "out of a good thought everything will flow by itself," Schoenberg also writes, "I was always of the opinion that this work is not to be judged by purely artistic criteria, for it is a purely functional work, whose purpose is to be used as propaganda. Where the Jewish national question is concerned, for me the political effect stands far above the artistic value. You do know that I wish to dedicate myself to the rescue of the Jewish nation. I had already perceived the situation correctly soon after the war, and have thought it through since in every respect. Since about 1921 [!] I have been intending to write a piece for the theatre as propaganda for my ideas."

Independent of such an intention, the work *Der biblische Weg* also documents Schoenberg's strikingly visionary artistic imagination. Written in 1926, which was before the time of the "Nuremberg Party Congress" (Nürnberger Reichsparteitage) and its parades, and long before the invention of the rockets carrying atom bombs, he anticipated both. The second and last scenes of the first act take place on a huge fairground and sports facility, upon which the youth of Israel parade with music, trumpet calls and the singing of a hymn; and this act concludes with a passionate address by the leader Aruns, who is given ovations of all sorts. In its entirety, however, it stands under a different motto: it is a feast of commemoration and solemn promise for the establishment of a new state, in which the Jewish people may live out their "divine idea" (Gottesgedanken). In the next act an invention is discussed, an apparatus which "can send to any point on earth and in any radius, beams that consume the oxygen in the air and that suffocate all life." With this the resistance of the strongest adversaries of the new state could be broken. Today, decades later, the parallel to the remote-controlled atom bomb is obvious.

Schoenberg's letters and writings show him as a fundamentally good and warm-hearted human being, open and friendly where he believed he could place his trust. Friends of his youth even report a decidedly happy nature. His strong personality was manifest and quite natural; nothing was further from his nature than to emphasize his artistic genius, or to play the superior human being. In intimate surroundings, when he did not have to be concerned with hostility, he was relaxed, naturally charming and almost always in a good mood. Where he saw need, he gave help inconspicuously and unselfishly. From decades of experience he knew what it was to be hungry, what a struggle it was to make ends meet for oneself and a family as a conductor of choirs, as a participant in Wolzogen's "Überbrettl" (a cabaret) in Berlin, and as the orchestrator of several thousand pages of operetta scores--all this at a time when there were no art prizes for young composers nor broadcasting companies to sponsor them. After World War I only two, or at the most three of the fifteen students who came to Mödling for instruction on two mornings each week paid him; all the others he taught without charge because he knew they did not have the financial means. He also was expected to compose chansons for the Berlin "Überbrettl." Even though his aim was not to be original, and certainly not to be offensive in his work for this rather notable literary carbaret, a true scandal came about during the performance of Gustav Falkes' "Sleepwalker" (Nachtwandler), which forced its discontinuation; possibly the scandal resulted from the sound of the unfamiliar accompaniment of piccolo flute, little drum, trumpet, and piano.

The good natured, warm-hearted human being underwent a change where music was concerned, and not only his own music. Then all levity ceased for Schoenberg; there was no compromise, no leniency or consideration either for himself or for others, and neither in spiritual attitude nor in practical questions. Neither money nor honors could make him deviate so much as a millimeter from his path when he recognized it as the right one. The integrity of his spirit was unshakable; it alone governed his conduct. In so acting, he created many enemies for himself, a matter which was of little importance to him where his beloved music was concerned. Consciously and without hesitation he faced his adversaries. For a short time after his arrival in the USA at the age of sixty, he found himself the center of attention. Interviews, long newspaper articles, and grand receptions by the New York art world made a celebrity

of the master of atonal music. The radio also got involved with an
interview (one carefully worked out beforehand). At its conclusion
Schoenberg's interviewer could not resist the temptation to ask an
impromptu question: "What do you think, Mr. Schoenberg, of
American music? When will it reach the quality level of Europe's?"
For many this cue might have seemed a splendid opportunity for
the composer to ingratiate himself and to pave his way for an easy
existence in the USA; not for Schoenberg. After reflecting a
moment, he answered, "Well, in about 300 years," and added,
because of the baffled face of his interviewer, "And why would you
suppose that American music could achieve this any faster than
European music, which needed that much time to reach today's
level of development?"

        Just such seemingly minor incidents as these reveal side-
lights that are characteristic of the creative artist and his relation to
the outside world. Often the complex personality of the artist becomes immediately and surprisingly clear when one becomes
acquainted with it through spontaneous reactions to more or less
accidental events or encounters. Thus also private pastimes
contribute to the image of the master. Schoenberg liked to play
ping-pong, and in his last Berlin apartment he had a room set aside
for it. His passion, however, was tennis, which he played with
fanatic dedication and about which he wrote in several essays. He
taught the first practical knowledge of the game to his children, and
when his son Ronny became the tennis champion of the thirteen-
year-olds in Los Angeles, and later also brought home several cups,
there was unimaginable happiness in the Schoenberg household.
Another of Schoenberg's hobbies was chess. He even invented a
new game with one hundred squares, which he called "coalition
chess" and described in very precise detail. At a little evening social
gathering--it was around 1930 in Berlin--he was just in the process
of showing and explaining this game to some friends when Dr.
Emanuel Lasker, the well-known world chess world master, was
announced. Hastily, Schoenberg packed up his chess set and hid it.
When I questioned him as to why he would not show it to Dr.
Lasker, he responded, "What can you be thinking of! Imagine if I
were to come to Lasker and he were to show me a book on harmony he had authored. . ." In his teaching of composition he liked
to draw parallels with the game of chess: "Just as the master chess

player must be able to think through several moves in advance, so the composer must be able to foresee and think through the development of a composition, and all the possible combinations of motives and themes; from the beginning he must envision the development of the whole."

He was not present to experience the wave of success his music enjoyed in Europe after 1945; he was more conscious of the animosities to which he saw himself subjected because of his music. Just how well he had understood his position, without any thought of improving it through the compromise of a return to tonality, becomes evident in "My Audience" (Mein Publikum), an essay published in 1930 in the Berlin "Cross Section" (Querschnitt). It begins with the words, "If I were asked to say something about my audience, I would have to confess: I don't believe I have one." His firmly rooted position becomes just as clear in a discussion with Dr. Eberhard Preussner and Dr. Heinrich Strobel, broadcast over Radio Berlin on March 30, 1931, which he concluded thus:

Mr. Strobel, do not underestimate the size of the circle which is forming around me. It will grow through the intellectual curiosity of an idealistic youth which feels itself more attracted by the mysterious than the commonplace. But come what may, I cannot think or say anything but what my task requires of me. Gentlemen, do not take this for arrogance. I would like to be more successful than I am. It is not at all my desire to stand there as a solitary stylite. But as long as I consider my own thinking and my own imagination to be valid, I will not be able to believe anything else than that such thoughts must be thought and must be spoken even if they can never be understood. I myself am not at all of the opinion that I am all that incomprehensible. But let us ask ourselves: should ideas of undeniable greatness, as for example those of someone like Kant, not have been conceived and not have been set down because even today honest people must admit that they cannot follow them? To one whom our God has bestowed the

destiny of saying unpopular things, to him He also
has given the ability to resign himself to the fact
that it is always the others who will be understood.

Along those same lines of thought, the estate also includes
remarks from Schoenberg's time in America. In a letter to the
European conductor Hans Rosbaud, with whom he was on friendly
terms, he deplored the fact that the understanding of his music still
suffered because he was not looked upon as a conventional and
entirely typical composer, but as a modern, dissonant twelve-tone
experimentalist. "I, however, wish nothing more ardently, if I wish
anything at all, than that people would look upon me as a better
version of Tschaikovsky--a little better, for God's sake, but that is
really all I ask for. Or at most, that people would know and whistle
my melodies." "But," as some notes from the same time read, "I do
not write for imbeciles. A composer who writes for the audience
does not think in music." The standards which Schoenberg had for
himself were equivalent to his demands upon the listener, who he
assumed would feel annoyed by the shallow and banal, which could
be understood immediately by any simpleton.

But Schoenberg also actively strove to educate the public
in the hearing of modern music. It was immediately after World
War I when, in November 1918, he founded the "Society for Musical
Private Performances" (Verein für musikalische Privataufführungen)
in Vienna for this purpose. (Incidentally, the establishment of this
institution and its survival until 1924 is today an almost incomprehensible manifestation of idealism on the part of Schoenberg and
his circle, from Alban Berg and Anton Webern to his youngest
students.) A brochure written by Alban Berg opens with these
sentences:

The society founded by Arnold Schoenberg in
November has the purpose of providing artists and
friends of the arts a true and accurate knowledge
of modern music. It is by no means the purpose
of the society to propagandize for any school or
to benefit the composers performed, but only to
serve its members by bringing illumination in place

of the hitherto obscure and problematic situation
of modern music. Therefore, this is not a society
for composers, but one exclusively for the public.
Should acceptance and enjoyment result from the
performance of some of the works and thus also
serve to advance the work and its author, such is
merely a by-product. In the compilation of the
programs, however, no consideration can be given
to achieving this, nor to avoiding the somewhat
inevitable opposite effect: our sole purpose is as
definitive performance as possible.

Every week a concert took place to which only members
were admitted: the press was excluded in order to avoid any
influence by the critics, and there were no prior announcements of
any of the programs. Schoenberg, Berg, and Webern supervised or
directed the rehearsals. A performance was only permitted after its
technical and musical   perfection was assured. One can perhaps
imagine the magnificent training resulting from this for every one
of us students. How ridiculous was the talk of the purely intellectual and mathematically contrived "writing-desk music" in view of the
practical work accomplished in such a way; in the first two years,
189 compositions received exemplary performances.

The thought of establishing such a society grew out of
Schoenberg's own experience. This was because for quite a long
time Schoenberg avoided going to concerts that included modern
works, because he found them "hideous." Nevertheless, when he
was forced to attend such a concert once, he had the opportunity of
following along in the score, which was held by a neighbor. At that
point he suddenly recognized that what was in the score was not at
all unclear or senseless, but that what the conductor and orchestra
were producing was faulty and did not at all reflect what was set
down in the score. It became clear to him how important a perfect
performance can be for the hearing and understanding of new
music. When Schoenberg once suggested to a conductor that he
perform his first *Kammersymphonie* (Chamber Symphony), the
conductor turned him down with the words, "Honestly, I don't understand your music." Schoenberg retorted, "I do not understand

why you have to be truthful just where my music is concerned! After all, you perform the classics without understanding them."

Schoenberg was a master of polemics. Again and again, as an artist and as a human being, he had to fight for his life. In open and veiled attacks on him, it was the musicians--especially composers and conductors--who were especially malicious. Yet Schoenberg himself attacked where selfish interests misused art, where "one dirty hand washed the other," or where incompetence and slovenly work was evident, bringing harm to the music. Besides hundreds of essays, the estate includes a whole stack of journals with comments on certain essays, partially written on the margins, but also in the form of long explanations which were pasted in or inserted loosely in the texts. There statements by Alfredo Casella, Ernst Krenek, Hindemith, Wellesz, and Adorno are subjected to sharp scrutiny; here Schoenberg almost never commented exclusively negatively, for he was a discriminating judge. Frequently, with regard to a negative commentary, he developed his own thoughts and concepts in a brillant and precise manner. The following is an example: after commenting on an essay about Schubert's song "Ihr Bild" by the musicologist Heinrich Schenker, he added: "The presentation [of musical thought] will never be accomplished on one level alone!!! The reason is simple: it is because a composition simply does not occur on just one plane. Schenker's *Urlinie* is (at best) a cross section through the whole. Yet one must make many such cross sections. The artfulness in art consists of the fact that one does not perceive the complexities; therein lies its simplicity. That the smallest details are simple is not due to the merit of the author; it is inevitable. For that matter, he did not compose these smallest components, but rather the whole. A piece consists of details only when it is taken apart."

Thus for Schoenberg negation often is not an end in itself, but a point of departure for the development and arrangement of his own thoughts concerning a given topic. Several of his own essays concern themselves with Stravinsky, Kurt Weill, Max Reger and others. He takes to task especially vigorously Riemann, the "Tainter of Sources" (Quellenvergifter), referring to Hugo Riemann, the musicologist and editor of the well-known dictionary. Schoenberg begins his contemplation and discussion of Ernst Kurt's book "Linear Counterpoint" (Der lineare Kontrapunkt) with these words:

"It has always been clear to me that there is something that looks and sounds like counterpoint, but is not counterpoint after all." All these essays and commentaries include a wealth of new thoughts, opinions and formulations concerning questions and problems, and even though they may be considered as musical contributions to the history of the recent past, they are so full of material concerning today's interests that they should be published soon. An article with the title "False Alarm" (Falscher Alarm) carries a later, undated addition: "I did not complete the article at that time because I found Pfitzner's brochure increasingly bad, so that I considered it superfluous to contradict it. Perhaps it would have been better after all? See also the comments in the brochure." The brochure under discussion is Pfitzner's "Danger of Futurists" (Futuristengefahr), a polemic treatise against atonal music, which was later reduced to absurdity by a brillant polemic of Alban Berg. An outline of a parody on Pfitzner (by Schoenberg) with the subtitle "Three Acts of Revenge from Palestrina" includes the remark: "For an 'Entertaining Evening' planned at the 'Society for Musical Private Performances' for which my sense of justice caused me also to include a few quips on myself." Schoenberg's sense of justice also induced him after 1945 to intervene spontaneously for Pfitzner in a letter to the Munich de-Nazification court, which the latter is said to have acknowledged with perplexed surprise.

There were, however, also renowned composers who, from the beginning, recognized the special importance of Schoenberg for the music of our century, and who held him in high esteem and admiration. In October 1919 Alfredo Casella and Maurice Ravel came to Vienna and played the first performance of the arrangement of Ravel's "La Valse" for two pianos in honor of Schoenberg at the "Society for Musical Private Performances." One will read two names with special surprise in connection with the innovator Schoenberg: George Gershwin and Giaccomo Puccini. Schoenberg became acquainted with Gershwin in Los Angeles, and on a tennis court at that. A true friendship developed between the two. Schoenberg rated Gershwin's music highly because of its strength of imagination and originality, and put him on the same level with Johann Strauss and Jacques Offenbach. The estate includes the moving eulogy that he gave for his friend.

During the fall of 1920 Puccini came to Vienna for the

performance of one of his works at the "Staatsoper" and he inquired immediately when and where he could hear music by
Schoenberg. He had to be told at this point that his wish could not
be realized for the composer was not to be found in the concert and
opera repertories of his native town since the public and the critics
ignored him completely. When Schoenberg learned about Puccini's
wish, he sent me to him at the Hotel Bristol in order to extend his
cordial regards and an invitation for the next concert of the "Society
for Musical Private Performances." The [Italian] master received me
exceedingly cordially, inquired thoroughly about his colleague and
his work, and expressed his regrets again that it was impossible for
him to hear Schoenberg's music. Since Puccini was about to depart,
he could not attend the concert at the society. It was not until a
few years after this that a meeting came about between them in the
Palazzo Pitti in Florence where Schoenberg performed with his
Vienna "Pierrot" ensemble during a concert tour of Italy. As
reported by Dallapiccola, Puccini had come to Florence solely for
the purpose of hearing the work and of following it in the score.
Thereafter he requested Casella, who was present, to introduce him
to Schoenberg. Casella took him to the green room and arranged
a meeting between the two composers; Puccini confessed that the
work had made a deep impression on him. Schoenberg never forgot
this noble attitude on Puccini's part and reciprocated by working a
vocal phrase from Puccini's *Manon Lescaut* into the score of his
own cheerful one-act work *Von heute auf morgen* (From Today to
Tomorrow).

    The documents that I found in Schoenberg's estate about
the musician, the composer, his calling and his destiny are just as
plentiful and many-sided as those about the human being Arnold
Schoenberg. Stacks of sketches make evident how he was impelled
to write and to compose, for both were direct expressions of life for
him. Especially these cursory sketches, the beginnings of many
compositions--inspirations of the moment that were jotted down,
forgotten again, and superseded by new ones--document the spontaneity of a creative process in such a compelling manner as is
seldom experienced. Spontaneity and abundance: here things
were drawn from plentiful resources. The fleeting character of the
notes betrays the speed of his writing. Composition here meant

simply the recording of that which had already taken shape in the mind and imagination. Concerning this an illuminating comparison of Schoenberg's comes to my mind: "The composer experiences the work as a whole in space, and transforms it into time when copying it down. The listener, on the other hand, experiences it in reverse, at first at the moment of performance, and only thereafter, retrospectively as it were, as an entity in a spatial overview." The swiftness with which Schoenberg composed completely reduces to absurdity the opinion that his music was calculated and mechanical-- at least for those who do not realize already, when listening to the natural flow of the music, the senselessness of such an assertion.

Schoenberg took issue with this quite concretely: the second and fourth movements of his string quartet in F-sharp minor op. 10 were each written in a day and a half. The composition of the half-hour monodrama *Erwartung* (Expectation) was completed within the brief period of 17 days. Of the twelve-tone works, the third string quartet was completed in less than four weeks. Of the one-act opera *Von heute auf morgen* Schoenberg wrote an average of twenty-five measures a day, consisting of the complete orchestral score with precise indications for instrumentation. Because Schoenberg did not orchestrate in retrospect; on the contrary, tone color, rhythm, melody, and harmony were for him rather a simultaneous part of musical inspiration. To get a true picture of the effortlessness of Schoenberg's creative process, one must consider the actual task of note-writing that is required for a modern full score; and seen in such a way, the time frame given is still further reduced. The choral interlude of the opera *Moses und Aron*, an extremely artistic double fugue a6 with orchestral accompaniment, was composed in six days; the entire second act with the *Tanz um das goldene Kalb* (Dance around the Golden Calf) was completed in full score in less than seven months. Of the double fugue, incidentally, the first sketch has been preserved. Included in it are thematic outlines of various contrapuntal stretti, and in cue words a detailed disposition of the course of the double fugue, its organization, and its dramatic characteristics. With it there is a note saying: "Total duration at the most four minutes, 48 measures at the most." The composition then consists of 32 measures, which proves again that Schoenberg had a perfectly clear idea of the entire work before he set out to write it down. In this connection a two-page sheet found in the

estate is characteristic, for it deals with the "pain of creation,"--a
term to be put in quotation marks since it was a psychological
condition that Schoenberg never knew. In this way one must also
understand a postscript under the manuscript for male choir of
op. 35 entitled "Solidarity" (Verbundenheit), of which the text and
music of the first two stanzas were written down in about two
hours, and the second three days later only "because company kept
him from doing it."

A letter directed to his friend Alban Berg about the work
on *Moses und Aron* is revealing as regards Schoenberg's manner of
composition and the origin of the texts for the music. He writes,
"The text is only completed while composing, at times even only
thereafter." This demonstrates that Schoenberg identified with
Mozart's requirement that the poetry must be an obedient servant
of the music. This also further allows us to recognize the function
of the words inserted into the music as dependent on it, a fact,
which--as a consequence--precludes a purely literary evaluation of
texts set to music. Especially when he was working on *Moses und
Aron*, it was again and again the text that held up the composer.
Proofs of this are the many textual drafts, which were rejected again
and again, especially for the third act. Moses' lament, which
concludes the second act, "O word, thou word, which escapes me,"
reflects the predicament of the author. The letter to Alban Berg
then continues, "Only if one has a clear vision of the whole is it
possible to create the text while composing or even thereafter; and
the artistry consists not only in keeping this vision alive at all
times, but also in intensifying it, enriching it, and expanding it while
working out the details! This should be recommended to all opera
composers." Concerned that external events forced interruptions of
the work again and again and that this could endanger the organic
coherence of the whole, Schoenberg comforts himself that there
must be a kind of "subconscious memory" involved, which somehow,
musically as well as textually, "brings him right back on track."
When he wrote that, he may have remembered an incident that
happened a few years back while he was composing the *Orchester-
Variationen op. 31*. When he took up the work after a longer inter-
ruption, he searched in vain for the sketches which included the
idea and course of the next variation. He then tried to figure out
the variation principle from the portion composed already, but

without success. At last he began to write out the variation from
the beginning in accordance with a new idea.   When he had
completed it and compared it with the portion composed earlier, it
turned out that he had invented the old idea all over again, that he
must have newly arrived at "the same logical thought" when he had
"given up on finding it through recollection."   The subconscious
memory was more dependable. Schoenberg the alleged formalist,
considered the subconscious always to be the primary element of his
work. "When more happens than one can conceive oneself, then it
can only happen on the subconscious level," he insisted and showed
it in many examples from Beethoven or Brahms. The 1932 lecture
at Radio Frankfurt, entitled "Brahms the Progressive" (Der fort-
schrittliche Brahms), includes many such subconscious musical ideas
of construction that Schoenberg found in this master. What is valid
for every normal person while speaking, when constructing subconsciously the grammatically correct word order and sentence forms--
for otherwise the result would be gibberish--also has validity for
musicians when they express themselves in their language, that of
music.

A composer is confronted with an especially difficult task
when working on a piece over some decades. When Schoenberg
wrote his first *Kammersymphonie* in 1904, he began at the same
time with the composition of a similar work;   the latter, however,
in contrast to the former, which was intended for solo instruments,
was conceived for a small orchestral group.   At first this work
progressed only to about the middle of the first movement; then it
was worked on five years later, and once more in 1916 without
being completed. It was not finished until 1939, that is 33 years
after its inception, at the suggestion of the conductor Fritz Stiedry,
who guaranteed the first performance in New York. Obviously the
already existing portion of the music had become alien to Schoenberg in the meantime. It had been written during his first, purely
tonal period without much reflection, with total trust in his own
concept of form, and in a style originating from other means of
expression but since abandoned because of new insights. As
Schoenberg wrote me, now it had to be completed "in the style in
which it had been composed." According to his own statement,
Schoenberg altered very little in the first of the two movements of
the work; only the ending and the instrumentation are new. Com-

pletely new, however, is the second movement, an "Allegro." Originally Schoenberg had more movements in mind, including a fifth movement, as is evident from the correspondence with Stiedry. The estate includes sketches of the third movement and a partially realized draft of 127 measures, an "Adagio" planned as an epilogue. Schoenberg's decision against continuing this work was testimony to his sense of responsibility towards his creative task, his consciousness that he was acting at the bidding of a higher power. In a letter to Stiedry, evidently written in the midst of his work on the third movement, it is stated: "The last movement is an 'Epilogue,' which, it is true, brings new material (derived from the preceding), but which is not absolutely necessary. The musical and 'physical' problems are presented thoroughly in the two completed movements; the final movement adds to it, so to speak, some 'contemplations.'" It was wholly crucial for Schoenberg to say merely what had to be said, what was worth saying and hence necessary. In himself and in others he hated empty talk, and he examined every thought for quality and content before he let it pass. So it was when Alban Berg wished to expand the piano sonata op.1, his final piece, at the conclusion of his years of study with Schoenberg: the first movement was to be followed by a slow one and a finale. Since he had been unable over a long period of time to come up with anything appropriate, Schoenberg finally advised him: "Well, then you have just said everything there was to be said." The work remained in one movement.

After all this, it is no longer surprising that Schoenberg was against the sensational and superficial as it had long manifested itself in the mania for premiere performances. True originality, however, is the organic characteristic of a work of art; it can never be intended a priori. This is what Schoenberg had in mind when he once mentioned, among the circle of his students, how baffled he was at the reaction of the public and press to his first non-tonal compositions. While composing he had not given a moment's thought to the creation of something especially original. It was only the resistance from the outside which brought this to his attention. Here perhaps one may look for the beginnings of Schoenberg the theoretician and teacher, who once said, "In every artist the desire will awaken for a conscious test of the new means and forms; he will wish to know consciously the laws and rules governing the forms which he received as if in a dream." Again, we see here the clear distinction between the creative values of the conscious and the subconscious. Concerning the topic of originality, I found in the estate the following notes on a slip of paper dated 1912, which is the beginning of the non-tonal period of work: "The mania for originality is degenerating into the fashionable. Artists only look for the new--and find it! But indeed not all such show genius?!? Hence, the new or original is not crucial as a manifestation of genius, but is only one of its most frequent characteristics. This is because we expect progress from that which has genius, and we think that it is progress that leads to higher things! But it does not have to be that way for we do not develop in a straight line."

Thus the questions of aesthetics are closely intertwined with this subject. They had already occupied Schoenberg when he wrote his *Harmonielehre*. There he had concerned himself with the concept of beauty, and he traced it back to the genuine, the true in the work of art. He rejected aesthetics as a criterion of art. Invention and expression, logic and flow of presentation are for him the actual artistic values. In 1923--the first steps within the concept of the twelve-tone technique had just been taken--Schoenberg wrote to J. M. Hauer that he would now be in a position to compose spontaneously and imaginatively as one does only in youth, but that he would nevertheless remain under a precisely identifiable aesthetic control. Busoni's little volume "Outline of a New Aesthetic of Music" (Entwurf einer neuen Ästhetik der Tonkunst), found in Schoenberg's library, is full of notes on the margins and added sheets with critical comments and his own thoughts about the topic. In April 1941 he was invited to a conference on aesthetic problems sponsored by the Cleveland Museum of Art and the Carnegie Corporation of New York. It cannot be determined whether or not he participated, but he occupied himself immediately with the theme of the conference, and dealt with it in his thesis "Aesthetics is Pure Science" (Ästhetik ist reine Wissenschaft), and he made an elaborate proposal for the establishment of a "Forum for Aesthetics and the Arts" (Forum für Ästhetik und Künste) to bring the arts and sciences into an interaction and counteract the alienation of life from nature and research from theory. This is another demonstration of the way Schoenberg's ever-active mind reacted immediately to whatever appealed to him, and the way he dealt with it imaginatively. In order to establish a connection between concepts as diverse as art and science, one must first clarify what separates one from the other. Thus a note that refers to Schoenberg's basic theoretical work "Musical Idea and Its Presentation" (Der musikalische Gedanke und seine Darstellung) reads: "Science strives to present its thoughts exhaustively and in such a manner that no question remains unanswered. On the contrary, art is content with a multi-faceted presentation, out of which the idea rises unequivocally without having to be articulated directly. Thereby a window remains open through which--from the rational point of view--intuition enters." And such a multifarious presentation of thought is evidenced in counterpoint, a concept within which the combination of voices is by no means an end in itself. The contrapuntal theme is so constructed that it already contains all these many shapes within itself, thus making possible the complex presentation of thought.

It is this multifarious presentation of complex thoughts that frightens away the intellectual "middlebrow" from Schoenberg's music, for it extends beyond his faculties of perception; this is because it addresses people for whom it is a pleasure to engage in deep thought and to wrestle with difficult problems. It is, though, a fundamental error to believe that the so-called atonality is responsible for the difficulty of understanding. The creative period of Schoenberg's youth which ends with the year 1908 and includes the "Second String Quartet in F-sharp minor, op. 10," was purely tonal. Nevertheless, because their own musical capacities had been exceeded by these tonal compositions, many experts as well as listeners revolted against them. When Schoenberg submitted his *Verklärte Nacht*, op. 4 to a Viennese musical organization for performance, his score was returned with the comment that it contained a chord that "does not exist at all." (It was the inversion of a ninth chord with the ninth in the bass, that is a five-note chord in an inversion not mentioned in the books on harmony.) Schoenberg reacted with humor, answering that he thoroughly agreed that one could not perform music that does not exist. After the premier performance in 1902 the press called the sextet a "calf with six feet." From that time it has become one of the most successful works of Schoenberg. The public reacted in a similarly negative fashion towards other tonal works of the composer, such as the E-Major Kammersymphonie and the aforementioned F-sharp minor Quartet which, about fifty years later, had to be repeated by request during a concert in Paris. Schoenberg was self-taught if one disregards the counterpoint instruction of not quite one year that he received from his brother-in-law-to-be, the composer and conductor Alexander von Zemlinsky. He had already begun to compose at the age of nine. At that time he studied by means of scores, through attending concerts and operas, and as an eager quartet player with his school friends. The estate includes a number of unknown compositions, among them many early songs without dates. They may possibly have been written before the "Six Pieces for Piano Four Hands" (Sechs Stücke für Klavier vierhändig), composed in 1894. A string quartet in D Major of 1897 (Faber & Faber, London) demonstrates an astonishing maturity of craftsmanship for a twenty-three-year-old, with a language schooled in Brahms but already showing some personal traits, especially in the middle movements. Moreover, from the year 1901 the seven chanson-like "Brettl Songs" (Brettl Lieder, i.e. cabaret songs) have been preserved. Such titles as "Gigerlette," "Galathea,"and "The Contented Lover" (Der genügsame Liebhaber) drawn from texts by Wedekind, Bierbaum and others and composed by the future master of modern music, afford us a few delighted chuckles.

From the non-tonal period are the three sheets of music which I found under a mass of loose sketches. They have the date of February 8, 1910 and include two completed pieces and a third, uncompleted one for soloistically scored chamber orchestra. Here is a discovery that might almost be considered sensational since its movements of aphoristic brevity (twelve or seven measures respectively) make it the first music of this type. Schoenberg's student and friend Anton Webern wrote his first pieces of like brevity during the same year, but without a precise date: "Four Pieces for Violin and Piano" (Vier Stücke für Geige und Klavier) and the "Six Orchestra Pieces op. 6" (Sechs Orchesterstücke). Evident from several of Schoenberg's notes is the intense interest with which Webern took note of everything composed by Schoenberg, and the fact that both cultivated a constant exchange of thoughts concerning their work and that Webern liked to take up the suggestions of his friend. A special reference by Schoenberg suggests that in this regard he was the dominant factor. The unfinished compositions left

behind or those just begun span over five decades of Schoenberg's
work. There are several tonal, atonal or twelve-tone string quartets,
chamber music of all kinds, and works for orchestra: for example
there is a score with over 250 measures from the year 1898, entitled
"Spring's Death" (Frühlings Tod) after Lenau, a symphony of 1937
conceived for four movements, a symphony in G minor begun in
1900, and the beginning of an opera based on Gerhard Haupt-
mann's "And Pippa Dances" (Und Pippa tanzt); there are also two
violin concertos, an orchestra passacaglia, and works for chorus
including oratorios.

Two of the oratorios and works for chorus are both of special interest and of primary importance: a symphony begun about
1912, for soli, mixed chorus, and orchestra, the "self-confession of
a human being of our time, with his spiritual and psychological
needs, who by wrestling with God finds Him and learns how to
pray"; and the later oratorio *Die Jakobsleiter* evolving from this,
unfortunately not completed. When several earlier attempts to
assemble texts for the aforementioned symphony from the Bible and
from the works of Dehmel, Tagore, and other poets, did not achieve
the desired result, Schoenberg wrote the text himself. The surviving
sketches of the symphony are of musicological interest in that the
"Scherzo" is based on the first pure twelve-tone theme which is
known to Western music--the first yet unconscious step in an inevitable development which was becoming more and more apparent.
Schoenberg took over portions of this symphony in the *Jakobsleiter*,
which is of approximately forty minutes' duration, and which com-
prises approximately half of the text which had been completed.
One of the five large sketchbooks also includes completed portions
of the second half, foremost among them the final chorus. The
manuscript score of the *Jakobsleiter*, begun in 1917, refutes the myth
of Schoenberg's "creative pause" before his twelve-tone period, for
the composition of the "Four Songs with Orchestra" (Vier Orches-
terlieder), the last free atonal opus written, falls into the years
immediately preceding 1915/1916, while the compositional stages of
the *Jakobsleiter* in the sketchbook extend from 1917 to 1918 and
from 1921 to 1922, which is into the twelve-tone epoch. The special
significance of this score lies partly in its completely novel means of
expression, which predate by decades today's developments of
electronic stereophonic music with its dispersed sources of sound.

Thus Schoenberg calls in the score for the so-called "Music in the
Distance" (Fernmusiken), for which he uses choruses as well as
orchestra, and which he locates partly some one to two meters
above the highest point of the main orchestra, and partly in the distance. The height and distance thereby differ, for the "Orchestra in
the Distance" (Fernorchester) marked F2 is further removed than
F1, and H2 is placed higher than H1. In addition, the various
bodies of sound are made independent of each other by the
instruction to the conductor that the respective "Music in the
Distance" should not be brought in at specific parts of measures but
should, as it were, float independently of the measure. Dotted lines
indicate the parts of the measure between which the distant sounds
are to be distributed. This is a completely novel and at the same
time truly creative acoustic sound conception, years before the
invention of broadcasting and the free distribution of sound sources
in a room, without which modern music can no longer get along
today.

       This is the most striking proof of the fact that true creators
of genius can hear sounds "which do not yet exist," and that their
realization often leads to advances in technical development of
instruments and their possibilities for use. But this is by no means
the only evidence or proof. Already in 1903, in the score of the
symphonic poem *Pelleas und Melisande*, the first glissandi for
trombones in music literature are found. The strings in Schoenberg's works are often forced to use novel fingerings for passages
which cannot be negotiated with fingerings of the classical violin
school, and which for that reason were declared unplayable. But
since the true composer also invents for the instrument, new ways
of performance were established. It is strange that to this day
nobody has taken note of the fact that Liszt's performance manner,
which governed piano technique for a long time--the left side of the
keyboard belonging to the left hand and the right side to the right
hand--was altered radically by Schoenberg, necessarily resulting from
the changed structure of his music. Something completely new are
the "spoken chords" in the stage work *Die glückliche Hand*, completed in 1913, where Schoenberg transferred the notation of "Sprech-
stimme"--used for the first time in *Pierrot Lunaire*--to the choral
idiom. The spoken word, inserted into music in a strict melodic and
even more rigorous rhythmic notation for the first time by Schoen-

berg in the *Gurrelieder* of about 1900, became so common that one
is no longer aware of its origin.   With Schoenberg himself it
experienced modifications through the flexible adaptations necessitated by the artistic requirements from one work to another.   One
of the most interesting of these can be found in the opera *Moses
und Aron* and in the incomplete first psalm of the group he authored himself.   There a new way of associating words and music
comes into being, in which the text sung by the chorus is also
spoken simultaneously by a speaker or speakers. This has the
advantage that one does not have to strain to hear the text, which
is always rather incomprehensible in multi-voiced choral singing, but
that one readily understands the text and can concentrate on the
music which is sung. The spoken word has anticipated the meaning,
which is important for the musical understanding, since words need
only a fraction of a moment for comprehension. A second advantage is of an artistic nature: with the juxtaposition of speaking and
singing, a new expressive element of the highest dramatic effectiveness has been achieved.

      It is self-evident that such new means of expression do cre-
ate considerable difficulties for the performers, often resulting in
the too-hasty judgment that the work cannot be done. As a reason
for one's own failure, the composer is readily held responsible; he
was, so to speak, just indulging his far-flung fantasies without
taking into consideration the possibilities for performance. Schoenberg did foresee that. There are letters and other documents in the
estate that   include detailed information concerning matters of
musical performance as well as those of stage technique. Schoenberg himself made colored sketches for the drama with music *Die
glückliche Hand*, which requires fantastic scenery, and he indicated
meticulously in the score his complex requests regarding the
lighting. When in 1930 this work together with the monodrama *Die
Erwartung* went into production at the Kroll-Opera in Berlin,
Schoenberg specified in a letter of many pages how the changes of
the set had to be accomplished with an open curtain, and he added
to this a stage model which he had constructed himself. For the
production of *Die glückliche Hand* he even prescribed the positions
and paths which the actors were to follow, addressed all special
problems concerning the production, and added at the end: "I am
not a friend of so-called stylized stage decorations (which style?)

and I like to see in the scenery the well-trained hand of a painter who makes a straight line straight and does not take children's drawings or the art of savage nations as his examples." And most characteristic: "The objects and localities have an active function in my pieces, and it is for this reason that they should be as recognizable as the pitches. If the spectator, like someone looking at a puzzle,[3] has to first ask himself what they mean, he meanwhile misses part of the music. That may be agreeable to him, but to me it is not desirable." Again and again the predominance of the music is addressed; everything is born of it and relates to it. Also very clear in this regard is a lengthy letter to Wilhelm Steinberg, the conductor of the first performance in Frankfurt of the comic one-act opera *Von heute auf morgen*: "My opera is a vocal work from A to Z," reads the basic requirement of the composer. "In acting as well as in singing, the singers shall always remain noble, never characterize at the expense of vocal beauty, never overact . . . They do not have to worry, my music does not need any help; it is so characteristic that if it is given correct musical interpretation, all the dramatic characteristics will appear by themselves." And this is followed by an extraordinarily graphic psychological description of the four persons in the action, which with its precise characterization leaves neither the director nor the performing artists any room for uncertainty. Finally, Schoenberg designs a detailed rehearsal schedule for the orchestra, all of it based on a profound knowledge of the problems of rehearsing such a work as well as of producing an opera. The letter ends with a short explanation of the idea of the work, which, together with the other points discussed, the conductor may present to all other participants. "I address myself to my colleague [the conductor] first, for if the music is good, one cannot go easily wrong with the rest." This is followed again by a warning to the director: "To do more would do harm because it has not been composed." The producer must simply derive the staging from the music, which includes everything: the dramatic as well as the comic, gesture and motion, dynamics and characteristic voice modulation.

A find of special value are the seven large and closely spaced pages that contain the quite precise directions for the opera *Moses und Aron*. They address separately the conductor, the instrumentalists, the singers, the decorators, the painters, and the lighting engineers; they concern themselves with the dancing around the "Golden Calf," the acting, the speaker of the part of Moses and the musical presentation. To the director Schoenberg grants liberty "as long as he uses it with discretion, moderation, and taste," and he adds, "All that serves to emphasize the idea is done well"--words which should be considered of general value for the rendition of a composition by Schoenberg. In regard to *Moses und Aron* he grants the main performers a special degree of freedom because "these two performers here have a task which can hardly be resolved without contributions of their own." Directions such as these document in a unique way the concreteness of Schoenberg's artistic intentions, the preciseness and acuteness with which he gave his visions shape, and the imagination he expected for their realization. They refute the fatal misunderstanding that he never considered the performance potential of the work. As in the comic opera *Von heute auf morgen* he also attached the greatest importance to beautiful singing in *Moses und Aron*: "The melodies are to be sung beautifully and characteristically. Foremost should be noble tone, the notes well connected, smooth transitions. The notes should always be well sustained, the vowels long, the consonants quick, legato. Characterization should never be achieved at the expense of beautiful sound production!" In a letter to Anton Webern dating back to the time when Schoenberg was working on the second act, he mentioned how much work he put into the exact realization of the "Dance Around the Golden Calf" in order to leave as little as possible to the directors and choreographers. "You know that I do not care much for dance. Its expressiveness, as a rule, is generally on a level not higher than the most primitive program music, and its 'beauty' with its petrified mechanics is odious to me. Up to now I have been able to devise such moves, which do at least achieve another level of expression than the customary hopping about of the ballets. Hopefully I shall progress further in this direction." In conjunction with this, nine large sheets of full score in pencil turned up in the estate, which probably represent the first continuous copy of the "Dance Around the Golden Calf"; five to six music staves contain precise indications of instrumentation. Very precise production directions are entered in ink, evidently later, and indeed in direct connection with the passages of the music that correspond in character and rhythm. One can assume that, in the spirit of his letter to Webern, Schoenberg would later have amended his directions considerably, especially concerning the choreography. In this letter he also mentions that he generally puts in the text when he writes out the score, this being the most laborious task for him. The first draft of the text still adhered to the form of an oratorio. Between this and the final text version there are no less than three different stage versions and numerous temporary drafts of portions of the work, with modifications and corrections of varying extent. For that matter, Schoenberg worked on the conception of the third act (as is widely known, it was never composed) in the USA. Two text versions exist for it, and one of them is, interestingly enough, cast completely in the style of a grand opera; it calls for two separate stage levels for big processions and, at the conclusion, for the two larger-than-life tablets that contain the law to be above the scene, immersed in radiant light. It may have appealed to Schoenberg to attempt such a solution with all the splendor of the operatic tradition, perhaps only in order to reject it more determinedly in favor of the solution eventually selected, which represents the thought more purely and clearly: in the judgement which Moses holds over Aron. The question of why Schoenberg did not complete the third act (so much discussed since the first performance), and the doubt as to whether he did not refrain from writing the composition because he thought that the work could not be performed, can now be resolved definitively, first because of completely unequivocal references in the letters which corroborate his intention to complete the work, and secondly because of a one-page sketch with the beginning of the third act and the entry: ". . . but do not forget to lay out here a movement consisting of five to six different sections." His precarious health, which deteriorated rapidly during the last years of his life, and the necessity of securing a livelihood for his family are the sole factors that deprived Schoenberg of the necessary time and concentration for far-reaching artistic projects.

Immense, nevertheless, is the amount that came into being during Schoenberg's time in America from 1933 to 1951 as regards compositions, literary works, and grandly conceived theoretical works whose significance cannot as yet be perceived. As a curiosity I should like to mention two small notebooks containing many sketches of purely tonal music for a motion picture. During the first years of his stay in Los Angeles many musicians from the movie industry enrolled as students with Schoenberg because they believed they could learn many interesting tricks of composition and orchestration directly from him. They were very disappointed when Schoenberg had them work in harmony and counterpoint instead. His friends brought it to the attention of the powerful movie producers of Hollywood that one of the foremost European composers now lived in the community, and that they should make use of the opportunity thus presented. A meeting with the appropriate executive from Metro-Goldwyn-Mayer did not come about until he had been shown an extensive article about Schoenberg in the "Encyclopaedia Britannica," with which he was very impressed. He proposed to Schoenberg that he write the music for Pearl S. Buck's movie "The Good Earth," which had just been put into production, and he even accepted the request for an enormous fee. The negotiations then failed because of Schoenberg's condition that not one note of his music could be changed. Even though Schoenberg anticipated the negative result, he occupied himself with this task that was so new to him, and sketched music for particularly salient scenes of the movie, which is now recorded in the two little books. The fact of the matter is that America had virtually no influence on Schoenberg either with its music or its general concepts of values. He lived there in "splendid isolation," a fact which is also evident from certain remarks in his letters. It is therefore understandable that he turned down the honorary doctor's degree which was offered to him by the University of California. Jazz made only sporadic inroads into his music: in a few measures of the opera *Von heute auf morgen* for the characterization of a scene, and in the second movement of his *Suite op. 29* for several instruments--a work dedicated to his wife Gertrud and one exceedingly cheerful in character. To an inquiry from the "Chicago Tribune" as to whether jazz had had any influence on German music, he answered in the negative with the remark, "No more than gypsy music at one time." For two works, both of which are strictly tonal, Schoenberg complied with special requests which were presented to him in the USA: he wrote the *Suite for Strings* which he wrote for American university orchestras in order to expose them to new modes of expression "without, for the present, subjecting students to the harm which may befall them through the 'poison of atonality,' as he then remarked somewhat ironically in the unpublished preface; and he wrote the op. 43 "Variations for Band" (Variationen für eine Bläserband), a very popular form of ensemble in the USA. "It is not one of my main works," he wrote to the conductor Fritz Reiner; "Everybody can see that, because it is not a twelve-tone composition. It is one of those works which one writes in order to delight in one's own virtuosity and, on the other hand, to give something better to perform to a group of amateurs, in this case wind bands. I can assure you, that from a technical point of view it is a masterpiece, I believe it is also original, and I know at the same time that it is inspired. This is true not only because I cannot write even ten measures without inspiration, but also because I wrote this piece with great pleasure."

It would constitute a treatise by itself were I to cite here the various remarks that can be found in the letters and essays by Schoenberg concerning twelve-tone composition, remarks that show "that these works are first and foremost works of a musical conception and not, as many assume, mathematical constructions," and that his statement "I cannot write ten measures without inspiration" amounts to a confession of universal validity.   In a letter to his brother-in-law Rudolf Kolisch he emphatically warns against the analysis of twelve-tone rows "because this leads only to what I always fought against: the realization of how it was done, while I always aimed for the recognition of what it is!" After all, the main task is to make good music. How it was done is a question of second or third importance. The spiritual star under which his entire work stood is revealed by a short marginal note in one of the large sketch books. There, at the beginning of the Adagio from the "Quintet for Winds" (Bläserquintet op. 25) is the sentence, "I believe Goethe would have to be quite satisfied with me." This sheds light on much: the position and mentality of Arnold Schoenberg the artist as well as the thinker, and the ethos and weight of his work.

Now there remains only the task of telling about Arnold Schoenberg as a teacher, even though it is not possible to separate those aspects that complement both a teacher and composer reciprocally; the human being cannot be isolated from the artist, nor either from the teacher. One is always at the same time the other.

In a copy of Schoenberg's *Harmonielehre* (1911), the one

which he gave to his wife Gertrud during their first year of marriage, a dedication is written on the title page: *"Harmonielehre* we shall not need. Because I have not learned it, I have written it, and even though you may wish to read it, it will not tell you what you do not know. 'One learns only what one knows anyway,' I said once. Thus it is that here the chapter 'Meter and Harmony' (Takt und Harmonie) is too short. Meter is the disposition of harmony, and the teaching of harmony is the teaching of form. The deepest meaning of this reveals itself only to the one who does not ask for it. He indeed has the answer before the question."

This, in its ambiguity, is a typical train of thought for Arnold Schoenberg. The sentence: "One learns only what one knows anyway," comes, on the one hand, from the self-taught person Schoenberg, and on the other from the creative artist, because the latter--the composer--is actually unteachable. If one shows him "how he must do it," and refers to the fact that others have also done it in that way, then this may be teaching about the arts, but not instructing the artist. For the true artist, one with originality, innate knowledge and talent are always stronger than preparatory training in the craft. Thus the task of the teacher towards the artist is clarified: he can teach the latter only what he knows anyway, but does not yet realize. In other words, the artist should learn how to listen to himself. Simultaneously then he will acquire the technique necessary to express himself. Thus it has to be understood that Schoenberg never showed his students how something was to be done, but only helped with the understanding of what it might be. And so it can be explained that his best students--we may think about Alban Berg, Anton Webern, Winfred Zillig, Nikos Skalkottas, Hanns Eisler and Richard Hoffmann--had their own style from the beginning, that in their music they never imitated what their teacher wrote, because he had always admonished them to follow only their own thoughts and to listen to themselves. When Schoenberg was forced to devise for himself a new means of livelihood during the fall of 1933 in the USA, he developed for the director of a Boston conservatory his ideas concerning the instruction to be given there. For this he harkened back to the composition courses he had given in Vienna during the winter of 1917/18, in which he made his students find out for themselves through discussion, analysis, reflection, and observation what the elements are upon which musical art forms are based. Among other things he mentioned the analysis of Bach works for students who had passed counterpoint; this would also be of interest to pedagogues because they especially have to help the students find themselves. It is only one more step from finding oneself to one's very own personal expression.

Schoenberg was already teaching at the age of thirty. Anton Webern was one of his first students. At the age of thirty-five Schoenberg wrote the tonal *Harmonielehre*, which is basically a part of his composition teaching, and today it is still as new and informative as it was when it was first published. It contains an abundance of thoughts of a pedagogical, aesthetic and artistic nature. From then on such thoughts return again and again, complemented, altered and, at the same time, touching on other related fields in notes, letters, essays and the various current outlines for larger projects. The "Policies for a Ministry of Culture" (Richtlinien für ein Kunstamt) presented to the Austrian government after World War I by the architect Adolf Loos, included Schoenberg as the author of the section on music. There it says: "The most important task for the 'Section for Music' is to secure the musical superiority of the German nation which is rooted in the talents of the people. This (superiority) should come from the tradition of earlier times, when the German grade school teacher was almost always the music teacher too, and who even in a smaller village was active as such and created in this way a reservoir large enough to provide for the highest levels. With the establishment of the modern public school, the teaching of music was reduced to barely sufficient instruction in singing. In another hundred years we will have lost this superiority." To this warning Schoenberg then adds recommendations for the establishment of special music schools at the elementary, junior, and high school levels, since the best possible solution, to incorporate musical instruction in the grade schools again, would be too difficult to realize and too costly. The first concept for the establishment of a "School of Education in International Styles" (Internationale Stilbildungs-Schule) originated during the twenties. Some years earlier Schoenberg had drawn up in detail the topics and conditions for acceptance into a seminar in composition, which at the end of 1918 he briefly implemented with the collaboration of Webern, Berg and some of the older students. The teaching conditions at American colleges and universities which are quite different from those in Europe, stimulated Schoenberg's pedagogical abilities anew, first and foremost in connection with his own teaching activities at the University of California (at Los Angeles), for which there is a detailed plan in the estate regarding the course of studies and the examinations. In a letter to the president of the University of Chicago he discusses at length the possibilities of organizing a music department.

. In the essays in which Schoenberg concerns himself with questions of composition, the same basic thought is presented again and again in various guises: that he not only passed on what he knew, but also what was needed by the prospective student; that he did not teach style, nor practical recipes for composition, and that he did not suggest that any student write in the atonal or twelve-tone style. I recall an essay by Ernst Krenek, which came out a few years after the last war, in which he reports on the development of modern music in the USA and on the influence which the European masters who had emigrated to America exerted in that respect. There he expresses his astonishment and even disapproval that during all the years Schoenberg taught there, he had avoided teaching twelve-tone composition. At first glance, this may seem surprising, but without a doubt it becomes understandable in the light of Schoenberg's attitude as outlined above. Actually, Schoenberg went even further when he explained that he considered it to his credit that he had never encouraged students to compose, but rather that he had given most of his hundreds of students to understand that he did not think much of their creative abilities. Such an uncompromising attitude may appear too harsh for some, but one glance at the immense number of composers today proves that Schoenberg, with his sense of responsibility and urge for truthfulness, was right; it was a good deed to have prevented the production of an artistic proletariat.

During the fall of 1926, the former Prussian Academy of the Arts received from Leipzig the application of a Miss Fuhrmann: she wished to enroll in Schoenberg's masterclass in order to learn how to compose in an atonal style. The executive secretary, Professor Amersdorfer, sent the letter to Schoenberg who answered as follows: "Concerning the application of Miss Fuhrmann I have to make the following remarks":

1. First and foremost, there is a serious

misunderstanding here: I do not teach 'atonal music' but just music. The time is certainly not ripe yet for teaching atonal music! It would only be bad if one did so, while, on the other hand, it is essential to teach people how to compose properly!

2. Generally, in my teaching I aim less toward instructing than toward advising them, and for this reason I prefer to have only students here who will find the opportunity to make practical use of that advice--that is composers, or at least those about whom one can hope that they may yet become composers.

3. I do not have any objection, however, to treating someone such as Miss Fuhrmann as an exception, and allowing her to sit in on such theoretical courses as I conduct for my students off and on. Miss Fuhrmann's inquiry, my dear Professor Amersdorfer, provided a welcome opportunity for me to make such comments. To whom shall I address my answers in the future? I am "officially" completely uninvolved! With best regards,

faithfully yours, Arnold Schoenberg

Schoenberg's own models were in the first place Bach and Mozart. Utilizing their works as well as those by Beethoven, Brahms, and others, he introduced his students into the mysterious world of composition:

Analysts of my music will have to realize how much I personally owe to Mozart. People who looked unbelievingly at me, thinking I made a poor joke will now understand why I called myself a "pupil of Mozart," must now understand my reasons. This will not help them to appreciate my music, but to understand Mozart. And it will teach young composers what are the essentials that one has to learn from the masters and the way one

can apply these lessons without loss of personality.[4]

(this is taken from Schoenberg's
original English version)

Thus it is stated in one of the perhaps most important essays by
Schoenberg (unfortunately so far only published in English), the
treatise *Brahms the Progressive*. There Schoenberg shows through
many musical examples that Brahms--by comparison to Wagner--was
unjustly considered to be conservative and outmoded; and he reveals
ingenious constructive principles of form in Brahms' music, which
even today must be considered most novel and progressive. As for
Bach, the four letters of this name are inserted repeatedly and
artfully as notes in Schoenberg's music, as a token of his respectful
homage. Schoenberg glorifies Bach as a "continuous revelation."
In the teaching proposal for the conservatory in Boston mentioned
above, concerning the analysis of Bach, he says in proud modesty:
"I do not believe that Bach's fugues can be examined more
thoroughly." In *New Music, Outmoded Music, Style and Idea*,[5] an
essay of 1946 (which like the Brahms essay has appeared as yet only
in English, even though its fundamental train of thought represents
an exceedingly illuminating document concerning the phenomenon
Schoenberg) one can read: "Bach sometimes operated with the
twelve notes in such a way that one could be inclined to call him
the first twelve-tone composer." Incidentally, one may already
gather from these facetiously spoken words that Schoenberg's
technique of composition with twelve tones represents much more
than a mere mechanical manipulation. In a separate essay "Bach
and the Twelve Notes" (Bach und die zwölf Töne), he elaborates his
train of thought more precisely with references to examples from
the *Well-tempered Clavier* : the fugue in b minor, no. 24 from the
first volume begins with a theme that includes all twelve notes.
However, what seems more important to him is the fact that this
fugue could more appropriately be considered chromatic than those
which are usually called such. The chromatically altered notes
occurring in it are clearly independent of tonal relationships and are
more like the unrelated pitches of a chromatic scale in the basic set
of a twelve-tone composition. In his teaching Schoenberg often
repeated, both orally and in written form, his conviction that Bach

must have known of some special secrets concerning the interrelations of tones. This secret knowledge made it possible for him, in contradiction to the theorists, to construct from a broken chord the different themes of the *Art of the Fugue* with its artful canonic imitations. Schoenberg speaks about miracles that no human mind could create. The artist is merely the mouthpiece of a power which governs his hand. Counterpoint was Bach's mother tongue, and he translated the will of that power into the language of human counterpoint. In these few sentences--going beyond Bach's theme-- Schoenberg's belief in the call of the true artist by a higher power is revealed, and, on the other hand his conviction that those who consider his music to be constructed and born out of intellect are in error. In Bach, as well as in Schoenberg, imagination has definite priority over intellect. In this connection Schoenberg believed that Bach's most famous son, Philipp Emanuel, had inherited from his father an immense knowledge of counterpoint, and that he could have become equally famous "had he not considered the style of his father to be outdated, and had he possessed his inventive expressiveness and his personality."

"Knowledge of the secrets of music cannot be taught. It is inborn or it does not exist. This is also the reason why Thomas Mann's Adrian Leverkühn knows nothing of the true nature of composition with the twelve tones. All he knows he was told by Mr. Adorno, who knows only what little I could tell my students. The true facts will probably remain secret knowledge until somebody appears who has inherited them because of his inborn talent. It is the same today as it was with Telemann, Philipp Emanuel Bach, and (Reinhard) Keiser: nobody takes the trouble to present new thoughts and ideas, but only a novel style. And this style is one whose principles exhaust themselves mostly in the negative, through prohibitions of chromaticism, expressive melodies, Wagnerian harmonies, romanticism, biographical hints, subjectivity, functional harmonic progressions, illustrations, leitmotivs, conformity with the mood or action on stage, the characteristic declamation of an operatic text, a Lied, a chorus--hence all that was considered to be good before. Along with these 'official' prohibitions one finds instead numerous negative attributes, such as: pedal points instead of worked-out bass lines with moving harmony; ostinatos and sequences instead of developed variations and fugatos for similar purposes; dissonances which veil the vulgarity of the thematic material; and objectivity (new objectivity) which consists of imprecise imitations, a kind of "rhubarb-counterpoint" which only sounds as if it were of some real significance."

Unfortunately an extensive work planned by Schoenberg, *Bach's Counterpoint*, has remained only an outline. Twenty-four handwritten pages with examples, every page with its own chapter heading, suggest the proposed content of the book which, in this rudimentary form, already foreshadows a wealth of new insights into the works of Bach. The so-called "Magic Row" found in the estate-- a twelve-tone row that Schoenberg invented one year before his death--also belongs in the context of Schoenberg/Bach and counterpoint. It is unusual in that it was not written in connection with a composition, but is what might be termed an abstract entity. It offers, as it says at the end of the description, "a larger selection of invertible counterpoints of various kinds . . . Certainly, one must invent the themes as one usually does, but one has more possibilities for discovering related forms which nevertheless sound quite different." According to one of Schoenberg's essays on Bach, such a row is comparable to a canon of two or more voices, which is notated as a single line but can yield different sounds. Here the close connection between counterpoint and twelve-tone music manifests itself, for the structure of the latter is also primarily linear and designed for a multi-voiced texture. And in both types of music "harmony (as a form-giving element) is not under discussion." "Closely related shapes which sound different," actually signify unity within diversity, and in that is found the essence of all great art.

As in twelve-tone music, so to in contrapuntally conceived music, Schoenberg is interested in making music without ever stifling its flow, yet doing so with respect for the severity with which the materials are kept in order and within the laws. This, however, presupposes contrapuntal thinking, which is able to make music subconsciously and to which technical adjustments born out of the intellect have become second nature. In a letter of 1932 Schoenberg wrote (in answer to a query), "Concerning the question of a new kind of counterpoint I can only refer you to those of my compositions that have appeared since about 1921. The theoretical I do not yet know, and in the purely compositional I am completely dependent on my intuition, my sense of form, and my musical instinct." And in an essay entitled "Heart and Brain" (Herz und Gehirn) one reads: "There are times when I am not prepared to write even one example of simple two-voiced counterpoint, as I expect it from advanced students in my classes. In order to write a good example of this type, I need the cooperation of inspiration. In this regard I am much weaker than some of my students, who write good counterpoint as well as bad without any inspiration at all."

Right after the completion of his *Harmonielehre* in 1911 Schoenberg set out to outline a textbook on counterpoint. The work that went into it, interrupted again and again, can be followed in detail because the estate includes all drafts and fragments up to the fourth and definitive version begun in 1942. It was to be in three volumes, but it progressed only through the first volume, which deals with simple counterpoint. Beyond this, however, many fugues and chorale preludes for the later volumes exist. How completely Schoenberg's musical and technical mastery are united in this area is documented by the fugue a5 which constitutes the centerpiece of the overture of a tonal suite for strings composed in 1934, a form of the orchestral suite which was created by Lully and was extremely popular until Gluck. We have here the first tonal composition that Schoenberg wrote in the twenty-eight years following the "Second String Quartet." An unpublished preface found in the estate contains much information about it. It was intended as a kind of teaching piece for American college orchestras, one that would have something to communicate to the students as well as to the instructors. It was intended to prepare them for modern performance techniques as well as for problems of rhythm, intonation, harmony, counterpoint and the development of phrases, and for forms that technically as well as spiritually belong to a higher plane of art than the primitive, unvaried, and undeveloped melodies that find favor with the mediocre of all countries and nations. This work counteracts the conservatism of those teachers who do not possess anything that is worth conserving--not even such skills as would enable them to write a fugue like the one in this work. The true teachers, however, the proclaimers and disseminators of culture, and hence the genuine and true leaders, will be given a chance to instill in their students a deep respect for artistic ability, and to make it clear to the students that a culture can only be sustained by growth, since like everything living it can only live as long as it grows, but it will shrivel up and die as soon as it ceases to develop. Consequently, the technical as well as the spiritual can only be worth conserving artistically when it signifies a first step towards new development, towards new life; only then and because of that is it worth conserving. Like so many others, these clear and urgently admonishing words of Schoenberg were spoken into the void. At the conclusion of his preface, he remarks that after what has been said, it may be superfluous to mention that this piece does not imply a renunciation of his existing atonal and twelve-tone works written thus far.

Most revealing of Schoenberg the teacher as well as Schoenberg the artist are his detailed explanations and commentaries on the arrangements of other masterpieces. In earlier times such arrangements were customary; one only needs recall the Vivaldi arrangements by Bach, or the Mozart arrangements of Handel. To the same extent that such compositional methods fell more and more into disuse, the standard that should be applied to them also fell into oblivion, and so it can hardly be surprising that the works in question by Schoenberg met with sharp opposition from critics and musicologists. His were based on musicological or aesthetic considerations in which it was overlooked that both are subject to constant change and have no claim on eternal validity-- and especially not when, as here, only compositional considerations are applicable as justifiable and correct standards. And to the latter the musician Schoenberg lays claim with authority. What he touched became music to him, and thus the eighteenth-century compositions that he received before World War I from Guido Adler with a request for basso-continuo realizations to be included in the *Denkmäler der Tonkunst in Österreich* likewise are not for him museum pieces to be archived in accordance with the newest state of science, but living music. Thus the answer he gives to the Viennese music critic Max Graf on the second page of the manuscript of Georg Mathias Monn's cello concerto is an answer which at the same time represents a theoretical doctrine of a master of the craft of composition. For that matter, at a much later time, at the end of 1932, Schoenberg transformed yet another work by Monn, whom he evidently valued highly, a harpsichord concerto in free adaptation as a *Concerto for Violoncello and Orchestra*. Since the first London performance in 1935 with the cellist Emanuel Feuermann, it has hardly been performed elsewhere, perhaps because of the considerable difficulties of the solo part. In a letter (see Chapter IV, p. 161, dated February 20, 1933) Schoenberg pronounces himself satisfied: it turned out to be a very brilliant piece in which he took great pains with the sonority. His main concern was to remove the flaws of the Handelian style to which this work adheres, somewhat as Mozart did with the *Messiah* when he removed "whole handfuls of sequences" and replaced them with true substance. "Then I endeavored to fight the other main deficiency of the Handel style: there the theme is always at its best at its first appearance, and it becomes more and more insignificant and inferior in the course of the piece. I believe that I have succeeded for the entire work in approaching the style of Haydn." He proceded even more radically with the transformation of Handel's *Concerto grosso op. 6, no. 7* into a "Concerto for Strings and Orchestra" (Konzert für Streicher und Orchester). In doing so he went further than Mozart and Brahms with their Handel arrangements, especially in the third and fourth movements. Here he perceived the thematic invention and development as much too weak, and gave a completely new structure to the movements. The "Andante" of the third movement became an "Allegretto grazioso," and the final movement was also completely transformed and extended.   The uncompromising attitude that reveals itself here concerning questions of artistic integrity and musical quality is not stopped by great names, openly pointing out weaknesses as such; it is characteristic of Schoenberg in every respect for he always set the highest as a goal for himself, set inexorably the highest standards. But at the moment when he set them, in conjunction with that task he also showed the path towards the solution and cleansed the air of the dust of centuries, which at times has settled upon old music, and which one is frequently obliged to hear along with the music.

The two extensive double fugues in "Prelude op. 44", and in the interlude of *Moses und Aron*, as well as the chorale arrangements in the opera, attest to how masterfully Schoenberg transformed old forms into the format of twelve-tone compositions by means of his musical imagination. Approximately 40 canons originated in the tonal sphere during several decades, and their often quite artful construction evokes the spirit of the great Netherlands masters of counterpoint. Most of these are incidental works for jubilees or festive occasions, in part encoded in riddle canons as the Netherlands masters liked to do, and often with his own, frequently cheerful words appropriate to the particular occasion.

When Schoenberg's adaptations are under discussion, those of Bach's works must be mentioned. They are three in number: two chorale preludes and the *Prelude and Fugue in E-flat Major* for organ, which Schoenberg set for large orchestra. They brought on the wrath of his adversaries and created doubt even with his well-wishers, because at just about that time (between 1920 and 1930), after a certain amount of vacillation, a new Bach concept had finally been adopted. The performance of Bach's music had been cleansed of all dynamic gradations (considered to be of Romantic origin), and austere black and white realizations had been accepted as the only authentic ones. And it was at just this moment that Schoenberg came along with his instrumentations for a big body of sound as developed during the Romantic nineteenth century. Certainly this was irritating. But completely overlooked was the way Schoenberg utilized this big orchestra in specific terms--not, as one might say, in the sense of multi-colored sound combinations, but only for the concrete clarification of Bach's multi-voiced texture. Schoenberg expressed himself on this issue in a detailed letter of 1930 to the conductor Fritz Stiedry. It was his position that we do not know anything about performance practice during Bach's time, nor about the treatment of the Bach organ. Our 'sound ideal' is not for 'luscious' tone color, but rather that tone colors should only clarify the course of the voices, thus making audible the countrapuntal texture as the carrier of the musical thought. We do not know whether or not the Bach organ could do that back then; today's organists, however, are incapable of it. "I do know this, and it is one of my starting points: our musical comprehension today demands the clarification of the motivic development in the horizontal as well as the vertical. It is not enough to trust in the imminent effect of the self-evident presupposed contrapuntal structure, but we want to perceive the counterpoint as coherent motivic interactions. The 'pleasant' effect which comes about just because of artful voice leading is not enough for us anymore. We need transparency in order to see through it." According to Schoenberg's conviction, all this is not possible without phrasing. "Phrasing, however, is not to be used for 'stressing the affective' as was the case during the age of pathos. But it has

1. to distribute correctly the relations of weight within the line,
2. to partly reveal and partly hide the motivic structure, and
3. to afford the mutual dynamic interrelationship of each voice to all others and to achieve transparency of the ensemble sound."

Thus reads the sentence which gives the key to the artistic intentions of Schoenberg's Bach instrumentations, and the letter closes with the lapidary sentence: "Consequently, I believe, the right to transcription becomes a duty here." Purely as a creative musician, he subjected himself to this duty to the music of Bach, which he always loved and admired so much. As such he dared to push aside musicological theses and speculations.

Schoenberg amended his views accordingly concerning the instrumentation of Bach's organ works in a detailed and substantiated exposition dealing with the problem of the organ. He says that, if he had to select the stops, he would do it only in such a way that all voices stand out clearly. "I am interested little in its colors; actually for me colors have only one use, to make clear the idea, the motivic and thematic subject, and possibly its expression and character." In other words: tone color was, as a rule, only of secondary importance for Schoenberg; it only had the function of realizing musical thought as clearly as possible. Thus he also thought that only a small number of colors, perhaps two to six, would be enough for him on an organ, and that is in agreement with the tendencies of modern (electronic?--trans.) organ building today. These colors, however, he added, would have to have the complete range of seven to eight octaves, and--each by itself--the capacity for dynamic expression from the softest pianissimo to the biggest fortissimo. Here out of creative need, a master assigns a clear task to modern instrument construction. Again and again throughout the years, Schoenberg took up this issue in his essays. In 1926, after he had heard and carefully inspected the "Trautonium" in Berlin--an instrument constructed by Dr. Trautwein and one of the first instruments with electronic tone production--he took issue with its design in the essay "Mechanical Music Instruments" (Mechanische Musikinstrumente). He pointed out, for example, that it should be not at all the purpose of such an instrument to imitate the tone colors of the various orchestral instruments, but that the development should rather go in the direction of creating an instrument with the widest possible range and virtuoso performance technique, whose tone colors could be developed out of the new technical possibilities and free of constraint. Meanwhile, this is actually the case with electronic music.

Still others of Schoenberg's writings are of undiminished and current interest. Even today one occasionally encounters the argument that atonal music creates insoluble problems of intonation, that for a string or woodwind instrument the tone d-flat, for example, is higher than c-sharp while the notation of non-tonal music does not take that into consideration, c-sharp and d-flat being identical. Now one might be content to refer to the music of, say, the 19th century where precisely the same arguments took place with the so-called enharmonic principle on the basis of the commonly applied tempered tuning valid in Western music. Schoenberg, however, tackled the question thoroughly in a letter to an American addressee, in which the initial statement can be found that the piano has only tempered tones and that therefore, c-sharp and d-flat are one and the same tone. Indeed, when he studied intonation with string players, he had always demanded tempered intonation, and a c-sharp and d-flat are in no way different but an exactly measured half step between c and d irrespective of harmonic questions. "And I do believe that a listener who 'combines other tones in his ear' than I have stated is not educated sufficiently, since to be musical means to have an ear within the realm of music and not the concepts of nature. A musical ear must have assimilated the tempered scale. And a singer who gives pure pitches is unmusical, as somebody could be immoral who acts 'natural' on the street." This implies at the same time that there are people with perfect pitch who do not have any relation at all to music, that is who are unmusical. "To have an ear in regard to music" is complemented by a sentence in Schoenberg's *Harmonielehre*: "The ear is the musician's complete understanding." A more apt refutation of the common view of Schoenberg as a technical designer is hardly imaginable. Perfect pitch is for him an ability which essentially consists of the abilities to recognize tones, to perceive, recall, and reproduce them, as well as to imagine the tones and their relationships to one another in one's imagination, with the so-called inner ear.

Except for the short essay in his book *Style and Idea* (Stil und Gedanke), Schoenberg did not allow anything to remain mererely theoretical about his concept of composing with twelve tones. This was entirely intentional, for he considered this manner of composition as a family matter, as he once said in jest. Once, when the fact was pointed out to him that Josef Matthias Hauer also composed with the twelve-tone system, he directed his student Erwin Stein to publish the thoughts which underly this concept in order to protect himself from the accusation of plagiarism, which, however, could hardly be raised if one compares the music of Schoenberg and Hauer: it has nothing in common but the twelve notes. As a consequence, Schoenberg never taught twelve-tone composition, either in Europe or in the USA. Only in individual cases, when the music of a young composer already showed a tendency towards the twelve-tone practice, did he help with some compositional hints where he deemed it necessary. All the more interesting, therefore, are the numerous remarks--mostly contained in letters--concerning this far-from-exhausted topic. Thus in a letter to his brother-in-law, the violinist Rudolf Kolisch, Schoenberg turned emphatically against the type of analysis that restricts itself merely to finding the twelve-tone rows in his works. Repeatedly he attempted to make Webern, Berg and also "Wiesengrund (Adorno)" understand this, "but in this they do not believe me."[6] "I cannot say it often enough: my works are twelve-tone *compositions* and not *twelve-tone* compositions." And in a note referring to Thomas Mann's *Doctor Faustus* he scoffs, "Leverkühn is one of these amateurs who believe that composing with twelve notes means nothing else than the continuous application of the basic set and its inversions. . . . But to believe that following this rule would bring forth a composition is as childish or amateurish as the assumption that the observance of other prohibitions would be sufficient to make music--the avoidance of parallel fifths and octaves, for example." Repeatedly the importance of subconscious as opposed to conscious creativity is emphasized. This is stated in the letter to

Kolisch mentioned above: "Even though I am not ashamed of a healthy constructive basis of a composition where I have created it consciously, albeit it is less good than if it were a result of instinct and was created subconsciously, I do not wish to be considered an engineer on the basis of slight manipulations of the row because that would imply too little of an effort on my part. I believe that I would have to contribute more to earn such a title. I am, however of the opinion that I am able to fulfill the even higher demands of those who have insight enough to make them." And at another place one finds the lapidary sentence: "But everything depends, as always in art, not on the material but on genius."

The above has also full validity for the teacher Schoenberg. "I have never had a theory in my life . . . I do not consciously create tonal, polytonal or polyplane music. I write what I feel in my heart, and what I finally put down on paper has passed through every fiber of my body before. Therefore, I cannot say in which style my next composition will be; this is because it will be determined by what I feel at a given point when I develop and work out my thoughts." I have often witnessed that a student brought a composition in an apparently very modern style to Schoenberg, who then eliminated with a few strokes the seemingly "interesting" but wrong notes, thus demonstrating that they merely represented a pseudo-modern dressing up of a poorly invented tonal piece. On the other hand, the father of non-tonal music and the inventor of the compositional twelve-tone technique down to the end of his life held in equal value his works from the tonal period and his later music. One evidence of that is his 1950 analysis of his string sextet *Verklärte Nacht* composed in 1899, which I found in the estate. Invention and expression, logic and flow of the imagination, wealth of musical ideas--these were the determining musical values for him. To trace them in the works of the great masters was what he taught his students most of all, but never purely compositional tricks. He was of the opinion that a true composer wrote music for the joy of it and for no other reason. Who only composes in order to please others, thinking at the same time about the listener, is not a true artist. The latter is motivated to say something irrespective of whether or not there may be somebody who likes it, even if he dislikes it himself. Mention must yet be made of a fundamental theoretical work which Schoenberg left behind besides a novel treatise on instrumentation and the compendium on counterpoint. The last version of these ideas, written down for the first time in 1917, has the title "Musical Thought and the Logic, Technique, and Art of its Presentation" (Der musikalische Gedanke und die Logik, Technik und Kunst ihrer Darstellung). This title makes it understandable that Schoenberg hardly said anything about his technique of composition with twelve tones. For him it was a "method of a more craftman-like nature which had a decisive influence neither on the form nor on the character of a composition." The incomplete manuscript of more than 200 pages was begun in 1934 and had been worked on with interruptions since that time. As can be perceived by a cursory glance, it presents, even in its present fragmentary form, one of the most significant musical-theoretical treatises of Western music.

The work of a genius is timeless. Nevertheless, every period perceives it differently, detecting in it new traits which correspond with the period, new significances, a new outlook. On the other hand, much of what is familiar and accepted is discarded as unimportant or even false, or attains another meaning in the light of altered perceptions. How often and how radically has the perception of Bach or of Mozart changed in the course of time! Similar developments can already be observed today concerning Schoenberg, even though not even three decades have passed since his death. Yet Schoenberg's case is different in that certain crucial characteristics are absent from his image to this day. One can still speak of the "unknown Schoenberg," since much of what has been said here about the human being, the musician, and the teacher is only gradually emerging in detail as well as in the larger context. To the degree to which the complexity of this personality emerges in its intellectual breadth--from the as yet unknown treasures that are in the estate--it promises to become still more fascinating. This will only be recognized when the complete materials of his writings have been made public. To explore fully the genius of Arnold Schoenberg in all of its depth, and to make it artistically fruitful, is left to the future as one of the most resplendent tasks of men of music.

Notes

1. Editorial additions or translations are given in parenthesis.

2. Schoenberg objected to the combination of the two nouns into *Handschuhtage*; the intended implication here would be "Seven sales days for cheap gloves." Rufer also cites the German double-noun *Wasserlandung* (water landing) as a second example of the type of construction to which Schoenberg objected.

3. Rufer cites as an example a picture-riddle *Bilderrätsel* "Where is the Hunter?"

4. Leonard Stein, ed., *Style and Idea, Selected Writings of Arnold Schoenberg.* University of California Press, 1984, p. 414.

5. Ibid, p. 117.

6. Theodor Wiesengrund-Adorno (1903-1969) was a significant German social philosopher who studied with Alban Berg. Even though he was a strong advocate of Schoenberg, the composer did not regard him highly. Adorno assisted Thomas Mann in musical matters concerning his novel *Doctor Faustus*, which created antagonism between Schoenberg and Mann. Adorno published his earlier writings under the name Wiesengrund-Adorno.

CHAPTER II

Arnold Schoenberg - Guido Adler

Guido Adler (1855-1941) was born in Eibenschütz, Moravia, the son of a physician. After the death of his father (1856), his mother settled with her six children in Iglau, where Gustav Mahler also spent several years of his youth. During 1864 the family moved to Vienna, where from 1868 on, Adler studied music theory and composition, earning an artist's diploma in 1874. Anton Bruckner was among his teachers. Subsequent studies in law during 1873 resulted in a law degree in 1878, and eventually Adler turned to the field of musicology. His mentor there was Eduard Hanslick, and after graduation from the University of Vienna in 1880 with a Ph.D in musicology, Adler joined the faculty of the German university in Prague (1885). In 1898 Adler returned to Vienna, succeeding Hanslick at the University of Vienna, and he remained at this post until his retirement in 1927.

Adler is considered the founder of modern musicology in Austria and one of the early pioneers of the discipline. His many achievements include the editorship of the *Denkmäler der Tonkunst in Österreich*,[1] the organization of several international meetings, and the publication of several books and numerous articles. After his death in 1941, his library was confiscated by the Nazis and scattered among several Austrian libraries.

Professor Hugh Hodgson (1893-1969), founder and chairman of the Music Department at the University of Georgia until 1960, became aware of the Adler collection through Harold Spivacke, chief of the music division at the Library of Congress, and approached Adler's son, Hubert Joachim Adler, concerning a possible purchase of his library for the university. On April 27, 1948, Hubert Adler granted an option to the University of Georgia to buy the library for $ 6500. The university acquired the library, and after considerable difficulties and delays the library arrived in Athens, Georgia, in twenty-two crates during May of 1950.

From another letter of Hubert Adler (July 13, 1950), Professor Hodgson learned about Guido Adler's personal letters

51

and other documents which had survived the vicissitudes of the war
in the custody of Adler's former student Professor Leopold Nowak.
Again, Professor Hodgson arranged for the necessary funds through
an Atlanta foundation which requested to remain anonymous.
During February 1951 the University of Georgia and Hubert Adler
finalized the contract concerning the personal Adler papers, and in
early April of 1952 the university received these documents.[2]

The personal papers, including letters and other materials,
were organized and compiled by Edward R. Reilly in a provisional
index.[3]

Guido Adler was a highly respected personality on the
international music and art scene, and it is for this reason that his
extensive correspondence includes exchanges of letters with many
major figures of the time. As yet only Adler's celebrated correspondence with Gustav Mahler, his lifelong friend, has been
published.[4]

Guido Adler's correspondence with Arnold Schoenberg extended over one decade, from 1903-1913.[5] Most of the 38 letters
and cards concern themselves with professional matters and center
around Schoenberg's basso-continuo realizations for the *Denkmäler
der Tonkunst in Österreich*[6] and Schoenberg's cello cadenzas[7] for
the violoncello concerto by Georg Matthias Monn (1717-1750).[8]

Six of Schoenberg's letters to Adler have been omitted here
because they are of a strictly social nature (October 1, 1904; March
1, 1909; February 21, 1913 and three undated items).

The first contact occurred when Schoenberg approached
Adler in a letter dated Nov. 16, 1903 (see p. 61) referring to Karl
Weigl,[9] from whom Schoenberg had heard that Adler had ex-
pressed himself favorably about Schoenberg's work.

The five letters dated May 26, 1904; June 1, 1904; October
27, 1904, November 11, 1904; and January 7, 1905 (on pp. 63, 67,
69, 71) concern themselves with the raising of money for the
Association of Creative Musicians in Vienna,[10] and in particular
for the combined performance of the Philharmonic Orchestra with
the orchestra of the Concert Verein, sponsored by the Association.
The composition performed was Schoenberg's *Pelleas und Melisande*,
a work requiring an unusually large orchestra, which had its premiere performance in Vienna on January 26, 1906 under the direction of the composer.

At present there seem to be no known Schoenberg letters to Adler between January 7, 1905 (p. 71) and February 9, 1910 (p. 75). Schoenberg's undated letter (p. 73) included a request for work on basso-continuo realizations for the *Denkmäler*. As a consequence, this undated letter must predate the letter of February 9, 1910 (p. 75) in which Schoenberg reported to Adler the progress of his basso-continuo realizations. This evidence suggests that Schoenberg's professional relationship with Adler must have commenced early in the year 1910 at the latest. The letter of February 9, 1910 also implies that Adler had given Schoenberg the privilege of selecting the works for which he was to provide continuo realizations, and--for the first time--mentioned that Adler intended to send compositions by Monn and other masters to him.

Schoenberg's letter of January 16, 1911 (p. 77) is rather brusque, complaining of ignorance as to what his obligations might be for further work, and requesting a long-overdue confirmation of the oral agreement. Then Schoenberg goes on to lecture Adler about the latter's consideration for Mr. Fischer.[11] At the least, he told Adler, this recognition should also have been extended to him. Lastly, Schoenberg reprimanded Adler concerning his harsh language during their recent phone conversation. From the Adler-Fischer correspondence (Adler Collection, University of Georgia) it can be learned that at that time Fischer was beset with illness and personal problems, and that Adler's responses and support for him were generous. By July of 1911 (letter of July 8, 1911, p. 79) all seems to have been well again between Adler and Schoenberg.

An undated letter on p. 81 in the sequence of this book, must have been written before 1912 because of the reference to Monn's cello concerto and to that composer's own harpsichord version, both of which were published in vol. 39, II, *Denkmäler*, pp. 52-91 (see note 6). On the same grounds it can be assumed that the four compositions referred to by Schoenberg in his letter, are the four compositions for which he provided the basso-continuo realizations in this volume of the *Denkmäler* (pp. 32-40 and 52-115).

Of considerable interest is the next letter which is also undated (p. 83); it must also have been written before 1912 for the same reasons as given above for the earlier undated letter. Following Schoenberg's list of questions (p. 83; Schoenberg's page numbers are identical with those of vol. 39, II, *Denkmäler*), it is possible to provide an answer to his item I concerning the "smallprint" rests in the violoncello and bass with this quote from Fischer's critical notes of vol. 39, II, *Denkmäler*, p. 120:

> Die zahlreichen Abweichungen von III innerhalb
> des Begleitkörpers sind mit kleinsten Typen in den
> Notentext mit aufgenommen.

> [The numerous variants in the accompanying parts
> of III (Monn's harpsichord version of his own cello
> concerto, Staatsbibliothek Berlin, Preussischer
> Kulturbesitz, Ms. mus. 14,630-8) have been in-
> corporated in this edition in the smallest type of
> print.]

Fischer's statement also covers Schoenberg's last sentence in this letter (his number III), referring to the notes in small print found in the upper strings, which come from the Berlin Manuscript and would only apply to the harpsichord version. In point I of his letter, Schoenberg seems to have understood Fischer differently and more from the point of view of a composer. By his indication in this letter, Adler conceded that it would be possible to handle the lower strings in a more deliberate way, at times even omitting them altogether in order not to cover up the solo cello.

The second point (II) in Schoenberg's letter is well taken and demonstrates his musical sagacity. In Monn's cello or harpsichord concerto the cello solo part and right hand of the harpsichord solo are virtually identical, and the very few small differences serve only to make the material more idiomatic in the respective solo instruments. On the eighth note of the measure in question, Schoenberg concluded that the harpsichord version would be the more appropriate one because it did not change the harmony on that value, and he paralleled the upper part of the solo harpsichord figuration accordingly in the right hand of the continuo part (*Denkmäler der Tonkunst*, vol. 39, II, p. 73, last measure):

Adler seems to have been very pleased with Schoenberg's work
(letter of January 11, 1912, p. 85, and the beginning of the letter
dated January 13, 1912, p. 85). It is, therefore, all the more surprising to take note of this letter by Carl Prohaska,[12] written only
three months later:

W / 30 / 4 / 12/

Hochverehrter Herr Professor! ich danke Ihnen
vielmals für die Übersendung des letzten Bandes
der *Denkmäler*. Ich habe mir Herrn Schoenbergs
Arbeit angesehen und begreife Ihren Unmut voll-
kommen. Ich hoffe bald Gelegenheit zu haben mit
Ihnen darüber zu sprechen.
Mit dem Ausdruck vorzüglicher Hochachtung
Ergebenst, C. Prohaska

[translation]   Vienna. April 30, 1912
Esteemed Professor:
I thank you very much for sending me the last
volume of the *Denkmäler*. I have looked over Mr.
Schoenberg's work and I understand perfectly your
displeasure with it. Hopefully, I will have the
opportunity to speak with you about it soon.
With highest esteem,
Faithfully, C. Prohaska

At first Schoenberg's move to Berlin in 1911 was not altogether successful. After Schoenberg's poorly attended lectures at
the Stern Conservatory, he made his living as a free-lance artist and
set out to establish a conducting career. In this he met with some
success because of his growing international reputation, and even
the Viennese public had a change of heart concerning his music.
Nevertheless, Schoenberg turned down an offer from the Academy
in Vienna because he could not overcome his resentment for the
rejection of his music before he had left Vienna for Berlin. See his
letter of August 20, 1912, p. 91. In that same letter Schoenberg
asked Adler for some more work for the *Denkmäler der Tonkunst in
Österreich* or a recommendation to the *Deutsche Denkmäler der
Tonkunst*. More important for him than this, however, was his
request to Adler for a recommendation to Professor Kretzschmar[13] concerning a vacant teaching position at the Berlin Academy of Music. Adler obliged and promised to approach Kretzschmar in person at an opportune time because he thought this to be
more advisable than to write (letter of September 3, 1912, p. 93).

At the same time Adler also expressed his regret that Schoenberg had turned down the offer from Vienna and advised him to swallow his resentment if another possibility presented itself. Nevertheless, Schoenberg rejected this advice (letter of September 7, 1912, p. 93) because he would not be able to curb his anger, and--this is quite surprising--he would not find it possible to cope with the new enthusiasm of the Viennese public, feeling the need rather for the disapproval to which he was accustomed and through which he was coming to know himself. In conclusion, Schoenberg referred to Adler's recommendation in this letter for his teaching of harmony and counterpoint, suggesting that it would be even more appropriate to be recommended as a teacher in composition.

There are several letters between Schoenberg and Universal Edition which shed some light on Schoenberg's situation shortly before the outbreak of World War I. Schoenberg seemed to have approached director Hertzka[14] of Universal Edition about the possibility of his return to Vienna. In a letter of August 26, 1914 Hertzka expressed his willingness to enlist the help of Adler and other influential personalities concerning Schoenberg's return to Vienna, and even promised to try to find a rent-free apartment for Schoenberg, along with his wife and two children, for the duration of the war. In his next letter (December 9, 1914) Hertzka reported about the situation concerning the two vacancies at the Academy of Music: when Heuberger[15] was still alive, one of the positions was filled by Dr. Joseph Marx.[16] The other position, left vacant after the tenure of Siegfried Ochs,[17] was not to be filled at that time. Hertzka also reminded Schoenberg that his efforts to create a position for him were unsuccessful because of Schoenberg's earlier refusal to accept such a position when it was offered to him by the Academy of Music. Lastly, Hertzka reported that there was not the least prospect that Schoenberg would be employed as a choral director of the *Singakademie der Konzerthaus-Gesellschaft*. In Hertzka's next letter (December 30, 1914) he tried to console Schoenberg, suggesting that the situation in Vienna and Berlin was quite similar, reminding Schoenberg again, however, that it was not the fault of Vienna nor the Viennese that he had turned down the position earlier. Hertzka went on to inform Schoenberg about the possibility of becoming a second opera conductor in Breslau, indicating that director Runge of the city-theatre there would be interested in a not-too-expensive younger and unusual musician, and that he would be willing to invite Schoenberg to Breslau for an interview, all expenses paid. Hertzka's recommendation of Schoenberg was a glowing one (as he related to Schoenberg in the same letter), portraying Schoenberg as a unique personality with an absolute talent as a conductor and with much potential as an opera conductor. Also, Hertzka continued, the experiment would not be too risky for Runge: if it should work out, it would be sensational, but otherwise Runge would have the satisfaction of having attempted something unique even if it turned out just not to be feasible.

Most of the remaining letters were concerned with the performance of the cello concerto by Monn with Casals[18] as the soloist on November 19, 1913 at the occasion of the twentieth anniversary of the *Denkmäler*, and the solo cadenzas to be written by Schoenberg for the Monn concerto.

On March 9, 1913 (p. 97) Adler extended an invitation to Schoenberg to write one or two cadenzas for Monn's cello concerto as requested by Casals. In his response to this request (letter of March 13, 1913, p. 99) Schoenberg agreed enthusiastically to these cadenzas because he had had this intention himself earlier. At the same time Schoenberg explored the possibility of utilizing the cadenzas in a practical edition of the concerto which he hoped to be able to offer to a publisher. In the next letter one day later[19] (March 14, 1913, p. 101), Schoenberg had already come up with definite proposals concerning the cadenzas, and since Monn's concerto did not provide a place for such cadenzas, Schoenberg included a written-out musical alteration of Monn's score as a possible place for the insertion of a cadenza in the third movement (see Facsimile I on p. 103).

Adler offered Schoenberg a honorarium for his cadenzas even if Casals should decide not to use them in the anniversary concert of the *Denkmäler* on November 19, 1913. Schoenberg, in turn, seized the opportunity to extract independently maximum fees from the Universal Edition and the *Internationale Musikgesellschaft* (letter of May 15, 1913, p. 115). Quite understandably, Adler must have been annoyed by such a proposition. This is borne out by Schoenberg's reaction in his letter of May 31, 1913 (p. 117), in which he considered Adler's offer of 300 crowns as inappropriate (after having requested 500 crowns in his letter of May 15, 1913), also rejecting vehemently Adler's reprimand that Monn had had to content himself with far less.

   In Schoenberg's letter of June 15, 1913 to Universal Edition, he offered director Hertzka the separate publication of his basso-continuo realization of the Monn cello concerto in G minor (published in 1912 in vol. 39,II of *Denkmäler*), together with his cadenzas for 10% royalities with an advance of 500 marks. If Hertzka were interested, he would also be willing to make a practical edition with a piano reduction and cello solo for another 300 marks and royalities. Meanwhile (letter of July 27, 1913), Hertzka had authorized Mr. Szell[20] to make such an arrangement, and he hoped Schoenberg would have a look at it. Schoenberg refused to do so and complained to Hertzka that he should have waited for the fourteen days agreed upon after having offered it to him; he would himself have accepted it, since he could hardly afford to lose the money. In conclusion, Schoenberg excused Hertzka and stated that he would not pursue the matter further. In his letter of September 25, 1913 Schoenberg informed Hertzka that he had been working very hard on the Monn concerto, that he was sending along the first movement, and that he would meet the deadline of the following Friday with the rest, urging Hertzka to send the honorarium agreed upon immediately because of a financial obligation he had to meet on September 29th. From a letter of September 27, 1913, we learn that Hertzka obliged and sent 685 marks by telegraph. This last letter also referred to an awkward piano passage which Mr. von Wöss had revised.[21] Schoenberg's reaction to this interference was alluded to in Hertzka's letter of September 30, 1913, and the piano passage was not changed. The edition was published in 1914, but without the cadenzas.

   Schoenberg's recollection of "an Andante in E-flat Major in 4/4" referred to under his point 4 in the letter of January 13, 1912 (p. 85) may refer to an Andante E-flat Major in 4/4 called aria, which appears as the third movement of a *Partita a tre con Violino obligato* by Franz Tuma.[22]

   Adler's letter of January 15, 1912 (p. 87) confirmed that Schoenberg's four figured bass realizations *Denkmäler*, vol. 39, II, were in print and that Schoenberg's other realizations, now with Dr. Fischer, had been deferred.

II.S-A.o.1

Wien 16. November, 1903

Sehr geehrter Herr Professor, von Herrn Dr. Weigl erfuhr ich, dass Sie sich in günstigem Sinne über meine Arbeiten geäussert hätten. Diese angenehme Nachricht veranlasst mich, das Meinige dazu zu thun, um einem Wunsche, den ich schon länger gehabt, näherzutreten; dem Wunsche, Sie persönlich kennen zu lernen. Indem ich unbescheidener Weise voraussetze, dass Ihr Interesse an meinem Werk so weit geht, dass Sie ein Theilchen davon auch auf dessen Autor übertragen könnten, erlaube ich mir die Anfrage, wann ich mir erlauben darf, Sie zu besuchen.

     Einer freundlichen Antwort entgegensehend,
     empfehle ich mich mit vorzüglicher Hochachtung
     ergebenst Arnold Schönberg

Wien IX. Liechtensteinerstrasse 68/70 - II/22

II.S-A.o.2

Arnold Schönberg
Wien IX. Liechtensteinerstrasse 68/70   17 / 2. 1904

Sehr geehrter Herr Professor, ich erlaube mir Ihnen mitzutheilen, dass am 19. d[ieses] M[onats] (Freitag) im Tonkünstler Verein mein Sextett "Verklärte Nacht" aufgeführt wird. Da das wechselseitige "Zeithaben" und "Verhindertsein" verhängnisartig bemüht scheint eine Zusammenkunft zur Vorführung der Gurrelieder zu verhindern, wäre es mir sehr angenehm, wenn Sie einstweilen, wenigstens dieses Werk kennen lernen wollten. Wenn auch dieses Werk höchstens sagt, was ich vor 4 oder 5 Jahren angestrebt habe, und ich auch längst darüber hinaus bin, so ist doch vielleicht Manches darin, dass mir nicht ganz unglücklich scheint. Indem ich hoffe, Sie nicht allzu sehr [zu] enttäuschen, empfehle ich mich in vorzüglicher Hochachtung
     ergebenst Arnold Schönberg

II.S-A.t.1

Vienna, November 16, 1903

Esteemed Professor: I learned from Dr. Weigl that you spoke favorably concerning my work. This pleasing news encourages me to do my best in seeking to realize a desire which I have had for some time: the desire to meet you in person. Allowing myself the presumptuousness of assuming that your interest in my work extends so far that you might transfer a bit of it also to its author, I permit myself to inquire when I may call on you.

Looking forward to a favorable reply,
I remain with cordial regards,
faithfully Arnold Schönberg

Vienna IX. Liechtensteinerstrasse 68/70 - II/22

II.S-A.t.2

Arnold Schönberg
Vienna IX. Liechtensteinerstrasse 68/70   February 17, 1904

Esteemed Professor: Permit me to inform you that my Sextet *Verklärte Nacht* will be performed on the 19th of this month (Friday) in the Tonkünstler Verein.[23] Since alternating procrastination and obstructionism seem fatefully bent on preventing cooperation for the performance of the *Gurrelieder*, I would be very pleased if in the meantime you would at least be willing to get to know this work. Even if the work suggests at best what I strove for four or five years ago, and even if I have long since gone beyond it, still there are things in it that seem to me to be perhaps not too unfortunate.

With the expression of my hope that you may not be too disappointed, I remain yours with highest esteem,
Sincerely Arnold Schönberg

II.S-A.o.3

Arnold Schönberg
Wien
IX. Liechtensteinerstrasse 68/70   26 / 5. 1904

Verehrter Herr Professor, folgenden Sachverhalt habe ich Ihnen im
Auftrage der Vereinigung zu melden. Herr Docent Rietsch ist der
Schwiegersohn des Herrn Jos[ef] Eberle. Bei dem letztgenannten
hatte eine Ver[eins] Deputation schnorrend vorgesprochen. Vom
Urtheile seines Schwiegersohnes macht Herr Eberle es abhängig ob
und was er der Vereinigung zuwenden will. Verehrter Herr
Prof[essor], Sie haben sich schon so viele Beine abgelaufen und
angeschrieben für unsere Zwecke. Darf ich es wagen Sie zu bitten
das Urtheil des Herrn Rietsch in unserem Sinne zu beeinflussen,
damit er im Familienrath seines ehrsamen Herrn Schwiegerpapas
unserer Sache nützt.
        Ihnen stets dankbar, empfehle ich mich
        Ihr hochachtungsvoll ergebener Arnold Schönberg

II.S-A.o.4

Vereinigung schaffender Tonkünstler in Wien
Zuschriften sind zu richten an den Schriftführer
Oskar C. Posa,
Wien, VI/1,
Damböckgasse 2.   Wien, den 1. Juni 1904

Verehrter Herr Professor, es wird Sie vielleicht interessieren zu
erfahren, dass die Philharmoniker (vorläufig noch unoffiziell!) ihre
Zustimmung zur Mitwirkung gegeben haben. Sie verlangen
allerdings ein enorm hohes Honorar, das die Kosten der Konzerte
ungemein höher stellt, aber das darf keine Rolle spielen. Bezahlen
wird es doch jemand; also kommt es auf die paar Tausend Kronen
mehr oder weniger nicht an.
        Es wird sich nun darum handeln Herrn Direktor Mahler
zum Entgegenkommen zu veranlassen, hauptsächlich, was die Ein-

II.S-A.t.3

Arnold Schönberg
Vienna IX.
Liechtensteinerstrasse 68/70   May 26, 1904

Esteemed Professor:
I must relate to you the following circumstances on behalf of the
association. Lecturer Rietsch[24] is the son-in-law of Mr. Jos[ef]
Eberle. The latter had been approached by an association dele-
gation begging Mr. Eberle for a contribution. Mr. Eberle will rely
on the judgement of his son-in-law concerning his decision if and
how much he will contribute to the association.[25]   Esteemed
Professor, you ran yourself ragged and wrote so much on our behalf.
Could I dare to ask you to influence the opinion of Mr. Rietsch in
our favor, so that he will be supportive of our concern at the family
council of his honorable father-in-law.
       Always grateful to you, I remain
       faithfully yours, Arnold Schönberg

II.S-A.t.4

Association of Creative Musicians in Vienna
Letters to be directed to the secretary
Oscar C. Posa
Vienna VI/1
Damböckgasse 2   Vienna, June 1, 1904

Esteemed Professor:
It will   perhaps interest you to learn that the Philharmonic
Orchestra has agreed (as yet unofficially) to participate. However,
they demand an enormously high honorarium, which raised the cost
for the concerts much higher, but this should not matter. Somebody will pay for it anyway, and so a few thousand crowns more or
less should not matter.
       The question is now how to prevail upon Director Mahler,
especially concerning the scheduling of rehearsals. I hope that this

theilung der Proben anbelangt. Ich hoffe, das wird nicht allzu
schwer sein und ein Wort von Ihnen [wird] dabei eine grosse Rolle
spielen.
    Jedenfalls ist es angenehm, dass wir dieser Sache ledig sind.
Das Geld wird sich sicher finden.
    Ich empfehle mich Ihnen mit vorzüglicher Hochachtung
ergebenst Arnold Schönberg

II.S-A.o.5

Arnold Schönberg
Wien
IX. Liechtensteinerstrasse 68/70   9 / 6. 1904

Verehrter Herr Professor, ich danke Ihnen herzlichst für die
freundliche Zuwendung der Theoriestunde. Es zeigt sich, dass Ihre
Empfehlung direct Wunder wirkt, denn die Herren (Vater und
Sohn) haben mich gleich vor unserer Abmachung [?] taxfrei zum
Professor ernannt, worauf ich mich für verpflichtet hielt ein etwas
höheres Honorar zu fordern. Als Bohème, in früheren Zeiten,
hätte ich übrigens diese Geschichte viel lustiger erzählt.
    Unsere Vereinigungs Angelegenheit steht insofern schon
wieder gut, als wir mit dem Concert-Verein ein gutes Abkommen
treffen können. Die Philharmoniker haben uns da entschieden
genützt; deren Zusage dürfte dem Concert-Verein Angst gemacht
haben.
    Ich empfehle mich Ihnen auf das Beste und zeichne mit
vorzüglicher Hochachtung ergebenst Arnold Schönberg

will be not too difficult, and a word from you could be of great importance in this regard.

At any rate, it is very pleasant that we are free of this concern. The money will certainly be found.

I remain yours with highest esteem,
faithfully Arnold Schönberg

II.S-A.t.5

Arnold Schönberg
Vienna
IX. Liechtensteinerstrasse 68/70   June 9, 1904

Esteemed Professor:
I thank you with all my heart for the kind mediation concerning the theory lesson. It proves that your recommendation works wonders, for the gentlemen (father and son) appointed me tax-free on the spot and before our settlement, to the rank of professor, whereupon I felt obliged to ask for a somewhat higher honorarium. As a Bohemian, in earlier days, I would have related this story much more humorously.

The matter concerning our association is well insofar as we could reach a good agreement with the Concert Society.[26] The Philharmonic Orchestra was definitely of use to us, for their agreement must have alarmed the Concert Society.

With best wishes I remain with deepest esteem,
most faithfully   Arnold Schönberg

II.S-A.o.6

Vereinigung schaffender Tonkünstler in Wien.
Zuschriften sind zu richten an den Schriftführer
Oscar C. Posa,
Wien, VI/1,
Damböckgasse 2.   Wien, den 27. October 1904

Sehr geehrter Herr Professor, ich werde veranlassen, dass Ihnen
Ihre Karten zugeschickt werden.
       Erlauben Sie nun, dass ich auf eine Angelegenheit zurück-
komme, die wir schon vor einigen Monaten besprochen haben.
Nämlich die Rothschild Affäre! Ich muss Ihnen dazu sagen, dass
wir zwar nach einer etwas künstlichen Berechnung bei einem
mittelmässigen Erfolg unsere Konzerte materiell gedeckt haben.
Aber für den Fall, als wir etwa einen vollständigen Misserfolg haben
sollten, sind wir ganz unterdeckt.   Dieses Risiko haben wir im
ersten Begeisterungstaumel gerne übernommen.   Nun aber, da die
Zahlungen sich häufen und die Eingänge nicht zahlreicher werden,
wird uns, obwohl wir noch <u>lange</u> nicht nothleidend sind, doch angst
und bange, wenn wir an einen eventuellen ungünstigen Ausgang
denken.
       Deshalb möchte ich Sie nun an Ihre uns seinerzeit für den
Fall einer derartigen Noth gemachte Zusage erinnern.   Sie verspra-
chen uns damals, etwa im Juli oder August Rothschild in unserem
Interesse anzugehen.   Heute nun ist--wenn nicht einige Allzuängst-
liche unseres Vorstandes die Courage ganz verlieren sollen--der
Zeitpunkt gekommen, wo wir sehr darauf angewiesen wären, eine
derartige möglichst hohe Subvention zu erhalten.
       Ich habe also den Auftrag, Sie, sehr geehrter Herr Profes-
sor, namens des Vorstandes zu bitten, in dieser Angelegenheit,
dasjenige zu unternehmen, was Ihnen, bei Ihrem Interesse für unser
Unternehmen, am geeignetsten scheint.   Es ist wohl überflüssig zu
erwähnen, dass es uns nicht nur <u>lieb</u> wäre, wenn sich eine derartige
Angelegenheit rasch entscheidet, sondern dass wir geradezu es <u>drin-
gend nöthig haben</u> bald,   sehr bald eine hoffentlich günstige
Entscheidung zu erfahren.   Ich bin ohnedies unter uns Allen Der-
jenige, der alles am rosigsten sieht.   Für die anderen stellt sich die
Zukunft viel schwärzer dar--hoffentlich behalte ich recht; aber was
geschieht, wenn die Anderen den besseren Blick gehabt hätten?!?

II.S-A.t.6

Association of Creative Musicians in Vienna
Letters to be directed to the secretary
Oscar C. Posa
Vienna VI/1
Damböckgasse 2   Vienna, October 27, 1904

Esteemed Professor:
I will arrange to have tickets sent to you.

Allow me now to return to a concern which we have already discussed some months ago, namely the Rothschild matter! Concerning this I must tell you that according to a somewhat cursory estimate we have covered the expense for our concerts if they are moderately successful. But in the event of total failure, we would be completely ruined. This risk we accepted gladly in our first enthusiastic frenzy. But now as more payments are due and receipts do not increase, we are, although still _far_ from needy, becoming terribly frightened when we think about a possible unfavorable outcome.

For this reason I would like to remind you of the promise which you made us concerning such a possibly unfavorable situation. At that time you promised us to approach Rothschild in July or August on our behalf. Now today--if some of the overly anxious members of our executive board are not to lose their courage completely--the time has come when we depend very heavily on receiving the highest possible subsidy.

In the name of the executive board I have now been instructed, esteemed Professor, to ask you to take such steps in this matter as you deem necessary in the light of your interest in our endeavor. I suppose that it is unnecessary to mention that it would not only be _good_ for us if such a matter could be settled quickly, but that it is _downright urgent_ to learn very soon, let us hope, of a favorable decision. At any rate, among all of us I am the one who views everything in the rosiest light. To the others the future appears blacker. I do hope that I am right, but what will happen if the others had the more realistic view?!?

Excuse us, Professor, for clinging to you! What we could do ourselves we have done, but now here our strength and influence have reached their limit. And since we have had the good fortune

Verzeihen Sie, Herr Professor, dass wir uns an Sie hängen! Was wir alleine thun konnten, haben wir allein gethan; aber hier versagen unsere Kräfte und unser Einfluss. Und, da wir nun das Glück gehabt haben, in Ihnen einen einflussreichen Gönner gefunden zu haben, der für unsere Sache nicht weniger warm empfindet, als wir selbst, so halte ich es geradezu für unsere Pflicht, diese Möglichkeit nicht ungenutzt zu lassen, und finde uns vollkommen entschuldigt durch die Liebenswürdigkeit, mit der Sie, durch Förderung unserer Absichten, unsere Anmassung bisher gutgeheissen haben.

Indem ich Ihnen im Vorhinein aufs herzlichste danke, empfehle ich mich aufs beste und zeichne in vorzüglicher Hochachtung ergebenst   Arnold Schönberg

Arnold Schönberg
Wien IX. Liechtensteinerstrasse 68/70

II.S-A.o.7

11 / 11. 1904

Verehrter Herr Professor, die erste freie Minute benutze ich um Ihnen in grösster Eile einstweilen auf herzlichste für Ihre gütige Fürsprache zu danken. Da wir uns doch heute bei Mahler sehen, hoffe ich Gelegenheit zu mehr daran zu finden.

Ich empfehle mich mit der vorzüglichsten Hochachtung
Ihr ganz ergebener Arnold Schönberg

Arnold Schönberg
Wien IX. Liechtensteinerstrasse 68/70

to have found in you an influential patron, who feels no less warmly
for our concerns than we do ourselves, I consider it absolutely our
duty not to leave this opportunity neglected; and I feel ourselves
completely absolved because of the kindness with which you, by
furthering our purposes, have approved of our presumption so far.

 Thanking you in advance with all my heart, I remain
with my best wishes and highest esteem.
Most faithfully Arnold Schönberg

Arnold Schönberg
Vienna IX. Liechtensteinerstrasse 68/70

II.S-A.t.7

November 11, 1904

Esteemed Professor: In greatest haste I take the first free minute
to thank you with all my heart for you kind intercession.[27] Since
we shall meet at Mahler's today, I hope for the opportunity to
express this much more fully.

 I remain yours with highest esteem,
  yours most faithfully Arnold Schoenberg

Arnold Schönberg
Vienna IX. Liechtensteinerstrasse 68/70

II.S-A.o.8

Arnold Schönberg
Wien IX. Liechtensteinerstrasse 68/70   7 / 1. 1905

Verehrter Herr Professor, wenn es sich um jenen R[othschild]
handelt der in der Renn[?]gasse sein Palais hat, so kann ich Ihnen
darüber nur das folgende berichten: Herr Grindl [?] und ich waren
dort; der Prokurist empfahl uns, die Vermittlung Mahlers zu
verwenden, da er uns sonst wenig Hoffnung machen könne. Wir
haben das Mahler mitgetheilt und er hat sich nun in der letzten
Zeit neuerdings bereit erklärt an R[othschild] demnächst heran-
zutreten. Das ist Alles, was ich darüber weiss. Die Sache liegt also
bei Mahler.
       Dem [?] andere[n] R[othschild] wurde ein Gesuch über-
reicht, auf das wir bisher keine Antwort haben.
       Herzlichen Dank für Ihre freundliche Fürsorge.
       Ich empfehle mich in vorzüglicher Hochachtung
                              Arnold Schönberg

II.S-A.o.9

Arnold Schönberg
Wien IX. Liechtensteinerstrasse 68/70   [no date]

Verehrter Herr Professor, ich muss Ihnen leider mittheilen, dass es
mir nicht möglich sein wird an dem (hoffentlich noch nicht
angekündigten) Vortrag in der Internationalen Musikgesellschaft
theilzunehmen--wenigstens nicht aktiv. Ich habe soviel zu thun, zu
arbeiten, dass, wenn ich jetzt Zeit hätte, ich sie benutzen müsste um
mich auszuruhen, weil ich sehr überarbeitet und nervös bin. Aber
ich habe noch immer weiter und auf lange hinaus zu arbeiten, also
muss ich weiter arbeiten, obwohl ich mich gern ein bischen erholen
würde. An eigene Arbeiten kann ich schon garnicht denken. Ich
hätte sehr viel Lust wieder einmal zu komponieren und komme
nicht dazu.
       Unvorbereitet oder ungenügend vorbereitet kann ich die
Sache absolut nicht machen. Und ich müsste gering eine Woche
opfern um mich auf das vorzubereiten, das ich eventuell gerne

II.S-A.t.8

Arnold Schönberg
Vienna IX. Liechtensteinerstrasse 68/70   January 7, 1905

Esteemed Professor:
If it concerns that particular R[othschild] who has his palace in the
Renn[?]gasse, I can report to you only the following: Mr. Grindl
[?] and I were there; the clerk recommended to us to use the
mediation of Mahler, for he could not give us much hope otherwise.
We told Mahler about this, and he has agreed lately to approach
R[othschild] shortly. This is all I know about this, and the matter
is now up to Mahler.
        The other R[othschild] was presented a petition for which
we have not received an answer as yet.
        Cordial thanks for your kind concern.
        I remain yours with highest esteem Arnold Schönberg

II.S-A.t.9

Arnold Schönberg
Vienna IX. Liechtensteinerstrasse 68/70[28]   [no date]

Esteemed Professor:
        I am sorry to have to inform you that it will not be possible
for me to participate in the lecture (hopefully not yet announced)
of the International Society of Music, or at least not actively. I
have so much to do, to work on, that if I had the time now I would
have to use it to rest; for I am very overworked and nervous. Yet
for a long time to come I face a continuing work-load. Therefore,
I have to keep on striving, even though I would rather like to
recover a little. I myself cannot even contemplate composing; I
would like very much to compose once again, but I do not get to it.
        Unprepared, or not sufficiently prepared, I absolutely
cannot do this task, and I would have to devote at least a week to
it to prepare myself for what I possibly might wish to say.

sagen würde.

Ich erlaube mir daher den Vorschlag zu machen, dass Sie die Sache fürs nächste Jahr lassen. Zemlinsky und ich könnten uns im Sommer eingehend vorbereiten und den Fragen vielleicht auch etwas tiefer nachgehen, als es jetzt möglich wäre. Und ich denke es wäre dann am besten, die Diskussion gleich am Anfang der Saison zu veranstalten, wo man dann mit frischen Kräften und beruhigten Nerven daran geht.

Ich hoffe, verehrter Herr Professor, Sie sind über meine Absage nicht bös. Aber, die Sache hat doch nur dann Sinn, wenn sie gut, gediegen gemacht wird, nicht journalistisch oberflächlich. Und ich fühle mich augenblicklich gar nicht geistig potent genug, als dass ich mit Beruhigung etwas derartiges mir Ungewohntes unternehmen könnte.

Ich empfehle mich Ihnen auf das Beste und bin mit vorzüglicher Hochachtung

Ihr ganz ergebener Arnold Schönberg

II.S-A.o.10

Arnold Schönberg
Wien IX. Liechtensteinerstrasse 68/70   [no date]

Sehr geehrter Herr Professor, ich habe heuer etwas weniger Schüler, was ich auf die vielen neuen und neuesten Konservatorien zurückführe, und möchte Sie deshalb ersuchen, Ihren Hörern gegebenenfalls zu empfehlen, bei mir Stunden zu nehmen. Sie wissen ja was man bei mir speziell in Kontrapunkt und Harmonielehre lernt. Abgesehen davon, dass ich wohl der einzige modernste Lehrer in Wien bin! Abgesehen davon bin ich ja doch einer der ganz Wenigen, die einem wirklich zeigen könnten wie ein Continuo auszuführen wäre. Ich meine vom Standpunkt künstlerischer Schönheit und musikalisch-formeller Durcharbeitung und Glätte. Ich glaube also, dass Ihre Empfehlung Ihren Schülern nichts Ungünstiges brächte.

Ausserdem möchte ich mir erlauben Sie an Ihre Absicht mir Continuo Bearbeitungen für die Denkmäler zu verschaffen,

In view of this, I am taking the liberty to propose to you the postponement of this project until next year. Zemlinsky and I could prepare ourselves thoroughly during the summer and possibly follow up these questions more thoroughly than would be possible now. And I think that it would then be best to arrange this discussion right at the beginning of the season when one can approach the task with renewed strength and calmer nerves.

I do hope, esteemed Professor, that you are not displeased because of my refusal. This task, however, makes sense only if it is done thoroughly and not in a superficial, journalistic way. And I feel at this time that I have not sufficient intellectual stamina to undertake something this unusual for me with confidence.

With my best I remain cordially with highest esteem your truly faithful Arnold Schönberg

II.S-A.t.10

Arnold Schönberg
Vienna IX. Liechtensteinerstrasse 68/70   [no date]

Esteemed Professor:
This year I have rather fewer students, a fact that I explain through the many new and even newer conservatories. For this reason I would like to request that, if the occasion arises, you recommend that your students take lessons with me. You already know what one will learn from me, especially in counterpoint and harmony-- apart from the fact that I am certainly the single most up-to-date teacher in Vienna--and apart also from the fact that I am one of the very few who could really demonstrate how a continuo ought to be realized; I mean here from the point of view of artistic beauty and musical workmanship and polish. Thus I believe that your recommendation would lead to nothing disadvantageous to your students.

Moreover, I permit myself to remind you of your intention to procure for me some continuo realizations for the *Denkmäler*.

erinnern.

Da ich heuer mehr freie Zeit habe, aber diese nicht zum Komponieren verwenden kann, sondern zum Geldverdienen ausnutzen muss, wäre ich wohl in der Lage, so was rasch zu machen. Ich hoffe, Sie sind so freundlich in dieser Hinsicht an mich zu denken und ich danke Ihnen im Voraus herzlichst dafür.

Mit ergebenster Hochachtung
ergebenst Arnold Schönberg

II.S-A.o.11

XIII. Hietzinger Hauptstrasse 113   9 / 2. 1910

Sehr geehrter Herr Professor, die Auswählung der zu bearbeitenden Stücke wird mir durch Ihre Bedingung: österreichisches! etwas erschwert. Öfters finde ich ein Stück dessen Thema man österreichisch nennen könnte, aber in der (meist sequenzierenden) Fortsetzung verliert sich das bald wieder. So habe ich dann bis jetzt nicht viel Entscheidendes gewählt. Ich war übrigens durch viele Besorgungen und geschäftliches verhindert sehr oft daran zu arbeiten. Immerhin habe ich bei einigen Stücken zu arbeiten angefangen und glaube, dass ich sie machen werde. Gerne hätte ich den Pack noch länger zur Auswahl. Vielleicht finde ich bei öfterer Durchsicht noch mehr. Vielleicht geht das doch. Wenn nicht so werde ich Ihrem Diener diejenigen Sachen übergeben, die ich bestimmt nicht machen werde. Bitte also um fr[eun]dl[iche] Nachricht wann Sie den Diener schicken wollen. Soll ich das was bis jetzt fertig gearbeitet ist gleich druckfertig machen? In dem Falle müssen Sie mir noch ein paar Tage Zeit lassen. Denn mit dem Bleistift (wie Sie es wünschen) schreibt man immer etwas weniger sorgfältig und ich liefere gerne gute Manuskripte um dann mit der Korrektur wenig zu tun zu haben.

Wenn Sie mir den Monn und anderes schicken wollen, wäre mir das sehr lieb. Abwechselung ist bei so was sehr angenehm. Mit hochachtungsvoller Empfehlung ergebenst
Arnold Schönberg

Since I have more free time this year, which I cannot utilize for composing but must rather use to earn a living, I would be in the position to do something like that rather expeditiously.

I do hope that you will be so kind as to consider me in this matter, and I thank you most heartily for it in advance.

With most devoted esteem, most respectfully
Arnold Schönberg

II.S-A.t.11

XIII. Hietzinger Hauptstrasse 113   February 9, 1910

Esteemed Professor:

Selecting the pieces to be worked on has been made somewhat more difficult by your stipulation that they be Austrian. Frequently I find a composition with a theme which could be considered Austrian, but this disappears soon in the (general sequential) continuation. Thus I have yet to select much of distinction. In any case, I was prevented from doing much work on it because of many cares and business concerns. Nevertheless, I have begun to work on several pieces, and I expect to complete them. I would like to keep the packet longer to make further selections. Perhaps with further examination I shall find even more; that may still be possible. If not, I shall turn over to your servant the things which I am certain I will not do. Therefore, please let me know when you intend to send the servant. Shall I prepare for printing what I have completed up to now? In that case you must give me a few more days; for in working with pencil (as you wish) one always writes somewhat less carefully, and I do like to submit good manuscripts so that I will have little left to do on the proofs.

If you can send me the Monn and other things, I would appreciate it very much. Where such things are concerned, variety is so very desirable.

With respectful esteem, most faithfully
Arnold Schönberg

II.S-A.o.12

Arnold Schönberg   Telefon   4
Wien XIII.   H 472
Hietzinger Hauptstrasse 113   16 / 1. 1911

Sehr geehrter Herr Professor; Montag gab ich Ihrem Diener drei
fertige Stücke. Heute liegt noch eins fertig bei mir; Herr Fischer
schreibt, dass der Diener es heute holen wird.

Früher schon, habe ich Ihnen, resp[ektive] Herrn Fischer
4 fertige und ein halbfertiges Stück gegeben. Dieses halbfertige
könnte ich ja noch rasch fertig machen. Jedenfalls möchte ich nun
endlich gerne wissen, <u>wie viel ich noch zu arbeiten verpflichtet bin</u>.

Ich verstehe nicht, warum Sie das nicht anerkennen wollen
(<u>obwo[h]l</u> wir es <u>mündlich</u> **ausgemacht** hatten) dass ich ja beiläufig
wissen muss, was ich noch zu arbeiten habe. Ich habe ja noch etwas
<u>anderes</u> auch noch zu tun und muss mit meiner Zeit haushalten!
Wenn ich mirs einteilen kann, bringe ich Vieles fertig. Aber ich
kann nicht gerade dann arbeiten, wenn man es verlangt. Ich muss
ja schliesslich auch leben. Und soviel Rücksicht, wie auf den Herrn
Fischer, hätten Sie wo[h]l auch auf mich haben können! Mein
Komponieren ist ja vielleicht doch auch [?] etwas wert!

Ich will es dahingestellt sein lassen, ob Sie berechtigt waren,
mir in so schroffem Tone zu antworten, als ich letzthin telefonierte.
Immerhin könnten Sie erwägen, dass ich ja abgesehen davon, dass
ich keiner jener jungen Leute bin, die noch studieren, immerhin
schon etwas geleistet habe, was man beachten darf. Auch wenn man
die Gegenwart nicht schätzt.

Hochachtungsvoll Arnold Schönberg

Bitte um Nachricht:
Was habe ich noch zu arbeiten?

II.S-A.t.12

Arnold Schönberg   Telephone 4
Vienna XIII.   H 472
Hietzinger Hauptstrasse 113   January 16, 1911

Esteemed Professor:
Monday I gave your servant three completed pieces. Today yet another completed piece is ready at my place. Mr. Fischer writes that the servant will pick it up today.

I have already previously given you, through Mr. Fischer, four completed and one half-completed piece. This half-completed one I could still finish up quickly. In any case I would like finally to know <u>how many more I am obligated to do</u>.

I do not understand why you will not recognize (<u>even though</u> we **agreed** orally) that I do need to know what else I have to work on. After all I still have <u>other things</u> to do, and must be economical with my time! And when I am able to organize my time, I can get so much done! But I cannot work exactly when one demands it of me. After all, I also have to live. And you could have extended as much consideration towards me as you did toward Mr. Fischer! My composing perhaps may also be of some value!

I will leave it undecided as to whether you were justified in answering me in such a harsh tone when I phoned you recently. You could, at least, have taken into consideration that, beyond the fact that I am not one of these young people who are still students, I have already accomplished something, a matter of which one should take notice even if one does not value the present.

Respectfully Arnold Schönberg

Please let me know:
What do I still have to work on?

II.S-A.o.13

Arnold Schönberg
Wien XIII. Hietzinger Hauptstrasse 113   8 / 7. 1911

Sehr geehrter Herr Professor, anbei die gewünschten Stellen. Bitte
zu wählen, was Sie brauchen können. Aus den Quartetten habe ich
einige Stellen bezeichnet. Wenn Ihnen davon etwas passt, so bitte
ich die Stelle zu bezeichnen, dann schreibe ich sie Ihnen heraus.
Meine Kammersymphonie hat Fried, deshalb konnte ich daraus
keine Stelle entnehmen.
          Ich muss Ihnen nochmals herzlichst danken für die Hilfe.
Ich bin sehr froh über Ihre freundliche Gesinnung und es tut mir
sehr wohl Ihnen dafür danken zu können.
          Ihr ganz ergebener Arnold Schönberg

II.S-A.o.14 [post card]
Arnold Schönberg
Wien XIII. Hietzinger Hauptstrasse 113   4. Nov. 1911

Sehr geehrter Herr Professor, es war mir unmöglich Ihnen zu
telefonieren. Gienge das nicht, dass vielleicht Herr Dr. Fischer, mit
dem ich ohnedies über Einiges plaudern möchte, mich besucht um
das Nähere abzumachen. Er kann Ihre Aufträge bringen und erhält
dann meine Antwort. Uebrigens: ich bin bereit die Sachen zu
machen, die ich habe. Allerdings hoffe ich noch immer, dass ich für
eines oder das andere ein besseres Stück werde einschieben können.
Herr Fischer trifft mich Dienstag und Freitag ab 2 Uhr zu Hause.
Er soll sich aber jedenfalls anmelden. In diesem Fall kann es auch
Vormittag sein. - Es wäre mir furchtbar schwer in den beiden
folgenden Wochen einen freien Nachmittag zu finden um zu Ihnen
zu kommen.
          Mit ergebenen Grüssen hochachtungsvoll Arnold Schönberg

II.S-A.t.13

Arnold Schönberg
ViennaX III. Hietzinger Hauptstrasse 113   July 8, 1911

Esteemed Professor:
Attached are the required passages. Please select what you may be
able to use. I have marked several passages from the quartets. In
case there is something here which suits you, please mark the
passage, and then I shall copy it out for you.[29] Fried[30] has my
Kammersymphonie, and for this reason I was unable to select a
passage from it.
    I would like to thank you again with all my heart for the
help. I am very happy about your kind sentiments and I am very
pleased to be able to thank you for them.
        Your very devoted Arnold Schönberg

II.S-A.t.14 [postcard]

Arnold Schönberg
Vienna XIII. Hietzinger Haupstrasse   November 4, 1911

Esteemed Professor:
It has been impossible for me to phone you. Would it not be
feasible perhaps, for Dr. Fischer, with whom I would like to talk
about several things anyway, to visit me in order to settle the
details? He can bring your instructions and then receive my answer.
By the way, I am willing to do the things I now have. I still do
hope, however, that I will be able to replace one or another with a
better piece. Mr. Fischer will find me at home on Tuesdays and
Fridays after two o'clock. Even so, though, he should make an
appointment. In this case it could also be in the morning. During
the next two weeks it would be frightfully difficult for me to find a
free afternoon to visit you.
        With devoted regards, respectfully Arnold Schönberg

II.S-A.o.15

Arnold Schönberg
Wien, XIII.   Telefon N. 4
Hietzinger Hauptstrasse 113   H.472   [no date]

Sehr geehrter Herr Professor,
ich sollte doch Fortsetzung erhalten, und Herr Fischer sollte zu mir
kommen? Ja ich bitte, muss ich unötigerweise Zeit verlieren. Ich
meine: müssen Sie mirs schwer machen?   Giebts da keine Er-
leichterungen? Ergebenst Arnold Schönberg

      Ich sende drei fertige Stücke. Eines, mit dem ich nichts
anzufangen weiss, weil da eine Unklarheit vorliegt, und weil es mir
gar nicht gefällt, sende ich retour.
      Es sind aber 4 Manuskripte
                  Ergebenst D. O.
respektive 5.

Denn das Cellokonzert hatte ich auch als Klavierkonzert!

II.S-A.t.15

Arnold Schönberg
Vienna III.   Telephone N. __4__
Hietzinger Hauptstrasse 113   H.472   [no date]

Esteemed Professor:
Was I supposed to receive the next installment, and was Mr. Fischer
supposed to see me? Indeed, I ask you, must I lose time for no
reason? I am wondering why you have to make this so difficult for
me? Is there no relief?
     Faithfully Arnold Schönberg

     I send three completed pieces. Another I return because
I do not know what to do with it due to an ambiguity, and also because I really do not care for it at all.
     There are, however, __4__ manuscripts
          Faithfully A. Sch. [the above]
     Actually __5__,

     Since I also have the piano version [Monn's own transfor-
mation into a harpsichord concerto] of the cello concerto!

II.S-A.o.16   [no date]
Verehrter Herr Professor: ein paar Fragen, die sich mir unterwegs
ergaben. Bitte um Antwort
    I.) Seite 54, II System   1. u[nd] 2. Takt ferner
        55   I   3. u[nd] 4 Takt
in <u>Basso</u> (V[io]l[on]c[e]ll[o] u[nd] B[as]so) sind Pausen klein ein-
gezeichnet.
    Verlangt es der "Stil" dass Vcll und Bso stets mit dem Con-
tinuo zusammen gehen?   Oder weisen nicht diese Pausen darauf
hin, dass (insbesondere bei einem Vcll Concert!) diese leicht
deckenden Instrumente gelegentlich wegbleiben? Ich würde ebenso
instrumentieren!!
    Wenn ich sie weglassen kann (bei meiner Ausgabe!) dann
müsste ich stellenweise den Continuo ändern. Ich bezeichne solche
Stellen mit folgendem Zeichen: ⊙   **freigestellt** [*]
    II) Mir kommt die Cello-figur Seite 73, II. System, Takt 3
unwahrscheinlich vor.   Ich halte dagegen die gleiche Figur (im
anderen Rhytmus) im Solo-Klavier für richtig! Sind Sie meiner
Meinung? Im Cello das scheint bloss ein Schreibfehler zu sein.

                                                  ja [*]
    III) Ich denke die kleinen Noten in den Streichern beziehen
sich hauptsächlich ausnahmslos [das letzte Wort in Adlers Hand]
auf das Klavier-Konzert?   **ja** [*]
[* Adler's comments]

II.S-A.o.17   6 / 11. 1911

Arnold Schönberg
Wien XIII. Hietzinger Hauptstrasse 113

Sehr geehrter Herr Professor, es ist hoffentlich kein allzugrosses
Malheur, wenn ich das Korrekturenlesen bis nach dem 28.Januar
verschiebe. Ich habe an diesem Tage hier ein Konzert und die
Proben und sonstigen Vorbereitungen dafür, nehmen meine ganze
Zeit in Anspruch.   Sollten Sie aber mit dieser kleinen Verschie-
bung nicht einverstanden sein, dann bitte ich um umgehende
Nachricht: ich tue dann was ich irgend kann um früher fertig zu
werden. Mit ergebenen und hochachtungsvollen Grüssen
                            Ihr Arnold Schönberg

II.S-A.t.16   [no date]
Esteemed Professor: a few questions which have occurred to me in
the meantime. Please reply.
    I.) Page 54, 2nd system, 1st and 2nd measures, furthermore
        55, 1st system, 3rd and 4th measures.
Rests are given in small print in the <u>Basso</u> (V[iolon]c[e]ll[o] and
B[as]so). Does the "style" require that the Vcl and Bass always go
together in   the continuo?   Or do these rests not suggest that
(especially in a cello concerto!) these instruments, which cover each
other so readily, may be omitted at times?   I would use such
instrumentation myself!!
      If I could omit them in my edition, then I would have to alter
the continuo at certain places. I mark these places as follows: ⊙
                                                   either way [*]
      II) I consider the cello figuration page 73, second system,
measure three, as unlikely. In contrast to this, I consider the same
figuration (in a different rhythm) in the solo clavier as correct.
Would you agree with me? In the cello part this seems to be only
a writing mistake.   **yes** [*]
      III) I think the notes in small print in the strings refer mainly,
without exception [the last two words are Adler's addition] to the
piano concerto.   **yes** [*]
[*] Adler's comments

II.S-A.t.17   November 6, 1911

Arnold Schönberg
Vienna XIII. Hietzinger Hauptstrasse 113

Esteemed Professor:
I do hope that it is not too much of an inconvenience if I postpone
the reading of the proofs until after January 28th. On that day I
have a concert here and the rehearsals and other preparations for
it occupy my entire time. Should you, however, not agree with
this little postponement, please let me know immediately, and I
will then do whatever I can to complete it earlier.
With devoted and respectful regards,
        Yours, Arnold Schönberg

II.A-S.o.1

XIX,1.
Cottage
Lannerstrasse 9   Wien 11. I. 12.

Sehr geehrter Herr!

Sende gleichz[eitig]: x Bd rekom: die 4 von Ihnen mit
B[asso] C[ontinuo] ausgearbeiteten Stücke mit dem Ersuchen um
Korrektur,be[sonders] mache ich auf die Stelle im Divertimento
letzte Seite(43) Zeile 1 u[nd] 2 wegen der Schlüssel aufmerksam.
Ihre Bearbeitung macht mir Freude, sie ist von Phantasie erfüllt.

Gerne hörte ich wie es Ihnen geht. Es thut mir leid, dass
Sie von Wien gingen - hoffentlich nicht für immer! Bitte um rasche
Erledigung. Herzlichst grüsst Ihr
                    auf[richtig] er[gebener] Guido Adler

II.S-A.o.18

Arnold Schönberg, Berlin-Zehlendorf-Wannseebahn
Machnower Chaussee, Villa Lepcke.   13 / 1. 1912

Sehr geehrter Herr Professor, ich wollte Ihnen schon vor längerer
Zeit schreiben. Insbesondere weil ich gehört hatte, dass Sie sich
sehr lebhaft für meine Angelegenheiten interessierten. Und auch
weil ich mich freute, dass, wie man mir schrieb, Ihnen meine
Continuos gefallen. Aber so viele Angelegenheiten, die ich
betreiben muss, ohne einstweilen günstige Resultate zu erzielen,
hinderten mich daran.

Was nun die Korrekturen anbelangt, so bitte ich Sie drin-
genst mir

1.) die Manuskripte zu senden. Ich kann ohne diese Vorlage
kaum arbeiten. Denn der Stich scheint, wie mir eine flüchtige
Durchsicht zeigte **äusserst** fehlerhaft zu sein. Fehler, die ich ohne
das Manuskript kaum enträtseln kann!!

2.) Dann: Herr Fischer wollte ja vor mir eine Korrektur
lesen! Hat er das nicht gethan??

3.) Ferner: die Korrekturbogen beginnen mit Seite 11. Folg-

II.A-S.t.1

XIX,1.
Cottage
Lannerstrasse 9.   Vienna, January 11, 1912

Esteemed Sir:
    I am sending together per x Bd. rekom[31] the 4 pieces
for which you realized the basso-continuo and would ask you to
proof them. I wish especially to direct your attention to a passage
in the Divertimento, last page (43) systems 1 and 2 because of the
clefs; your realization gives me pleasure, it is filled with imagination.
    I would like to know how things are going with you. I
am very sorry that you left Vienna--but hopefully not forever!
Please take care of this quickly.

Sincerely your truly devoted Guido Adler

II.S-A.t.18

Arnold Schönberg, Berlin-Zehlendorf Wannseebahn
Machnower Chaussee, Villa Lepcke   January 13, 1912

Esteemed Professor:
I intended to write to you some time ago, especially after having
heard that you had taken a very lively interest in my activities--and
also because I was glad that, as someone wrote me, my continuos
please you. But I was prevented from doing so to by so many
matters which I had to pursue, thus far without success.
    Concerning the proofs I ask you urgently to
    1.) send me the manuscripts. Without these I can scarcely
manage, because the proofs, as I gathered from a hasty glance at
them, seem to be full of mistakes--mistakes which I can hardly
resolve without the manuscript.
    2.) Then: Mr. Fischer intended to read the proof before me.
    Did he not do so??
    3.) Furthermore, the sheets of the proof begin on page 11;

lich geht noch ein cirka 10 Seiten langes Stück voran. Ist das keines der von mir bearbeiteten?

4.) Ich habe ja viel mehr als vier Stücke bearbeitet.Ich weiss die Zahl nicht genau, aber 6 sind es, glaube ich, mindestens. An eines mit einem Andante in Es dur (4/4) erinnere ich mich und auch an eines in C-Moll. Aber es müssen noch mehr sein. Bekomme ich die noch zur Korrektur, oder werden die einstweilen nicht herausgegeben?

Vielleicht sind Sie so freundlich, mir diese Fragen zu beantworten.

Ob ich je wieder nach Wien zurück komme hängt wohl in erster Linie davon ab, ob sich mir jemals in Wien die Möglichkeit leben zu können bieten wird. Einstweilen sieht es wohl nicht danach aus. Sie sehen: ausser meinem Freund Schreker, der den kleinen Chor aufführte, findet es niemand in Wien für nötig, etwas von mir zu bringen. Dagegen habe ich zahlreiche Aufführungen im Ausland: in Paris, München, Berlin, Leipzig, Budapest u[nd] Prag. In Prag dirigiere ich am 29. Februar (könnten Sie vielleicht hinkommen?) ein ganzes Konzert, mit meiner Pelleas Symphonie.

Ich hoffe bald Antwort und die Manuskripte zu erhalten, dann erledige ich die Korrekturen in wenigen Tagen.

Indem ich Sie hochachtungsvoll grüsse bin ich

Ihr ergebener

Arnold Schönberg.

II.A-S.o.2

15. 1. 12

Sehr geehrter Herr!

Sende gleichz[eitig] unter x Bd rek: die gewünschten M[anu]sk[rip]te u[nd] ersuche ehemöglichste Erledigung der Korr[ekturen]. Eine Korr[ektur] ist schon gelesen u[nd] Sie haben die 2. Korr[ektur]. Die anderen von Ihnen bearbeiteten Stücke sind d[er]z[eit] nicht in m[einer] Hand, sondern bei Dr. Fischer. Sie sind vorläufig zurück gestellt worden. Sie haben 4 Stücke im Drucke, andere 4 sind von Labor bearbeitet, deshalb die ungleichen Papiere. Übrigens ist die Reihenfolge noch nicht definitiv. -

Es betrübt mich zu hören dass Berlin vorläufig die Hoff-

consequently, a piece of approximately 10 pages must precede it. Is this not one which I have worked on?

4.) Actually I have worked on many more than four pieces. I do not know the exact number, but I believe there are at least six. I do remember one with an Andante in E-flat Major (4/4) and one in C Minor. But there must be still more. Will I still receive them for proof reading, or are they not to be published at present?

Perhaps you will be so kind as to answer these questions for me.

Whether I ever return to Vienna will depend above all on whether or not I am ever again offered the opportunity to make a living in Vienna. At present it does not appear so. You see, except for my friend Schreker who performed the little chorus, nobody in Vienna considers it necessary to perform anything I have written. On the other hand, I have many performances abroad: in Paris, Munich, Berlin, Leipzig, Budapest and Prague. In Prague, February 29th I shall conduct an entire concert with my *Pelleas* Symphony (could you come perhaps?)

I hope to receive a reply and the manuscripts soon; I shall then take care of the proofs within a few days.

With respectful regards, I remain
Your devoted Arnold Schönberg

II.A-S.t.2

January 15, 1912

Esteemed Sir:

I am sending together by x Bd rek: the requested manuscripts, and I request that proofing be done as quickly as possible. The first proof has been read and you have the second proof. The other pieces you worked on I do not have at hand at the moment, for Dr. Fischer has them. For the time being they have been postponed. You have four pieces in print, and another four have been done by Labor;[32] hence the different kinds of paper. The order, by the way, is not definite yet.

It grieves me to hear that at present Berlin does not come up to your expectations. It will be hardly possible for me to come

nungen nicht erfüllt. Nach Prag dürfte ich schwerlich kommen, da
ich zu dieser Zeit [hier] angebunden bin. Danke für die Einladung.
Ihre Grüsse herzlich erwidernd
                    aufrichtig G[uido] Ad[ler]

II.A-S.o.3

S[ehr] g[eehrter] H[err]!
Wenn es möglich wäre, dass Sie die Korr[ekturen] früher besorgten,
so wäre dies sehr dankenswert. Wir sind mit dem Termin in arger
Klemme. Ich möchte Sie möglichst schonen, allein bitte das Mög-
lichste zu thun.
            Freundlich grüsst
                    Ihr Guido Adler
22. 1. 12

II.S-A.o.19

Arnold Schönberg, Berlin-Zehlendorf-Wannseebahn
Machnower Chaussee,
Villa Lepcke.   6 / 2. 1912

Sehr geehrter Herr Professor: in grösster Eile teile ich Ihnen mit,
dass ich die Korrekturen morgen abschicke. Es wird mir ausserordentlich schwer sie jetzt zu machen, denn ich habe soviel zu tun,
dass ich nicht weiss, wo beginnen. Aber ich nehme das trotzdem als
erstes vor, um Sie nicht böse zu machen. - Mein Konzert, das am
28/I. hatte stattfinden sollen, musste auf den 4.II. verschoben
werden, was unsägliche Mühe und viel Zeit kostete. Das [ist] der
Grund, warum ich nicht schon in der vorigen Woche die Sache er-
ledigen konnte. Nun ist das Konzert vorbei. Es hatte viel Erfolg.
            Ich bin mit hochachtungsvollen Grüssen
                    Ihr ergebener Arnold Schönberg

to Prague because I am tied up here at present; but thanks for the invitation.

Returning your regards cordially,
I am sincerely yours,
Guido Adler

II.A-S.t.3

Esteemed Sir:
If it were possible for you to take care of the proof reading earlier, we would be most thankful. We are in a real fix with the deadline. I would like to spare you as much as possible, but please do what you can.

Kind regards, Yours Guido Adler

January 22, 1912

II.S-A.t.19

Arnold Schönberg, Berlin-Zehlendorf-Wannseebahn
Machnower Chaussee, Villa Lepcke.   February 6, 1912

Esteemed Professor:
In greatest haste let me inform you that I shall mail the proofs tomorrow. It is extremely difficult for me to read them now, because I have so much to do that I do not know where to begin. But I shall do them first in order not to displease you. My concert, which was to have taken place on January 28th, had to be postponed to February 4th, and this created an incredible burden and took a lot of time. This is the reason why I was not able to take care of this matter during the past week. Now the concert has taken place. It was very successful. I remain with respectful regards, faithfully yours,

Arnold Schönberg

II.S-A.o.20

Arnold Schönberg, Berlin-Zehlendorf-Wannseebahn
Machnower Chaussee,
Villa Lepcke.   20 / 8. 1912

Sehr geehrter Herr Professor, es wird Ihnen bekannt sein, dass ich
nach Wien an die Akademie berufen war, aber im letzten Moment
abgelehnt habe. Meine Hauptgründe waren die Abneigung gegen
die Wiener Verhältnisse, mein noch lange nicht besänftigter Groll
gegen Wien und die mir nicht zusagende Stellung, die man mir
geboten hat. Materiell sowo[h]l, wie künstlerisch. Ob ich daran
Recht getan habe, kann ich nur mit dem Gefühl beantworten, nicht
mit dem Verstand verantworten. Allerdings erhoffe ich mir von
meinen hiesigen Aussichten Besseres, als man mir in Wien geboten
hat. Jedenfalls aber war meine Abneigung gegen die "Stadt der
Lieder von umgebrachten Künstlern" zu gross, als dass ich sie hätte
überwinden wollen.

       Nun muss ich aber hier in Berlin natürlicherweise den
Kampf für den Gelderwerb aufs Neue aufnehmen   und   deshalb
möchte ich Sie fragen ob ich nicht wieder für die österreichischen
Denkmäler der Tonkunst arbeiten könnte. Oder wenn da augenblicklich nichts frei ist, ob Sie nicht veranlassen können, dass ich
eingeladen werde, bei den Deutschen Denkmälern mitzutun.

       Oder aber (und das wäre mir das Wichtigste) ob Sie nicht
Prof. Kretzschmar, den Direktor der hiesigen Hochschule auf mich,
auf mein Harmonielehrbuch und meine Compositionen aufmerksam
machen und ihn fragen wollten, ob er mich denn nicht an die
Hochschule für die Kompositions-Meisterklassen, die ja ohnedies
unbesetzt sind, berufen wollte. Ich habe den Eindruck, dass Sie
Herr Professor, da Sie mich schon vor mehr als 5 Jahren in Wien
vorgeschlagen haben, an meiner Eignung für Derartiges nicht
zweifeln.

       Wenn Sie eines dieser Dinge tun wollten um das ich Sie
hier bitte, so wäre ich Ihnen sehr dankbar.

       Gerne wüsste ich, ob Sie meine Harmonielehre schon ange-
sehen haben und was Sie dazu sagen.

       Ich hoffe Sie befinden sich (und Ihre Familie) wohl und
[ich] empfehle mich mit ganz ergebenen Grüssen
       Ihr Arnold Schönberg

II.S-A.t.20

Arnold Schönberg, Berlin-Zehlendorf-Wannseebahn
Machnower Chaussee,
Villa Lepcke.   August 20, 1912

Esteemed Professor:
You may be aware that I received an offer from the Academy in
Vienna, but that I turned it down at the last moment. My main
reasons were my dislike of the conditions in Vienna; my long-time
resentment towards Vienna; and the unappealing position that was
offered to me--unacceptable materially as well as artistically.
Whether or not I made the right decision I can only answer with my
feelings, not my intellect. I do, however, hope for better prospects
here than have been offered to me in Vienna. At any rate, my
aversion towards the "City of Songs by Murdered Artists" was too
great for me to overcome.
        But here in Berlin, naturally, I have to resume the struggle
for a livelihood, and it is for this reason that I would like to ask you
if I might not work again for the *Denkmäler der Tonkunst*; or, if at
the moment there is nothing available there, whether you might not
arrange for me to be invited to work with the German *Denkmäler*.
        Or else (and this would be the most important thing of all
for me), whether you might be willing to direct the attention of
Professor Kretzschmar, the director of the local Hochschule, to me
as well as to my *Harmonielehre* and my compositions, and whether
you would ask him if he might be willing to invite me to the
Hochschule for the master classes in composition, which happen to
be vacant at present. Since you, Professor, already recommended
me in Vienna some five years ago, I am under the impression that
you have no doubts concerning my qualifications.
        If you would be willing to do one or another of the things
I have requested above, I would be most grateful to you.
        I would like to know if you have already had a look at my
Harmonielehre, and what you have to say about it.
        I hope that you (and your family) are well, and I extend to
you my most devoted regards,
        Yours, Arnold Schönberg

II.A-S.o.4

Villa Waldessaum
Obertressen, <u>Aussee</u>
in Steiermark   3. 9. 12

Sehr geehrter Herr!
    Gern werde ich Ihnen eine B[asso] C[ontinuo] Bearbeitung
zuweisen u[nd] d[as] sobald ich nach Wien zurückkehre.
    Ich bedaure d[a]ss Sie das Wiener Angebot nicht angenom-
men haben - ich glaubte, es sei nur eine Anfrage gewesen. Vielleicht ersticken Sie Ihren Groll, falls eine Möglichkeit sich ergeben
sollte.
    Mit G[eheim] R[at] Kretzschmar will ich bei günstiger Ge-
legenheit die Sache besprechen - schriftlich lässt sich so was nicht
einleiten. Es ist Ihnen bekannt dass ich Sie s[einer]z[eit] als Lehrer
für Harmonielehre u[nd] Kontrapunkt vorgeschlagen hatte wenigstens glaube ich mich zu erinnern. Mit der Lektüre Ihrer H[armo-
nie]l[ehre] kam ich nicht recht vorwärts: Manches sagt mir zu,
Anderes stösst mich ab. Ich wurde in der Durchsicht durch ein
Unwohlsein unterbrochen u[nd] musste dann Anderes vornehmen.
Also bitte um Geduld.
    Meine Familie befindet sich wo[h]l und ich hoffe das Glei-
che bei Ihnen.
    Mit bestem Gruss Ihr aufrichtig ergebener   Guido Adler

II.S-A.o.21

Arnold Schönberg, Berlin-Zehlendorf-Wannseebahn
Machnower Chaussee,
Villa Lepcke.   7 / 9. 1912

Sehr geehrter Herr Professor, ich danke Ihnen herzlichst für Ihren
sehr freundlichen Brief und für Ihre Zusagen. Leider ist mein
"Groll" gegen Wien nicht (wie Sie es verlangen) leicht zu ersticken,
denn er hat einen zu langen Atem. Aber ich muss sagen, abgesehen
davon: ich hielte es nicht für gut, wenn ich bald nach Wien zurück-
komme. Ich überschätze gewiss nicht das Mass an Begeisterung,

II.A-S.t.4

Villa Waldessaum,
Obertressen, <u>Aussee</u>
In Steiermark   September 3, 1912

Esteemed Sir:
    I shall be pleased to assign you a new continuo realization,
and will do so as soon as I return to Vienna. I am very sorry that
you did not accept the offer from Vienna; I had thought it was only
an inquiry. Perhaps you will be able to swallow your resentment
should a possibility present itself.
    At an opportune time I shall take up the matter with
Privy Councillor Kretzschmar; such a subject cannot be pursued in
writing. You are aware that I proposed you at one time as a
teacher for harmony and counterpoint--at least I think I recall doing
so. I have not made much progress with the reading of your
Harmonielehre. I agree with some points, others I find questionable.
I was interrupted in my reading because of an indisposition, and
then I had to concern myself with other matters. Therefore, please
be patient.
    My family is well, and I hope the same with yours.
    With best regards,
    your truly faithful   Guido Adler

II.S-A.t.21

Arnold Schönberg, Berlin-Zehlendorf-Wannseebahn
Machnower Chaussee,
Villa Lepcke.   September 7, 1912

Esteemed Professor:
    I thank you most cordially for your kind letter and your
promise. Unfortunately, it is not easy for me to "swallow my
resentment" towards Vienna as you desire, for it is too long-lived.
I must say, however, that apart from this, I would not consider it a
good thing to return to Vienna any time soon. I do not at all over-

das man jetzt für mich hat. Aber selbst die wäre mir schädlich.
Ich habe augenblicklich anderes mit mir abzumachen. Ich könnte
jetzt ein so lautes Lob, wie ich es manchmal aus Wien höre, gar
nicht vertragen. Ich will nicht eingeschläfert werden, sondern wach
bleiben. Ich will mir darüber klar werden, ob ich was und wer ich
bin. Und da will ich eher Tadel als Lob hören. Nicht weil ich auf
den Tadel mehr gebe. Aber ich bin nur gewohnter an ihn und weiss
dass ich mich um ihn nicht zu kümmern habe und dadurch komme
ich zu mir. Und das brauche ich augenblicklich!

Herzlichst danke ich Ihnen auch noch für Ihre Absicht, den
Herrn G[eheim] R[at] Kretzschmar auf mich aufmerksam zu
machen. Nur hoffe ich, dass Ihre Bemerkung, Sie hätten mich
s[einer]z[eit] auch [?] sehr für Harmonielehre und Kontrap[unkt]
empfohlen, nicht besagen will, dass Sie mich ihm auch nur für diese
Fächer empfehlen. Denn: in meiner wesentlichsten Eigenschaft
bin ich ja doch (so hoffe ich) Komponist, muss also doch Komposition am besten unterrichten können. NB: [nota bene] welcher
moderne Komponist (höchstens Strauss und Pfitzner ausgenommen)
wäre denn geeigneter dazu als ich, der ich, um ein Wort O.J. Davids
zu variieren (ein "gelernter Deutschböhme") ein gelernter Brahmsia-
ner, oder Beethovenianer oder Mozartianer bin. Aber ich denke
mir, wenn Sie aus meiner Harmonielehre das Kapitel (es ist ganz
kurz) über Choralharmonisierung lesen wollten, würden Sie leicht
entnehmen können, dass ich einen nicht ganz gewöhnlichen
Einblick in formale Fragen habe. Es wäre mir sehr sehr angenehm,
wenn Sie sich diese geringe Mühe machen wollten.

Ich danke Ihnen nochmals herzlichst und bitte Sie, mich
Ihrer Familie zu empfehlen.

Mit ganz ergebenen Grüssen
Ihr Arnold Schönberg

estimate the measure of enthusiasm for me now, but even that would be detrimental for me. At present I have come to terms with myself, and I could not really cope with such overt praise about which I hear on occasion from Vienna. I do not wish to be lulled to sleep, but to remain alert. I want to clarify for myself whether I do amount to something, and who I really am. And thus I would rather hear censure than praise. Not that I would prefer censure, but I am more used to it and know that I need not concern myself with it. By means of it I am able to find myself, and that is what I need at present.

I thank you also heartily for your intention to call Privy Councillor Kretzschmar's attention towards me. I only hope that your remark that you had recommended me at one time especially for harmony and counterpoint does not mean that you will recommend me only for these subjects. The reason is this: that, as I truly hope, my real calling is as a composer; hence I ought to be most suited for teaching composition. NB [nota bene]: which modern composer (with the possible exception of Strauss and Pfitzner) would be more suitable than I, who, to vary a remark by O.J. David (an "educated German-Bohemian"), am an educated Brahmsian, Beethovenian or Mozartian? But I think, if you would be willing to read the chapter in my *Harmonielehre* on chorale harmonization (it is quite short), you could easily conclude that I have considerable musical insight on questions of form. It would please me very much if you would be willing to make this little effort.

Again, I thank you with all my heart, and ask you to remember me to your family.

   With cordial regards,
   your Arnold Schönberg

II.S-A.o.22

Arnold Schönberg, Berlin-Zehlendorf-Wannseebahn
Machnower Chaussee,
Villa Lepcke   5 / 3. 1913

Sehr verehrter Herr Professor, ich hoffe, man hat Ihnen ausgerich-
tet,* aus welchen Gründen es mir zu spät worden ist, Sie Sonntag
(23) noch zu besuchen. Aber ich bin in cirka 3 Wochen wieder in
Wien um ein Novitäten-Konzert des Akad[emischen] Verb[andes]
zu dirigieren. Da hoffe ich dann das Versäumnis, zu dem mich
diesmal Zeitmangel zwang, gut zu machen.
    Jedenfalls danke ich Ihnen vielmals für Ihre Freundlichkeit
und würde mich sehr freuen, wenn Ihnen mein Werk gefallen sollte.
    In vorzüglicher Hochachtung
    Ihr ergebener Arnold Schönberg

* Die Schwägerin des Direktor Herzka sagte mir zu!!
Ich weiss ihren Namen gar nicht einmal.

II.A-S.o.5

XIX/1
Cottage
Lannerstrasse 9.   Wien 9. 3. 13

Sehr geehrter Herr!
Ich bedauerte sehr d[a]ss Sie nicht kommen konnten sah ein, d[a]ss
Sie zu arg in Anspruch genommen sind (bes[onders] die Korrekturen, wie ich hörte!) desto mehr freute mich der Abend u[nd] Ihr
Erfolg dem ich mich herzlichst anschliessen konnte. Einiges in
Dichtung und Musik blieb mir unklar - vielleicht giebt sich das bei
der zu erwartenden Wiederholung. Wenn ich nur in Wien bin! Ich
dürfte unmittelbar nach Ostern verreisen - Alles ist noch unbe-
stimmt. Hoffentlich kann ich Sie in Wien sehen. Auf alle Fälle
teile ich Ihnen mit, d[a]ss Casals das V[iolon]c[ello] Konzert von

II.S-A.t.22

Arnold Schönberg, Berlin-Zehlendorf Wannseebahn
Machnower Chaussee,
Villa Lepcke   March 5, 1913

Esteemed Professor:
I hope that you have been informed* why it was too late to visit you
on Sunday the 23rd. In about three weeks, however, I shall be in
Vienna again in order to conduct a concert of new works of the
Academic Society. At that time I hope to make good on what was
not possible at this time because of lack of time.
        In any case, I thank you very much for your kindness, and
it will please me very much if my work pleased you.
        With great esteem
        Your Arnold Schönberg

* I liked the sister-in-law of Director Herzka.
  I do not even know her name.

II.A-S.t.5

XIX/1
Cottage
Lannerstrasse 9.   Vienna, March 9, 1913

Esteemed Sir:
I was very sorry that you could not come, but understood that you
are too taken up with obligations (and especially, as I heard, with
the proofs!). I was therefore the more pleased about the evening
and your success, in which I was able to join heartily. Certain
things in the poetry and music remained vague to me; perhaps this
will change with the expected repeat performance. If only I am able
to be in Vienna! I expect to go on a trip right after Easter--every-
thing is still undecided. Hopefully I can see you in Vienna. In any

Monn bei einem histori[schen] Konzert (aus Anlass des 20 j[ähri-
gen] Bestandes der D[enk]M[äler] [der] T[onkunst] im November
hier spielen wird. Er wünscht eine oder zwei Kadenzen. Da Sie
das Werk genau kennen, den B[asso] C[ontinuo] gearbeitet haben
u[nd] selbst Cellist sind, so kamen wir (Casals u[nd] ich) darauf, Sie
zu ersuchen, die Kadenz oder Kadenzen zu schreiben. Stimmen Sie
ein?

Wegen anderer D[enk]M[äler] ausführungen des B[asso]
C[ontinuo] möchte ich dann auch mit Ihnen sprechen.

Ein ehemaliger Schüler, Prof. Bezecny in Prag, schreibt mir,
d[a]ss ihm Pierrot L[unaire] gefallen habe - nun beneide ich ihn
darum! Möchte so gern gerecht sein - muss aber immer wahr
bleiben, in Empfinden u[nd] Mitteil[un]g. Könnte sich dies ändern?
- ich meine, meine Apperzeptionsart!

Seien Sie, mein lieber Schoenberg herzlich gegrüsst von
Ihrem aufrichtig ergebenen Guido Adler

II.S-A.o.23

Arnold Schönberg, Berlin-Zehlendorf-Wannsebahn
Machnower Chaussee,
Villa Lepke.   13 / 3. 1913

Sehr geehrter Herr Professor, Ihr Vorschlag, dass ich zu dem Cello
Konzert von Monn Kadenzen machen soll, interessiert mich umso-
mehr, als ich diese Absicht selbst schon hatte. Ich bin also gerne
bereit, daszu tun, nur würde ich wissen wollen, ob ich berechtigt
bin, das Cello Konzert dann einem Verlag zu übergeben und
meinen Continuo dabei mitzubenützen. Ich stelle mir vor, dass es
hier wohl kein Hindernis geben sollte, da ja die Publikation in den
Denkmälern weniger praktischen, als vielmehr literarisch-histori-
schen Zwecken dient, die durch einen regulären Verlag nicht
tangiert werden.

Ich wäre Ihnen sehr dankbar, wenn Sie mir recht bald Ihre
Meinung darüber mitteilen wollten. Zu berücksichtigen ist ja dabei

case let me inform you that Casals will perform the violoncello concerto by Monn at a historic concert here in November [19th] on the occasion of the twentieth anniversary of the *Denkmäler der Tonkunst in Österreich*. He requests one or two cadenzas. Since you know the work very well, have realized the continuo, and are a cellist yourself, we agreed (Casals[33] and I) to ask you to write the cadenza or cadenzas. Are you willing?

Concerning further continuo realizations for the *Denkmäler*, I would like to speak with you then also.

A former student, Prof. Bezecny[34] from Prague, wrote me that he liked *Pierrot Lunaire*. Now I envy him for this! I would like to be just, but must always remain <u>truthful</u> in what I feel and communicate. Is it possible that this may change--that is to say, my way of perceiving things?

Accept now, my dear Schönberg, cordial regards from your truly faithful Guido Adler

II.S-A.t.23

Arnold Schönberg, Berlin-Zehlendorf-Wannseebahn
Machnower Chaussee,
Villa Lepcke.   March 13, 1913

Esteemed Professor:
Your suggestion that I write cadenzas for Monn's Cello Concerto is of all the more interest to me since I had already intended to do so myself. I am, therefore, quite prepared to do it, but only would like to know if I will be entitled <u>then to give the Cello Concerto to a publisher</u> and to utilize my continuo with it. I would think that there would be no objection to this, since publication in the *Denkmäler* serves less for practical than for literary-historical purposes, and would not be affected by commercial publication.

I would be very grateful to you if you would let me know your opinion right away. Perhaps my not unjustifiable desire to

vielleicht mein nicht unberechtigtes Bedürfnis eine solche Arbeit zu publizieren wenn sie zu meiner Zufriedenheit ausgefallen ist.

Ich freue mich sehr über Ihre Zustimmung zu meinen Gurre-Liedern. Vielleicht interessiert es Sie zu hören, dass die nächste Aufführung in Berlin am 27. Mai unter meiner Leitung stattfindet.

Ich empfehle mich Ihnen mit
vorzüglicher Hochachtung und
Ergebenheit. Arnold Schönberg

II.S-A.o.24

14/3. 1913

Sehr geehrter Herr Professor, wenn Casals sich für eine kurze Kadenz entscheidet, werde ich noch eine neue machen und dann in der "praktischen Ausgabe" beide veröffentlichen. Mir scheint es fraglich, ob man nicht da dem Bedürfnis des Virtuos[os] die Entscheidung überlassen soll und nicht dem historischen Gesichtspunkt. Wie mir scheint (da Sie ja meinen Entwurf Casal[s] senden wollen) sind Sie ja auch dieser Meinung.

Ich hoffe Ihnen morgen einen Entwurf zur Kadenz des 3. Satzes (die ich demnach einstweilen auch länger mache) senden zu können.

Ich muss erwähnen: In der Denkmäler-Ausgabe ist keine Kadenz vorgesehen. Es findet sich nirgends die gewisse "⌒Cadenza" Bezeichnung. Wollen Sie mir bitte mitteilen, ob ich nach Ihrem Dafürhalten geeignete Stellen gewählt habe. Für den letzten Satz

publish such a piece, if it turned out to my satisfaction, is to be taken into consideration.

I am very pleased at your positive reaction to my Gurre-Lieder. Perhaps you will be interested to hear that the next performance will take place in Berlin on May 27th under my direction.

I remain yours with great esteem
and faithfulness. Arnold Schönberg

II.S-A.t.24

March 14, 1913

Esteemed Professor:

If Casals decides in favor of a short cadenza, I shall write another one and publish both in the "practical edition." I ask myself if this decision should not be governed by the needs of the virtuoso rather than the historical viewpoint. Since you are willing to send my draft to Casals, it seems to me that you are of the same opinion.

Tomorrow I hope to be able to send you a draft for the cadenza of the 3rd movement, which I shall in the meantime also lengthen.

Something I need to mention: in the *Denkmäler* Edition no cadenza is provided for. Nowhere is the customary " ⌒ Cadenza" indication to be found. Would you please tell me if, in your

fand ich folgende Stelle (siehe den beiliegenden Zettel).

[Equivalent passage in the *Denkmäler,* vol. 39, II, p. 90, I,
mm. 5-9, for Facsimile I]:

Nun etwas anderes: in der letzten Nummer der "Signale"
(eines Expressblattes) greift der Herr "Professor" Dr. Max Graf (als
Mann der "Wissenschaft" verkleidet; einer Wissenschaft, von der

opinion, I have selected the appropriate spot (see the attached sheet).

Facsimile I.
From the original in the Hargrett Rare Book Library,
University of Georgia Libraries. Reprinted by permission.

Sie selbst genau wissen, wie weit die her ist) meine Monn-Bear-
beitung und auch Sie unglaublich heftig an. Ich dachte zuerst daran
zu erwidern, tue es aber doch nicht, denn mit den Leuten à la Graf
gebe ich mich nicht mehr ab. Ausserdem ist es mir ganz klar, dass
Graf Hintermänner hat (ich vermute Schenker und Violin, die ja
stets das ehrenvolle Amt ausübten Recensenten gegen Künstler
aufzuhetzen und ihnen ihr "Material" zur Verfügung zu stellen),
denn Graf ist nicht imstande einen Continuo von einem Kurszettel
zu unterscheiden.*   Das weiss ich aus der Zeit, wo er mir im
Cafehaus meine Meinung über musikalische Fragen abgeknöpft hat
um sie dann verstümmelt in der Zeitung für seine auszugeben.

Wenn Sie aber, da Sie ja auch angegriffen sind antworten
wollen (ich halte es für nicht dringend) so wäre ich bereit eine Wi-
derlegung der gänzlich haltlosen Angriffe in Briefform (druckreif)
an Sie (quasi als Rechtfertigung, Ihnen gegenüber) zu schreiben und
hielte es dann für zweckmässig, wenn Sie diesen Brief in Ihrer
Erwiderung wörtlich abdrucken liessen.

Selbstverständlich: ich vertrete alles was dort steht, bis auf
eine Stelle, die ein mir schwer begreiflicher Druckfehler oder eine
schlecht korrigierte Stelle im Manuskript sein muss, denn die hat
tatsächlich kaum Sinn und ich kann mich gar nicht erinnern, das
geschrieben zu haben. Vielleicht das aus Versehen stehen geblie-
bene Rudiment einer Absicht, die ich dann fallen liess. Es handelt
sich um (Seite 39, I. System, Takt 3) dieses eingeschichtige [einge-
strichene] cis in der linken Hand des Continuo. Das kann nur ein
Ueberersehen sein. - Sonst ist alles andere, wie ich zeigen werde
und durch Beispiele von Meistern, (Bach etc) beweisen kann (das
Material habe ich bereits) vollständig in Ordnung.

Bitte Seien Sie so freundlich mir Ihre Ansicht darüber zu
sagen. Ich, wie gesagt, lege kein Gewicht darauf, zu erwidern.
Denn mit einem Kerl, der so ordinär ist, eine so gute Sache, wie das
Continuo ist (selbst wenn er Recht hätte bleibt doch noch eine
Menge anerkennenswertes) bloss aus Rache für einen ihm nicht
gegebenen Händedruck so zu beschimpfen, möchte ich nichts zu tun
haben.

Ich bin mit vorzüglicher Hochachtung Ihr Arnold Schönberg

* oder wie Kraus sagen würde: einen Kontrapunkt von einer
  Sommersprosse

Now another thing:[35] in the last issue of *Signale* (a weekly paper), "Professor" Dr. Max Graf[36] (disguised as a man of "scholarship"--and of whose worth you are precisely aware) attacked my Monn realization, and also you with incredible violence. At first I intended to respond, but I shall not do so because I do not intend to have anything more to do with people of Graf's type. Furthermore, it is obvious to me that Graf has "behind the scenes" collaborators (I suspect Schenker and Violin,[37] who have always had the honorable role of inciting critics against artists and of supplying them with their "material"), since Graf is unable to distinguish between a continuo and a market report.* This I have been aware of since that time in the Coffee House when he stole my views on musical questions in order to claim them as his own in mutilated form in the newspaper.

If, however, you wish to respond (and I do not consider this urgent), since you were also attacked, I would be willing to write a rebuttal to the <u>completely unfounded attacks</u> in the form of a letter (ready for the press) directed to you (as a kind of vindication towards you); and I would think it then appropriate if you would have this letter printed verbatim along with your response.

Of course, I take responsibility for everything found [in the manuscript realization for the continuo part] except for one place which seems to me either an incomprehensible misprint or a poorly corrected place in the manuscript, since it really hardly makes any sense, and I cannot recall at all having written it.[38] Perhaps it was the remnant of an idea which I had discarded, but which had been left in by mistake. I refer to the c# above middle c in the left hand of the continuo (page 39, 1st system, measure 3). This can only be an oversight. Otherwise, everything else is completely in order as I will prove through examples (I already have of the material) from the masters (Bach etc).

Please be so kind as to let me know your views. As I said before, I do not consider it important to reply. I really would prefer to have nothing to do with a fellow so common that merely out of pique over a withheld handshake he would cast aspersions upon so excellent a job as that continuo (and even if he were correct, there would still be much of it worthy of note).

I remain with highest esteem, Yours,   Arnold Schönberg
* or, as Kraus would say: a counterpoint from a freckle

II.A-S.o.6

Denkmäler der Tonkunst in Österreich
Leiter der Publikationen;
Universitätsprofessor Dr. Guido Adler
in Wien XIX/1 Cottage, Lannerstrasse 9.

18. März, 1913

Sehr geehrter Herr,
es freut mich zu hören, dass Sie geneigt sind, zu dem Cello-Conzert
von Monn Kadenzen zu schreiben. Ich erlaube mir zu bemerken
dass die leitende Kommission mit Rücksicht auf Ihre Verwendung
in dem historischen Konzert, welches am 19. November d[ieses]
J[ahres] aus Anlass des zwanzigjährigen Bestandes der "Denkmäler"
stattfinden soll, gerne bereit ist, hierfür ein Honorar zu begleichen.
Die "Denkmäler" - Kommission hat in der letzten Zeit eine Art
Übereinkommen mit der Universaledition getroffen, dass praktische
Ausgaben von einzelnen Werken von dieser herausgegeben werden
können (unter gewissen Modalitäten). Sie können sich also des
Konzertes halber mit der Universaledition ins Einvernehmen setzen
und ich bin gerne bereit die Herausgabe zu befürworten. Natürlich
müssten Sie dann das ganze Konzert mit Vortragszeichen versehen
und dies so bald wie möglich, damit Mr. Casals, der dieses Konzert
spielen wird, mindestens im Mai in den Besitz Ihrer Bearbeitung
kommen kann. Denn Casals hat den Wunsch ausgesprochen, die
Bearbeitung möglichst bald zu erhalten.
     Leider kann ich Ihrem Konzert in Wien nicht beiwohnen
da ich morgen für etwa zwei Wochen verreise. Briefe werden mir
nachgesendet, wenn darauf steht "dringend." Für die Berlin Aufführung der Gurrelieder besten Erfolg!
     Mit freundlichem Gruss in
     aufrichtiger Ergebenheit,
     Ihr Guido Adler

II.A-S.t.6

Denkmäler der Tonkunst in Österreich
Leiter der Publikationen:
Universitätsprofessor Dr. Guido Adler
in Wien, XIX/1, Cottage, Lannerstrasse 9.

March   18,   1913

Esteemed Sir:[39]

I am glad to hear that you are thinking of writing the cadenzas for
the cello concerto of Monn. I take the liberty of mentioning the
fact that--in consideration of their use in the historic concert which
will take place on November 19th in commemoration of the
twentieth anniversary of the *Denkmäler*--the governing commission
is pleased to pay an honorarium for them. Lately the *Denkmäler*-
Commission entered into an agreement with Universal Edition,
whereby performance editions of individual works can be published
by the latter under certain conditions. You may wish, therefore, to
get in touch with Universal Edition concerning the concerto, and I
will be pleased to support the edition. Of course, you would have
to provide the entire concerto with performance indications, and
this as soon as possible so that Mr. Casals, who will perform the
concerto, will have in hand your arrangement at least by May;
Casals has indicated his wish to receive the arrangement as soon as
possible.

Unfortunately I cannot attend your concert in Vienna because I am leaving town tomorrow for about two weeks. Letters
will be forwarded if marked "urgent." All success in the Berlin
performance of the *Gurrelieder*!

With cordial regards
in true devotion your
Guido Adler

II.S-A.o.25

Arnold Schönberg, Berlin-Zehlendorf-Wannseebahn
Machnower Chaussee, Villa Lepke.　　　　　　　　10 / 4. 1913

Sehr geehrter Herr Professor, ich habe versucht für Casals eine
Cadenz zu bauen. Einstweilen für den ersten Satz. Ich bitte Sie
nun, ehe ich weiter arbeite diesen Entwurf (denn es ist bloss ein
Entwurf, es muss an einigen Stellen noch glatter werden und ich bin
auch zu Änderungen bereit), Casals, dessen Adresse ich nicht kenne
zu schicken und ihm folgende Fragen vorzulegen (Er kann mir
eventuell direkt französisch antworten)

I.　　　Ist dieser Entwurf genügend dankbar und schwer?
II.　　Ist alles ausführbar? (Ich kann es natürlich nicht?)
III.　　Ist es vielleicht (mir fehlt hier doch selbst jedes Urteil)
　　　　nicht etwas konventionell
IV.　　Ist es lang genug?
V.　　Soll die im III. Satz länger oder kürzer werden?

　　　　Von Ihnen hätte ich noch gerne Antwort auf folgende
Fragen:

I.　　　Bekomme ich das Honorar vom Verleger, oder von der
　　　　Intern[ationalen] Mus[ik Ges[ellschaft]
II.　　Wie hoch ist dieses Honorar? (Es dürfte doch nicht allzu
　　　　niedrig sein, da ich schon recht viel Zeit darauf verwenden
　　　　muss.)
III.　　Falls das Honorar von der Intern[ationalen] Mus[ik]
　　　　Ges[ellschaft] bezahlt werden sollte: habe ich das alleinige
　　　　Verlagsrecht oder wie steht diese Frage sonst?

　　　　Den Entwurf bitte ich Herrn Casals mir umgehend zurück-
zuschicken, damit ich an der 2ten Cadenz arbeite und die fertig
stellen kann.
　　　　Ich empfehle mich Ihnen mit
　　　　vorzüglicher Hochachtung
　　　　　　　ergebenst　Arnold Schönberg

II.S-A.t.25

Arnold Schönberg, Berlin-Zehlendorf-Wannseebahn
Machnower Chaussee, Villa Lepke.   April 10, 1913

Esteemed Professor:

I have attempted to create a cadenza for Casals--for the moment one for the first movement only. I would like to ask you before working further on this draft (and it is merely a draft, for at some points it needs to be made smoother, and I am also willing to make changes) if you would now send this draft to Casals, whose address I do not know, and if you would ask him the following questions (perhaps he can answer me directly in French):

I.   Is this draft sufficiently rewarding and demanding?
II.   Can everything be executed (naturally, I cannot do it myself)?
III.   Is it possibly somewhat too conventional (I myself cannot judge concerning this)?
IV.   Is it long enough?
V.   Should the cadenza for the 3rd movement be longer or shorter?

        I would also like to have your own answers to the following questions:

I.   Will I receive the payment from the publisher or from the International Musical Society?
II.   How much will this payment be? (It should not be too low since I am having to spend a lot of time with it).
III.   In the event the payment is to come from the International Music Society, would I have the sole right to publication, or what would the status of this be?

        I would like Mr. Casals to return the draft promptly to me so that I can work on the second cadenza and complete both.
        I remain yours with the highest esteem,
                faithfully Arnold Schönberg

II.A-S.o.7

Denkmäler der Tonkunst in Österreich
Leiter der Publikationen:
Universitätsprofessor Dr. Guido Adler
in Wien, XIX/1, Cottage, Lannerstrasse 9.   12. 4. 13

Sehr geehrter Herr!
Die Kadenz [und] Brief habe [ich] mit Dank erhalten. Ich glaube
d[a]ss sie zu lang ist, nur einige Takte genügen. In der damaligen
Zeit war noch nicht eine Kadenz im Mozart'schen Sinne üblich. Ich
will sie aber an Mr. Casals schicken. Wenn Sie für den letzten Satz
noch eine schreiben wollen, so begnügen Sie sich mit wenigen
Strichen.- Auch wenn Ihre Kadenzen nicht gespielt werden, so bin
ich gerne bereit, Ihnen ein Honorar anzuweisen. Sie bleiben Ihr
Eigenthum. Ansonsten wenn dann eine entsprechende Einrichtung
des Cellokonzertes in der Univ[ersal] Ed[ition] erscheint, wobei
eventuell Ihre Kadenzen ? [Wort nicht zu entziffern] Aufnahme
finden könnten.
    Ich bin vor einigen Tagen zurückgekehrt u[nd] habe von
den bedauerlichen Vorfällen bei Ihrem Konzert gehört.

        Mit freundlichen Grüssen bin ich
        Ihr aufrichtig ergebener Guido Adler

Mit der Absend[un]g der Kadenz an C[asals] werde ich warten bis
die 2. kommt.

II.A-S.o.8

XIX/1.
Cottage
Lannerstrasse 9.   Wien 16. 4 13

Sehr geehrter Herr!
Wenn Sie eine ausgeführtere Cadenz zum letzten Satz schreiben

II.A-S.t.7

Denkmäler der Tonkunst in Österreich
Leiter der Publikationen:
Universitätsprofessor Dr. Guido Adler
in Wien, XIX/1, Cottage, Lannerstrasse 9.   April 12, 1913

Esteemed Sir:
I received with thanks your letter and the cadenza. I believe that it
is too long; just a few measures would be sufficient. A cadenza of
the Mozart type was not yet customary at that [Monn's] time.
However, I shall send it to Mr. Casals. In case you wish to write
one also for the last movement, be content with a few bars. I will
be pleased to grant you an honorarium even if your cadenzas are
not to be performed. They will remain your property. Moreover if
an appropriate version of the Cello Concerto should appear then by
Universal Edition, your cadenzas [word unintelligible] could perhaps
be included.
        I returned a few days ago and heard about the deplorable
incidents during your concert.
                With cordial regards
                your faithfully devoted Guido Adler

I shall postpone sending the cadenza to Casals until the second one
arrives.

II.A-S.t.8

XIX/1
Cottage
Lannerstrasse 9   Vienna, April 16, 1913

Esteemed Sir:
In case you wish to write a more elaborate cadenza for the last

wollen, dann ist die von Ihnen ausgewählte Stelle u[nd] vorgenom-
mene harmonische Änderung richtig u[nd] zu benutzen. Allein
diesbe[zügli]ch nicht in den Intentionen des Komponisten. Der
Virtuose soll sich damit begnügen auf dem 2. u[nd] 3. Viertel von
Takt 2, System 2, Seite 90 also auf A u[nd] fis einige verzierende
Noten anzubringen. Ich bin der Meinung, dass eine grosse Kadenz
sowo[h]l unhistorisch wie künstlerisch nicht ganz berechtigt ist.
Sicherlich wird Ihre Kadenz an sich interessant werden u[nd] Mr.
Casals kann sich ja dann entscheiden, was er thut, Sie können bei
der Veröffentlichung beide Arten vorlegen. Ich sehe also Ihrer
freundlichen [?] Einsendung entgegen u[nd] werde dann alles an
C[asals] leiten u[nd] in Ihrem Sinne ihn auch an Sie verweisen.
        Der Casus "Signale" war mir bisher nicht bekannt. Ich
kenne noch nicht die letzte N[umme]r, glaube nicht dass ich
antworten werde. Ihnen steht es natürlich frei. Das einschichtige
[eingestrichene] cis ist natürlich ein Druckversehen. Ich glaube die
richtigen Hintermännner dieses Biedermannes zu errathen. Ich will
mir die N[umme]r kommen lassen. Ganz gut, wenn Sie das Pulver
trocken u[nd] bereit halten.
        Seien Sie herzlich gegrüsst von
        Ihrem aufrichtig ergebenen Guido Adler

II.S-A.o.26

Arnold Schönberg Berlin-Zehlendorf-Wannseebahn
Machnower Chaussee, Villa Lepcke.   9 / 5. 1913

Sehr geehrter Herr Professor, Ihre Karte erhielt ich [vor] ein paar
Stunden, nachdem ich die Entwürfe für die Kadenzen an Sie
abgeschickt hatte. Bitte wollen Sie mir fr[eun]dl[icherweise] mitteilen, ob Sie sie bekommen haben. Sobald ich Nachricht von Casals
habe, ob er die Kadenzen akzeptiert, mache ich mich an das übrige:
Bezeichnung der Vortragsarten. (Oder ist das blos für den Druck
nötig?)
        Wann ist denn das Konzert?
        Haben Sie Casals meine Fragen vorgelegt?

movement, then the location and change of harmony you have chosen are correct and useable. Considered by itself, it does not fit the intentions of the composer. The virtuoso should be content to add a few ornamental notes to the second and third quarter, that is on A and f-sharp in measure 2, system 2, page 90. I am of the opinion that an extended cadenza is not entirely justifiable, either historically or artistically. Surely your cadenzas will be interesting in themselves and Mr. Casals can decide then what to do; you can present both versions in the publication. Therefore, I do look forward to your kind [?] mailing, and I shall forward everything to Casals, and refer him to you in accordance with your wishes.

The *Signale* matter was heretofore unknown to me. I am not yet acquainted with the last issue, and I do not think that I will respond. Of course, you are at liberty to do so. Obviously, c-sharp above middle c is a misprint.[40] I have a hunch as to who the real people behind this "honest" man [Biedermann] are. I shall obtain this issue. It is quite right that you keep your gunpowder dry and in readiness.

Cordial regards from your faithfully devoted Guido Adler

II.S-A.t.26

Arnold Schönberg Berlin-Zehlendorf-Wannseebahn
Machnower Chaussee, Villa Lepcke.   May 9, 1913

Esteemed Professor:
I received your card a few hours ago after I sent the drafts of the cadenzas off to you. Please, be so good as to let me know if you received them. As soon as I have word from Casals as to whether or not he accepts the cadenzas, I shall go on with the remaining task: markings for performance (or is this only necessary for the printing?)

When will the concert take place?
Have you forwarded my questions to Casals?

Die kurzen Kadenzen kommen mir etwas dürftig vor. Aber [es] ist
schwer, etwas so kurzes mitten in einen Satz hineinzusetzen so dass
es vorher richtig unterbricht, dann nachher wieder gut weiter geht
was im Fluss nicht stört. Bei den längeren, wo man sich ausbreiten
kann, ist das leichter.
    Wenn Casals Wünsche hat, bin ich gerne bereit sie zu
berücksichtigen.
    Ich empfehle mich Ihnen mit vorzüglicher Hochachtung
           ergebenst Arnold Schönberg

Ps Graf antworte ich nicht!

II.S-A.o.27

Arnold Schönberg Berlin-Zehlendorf-Wannsee Bahn
Machnower Chaussee, Villa Lepcke.   15. Mai 1913

Sehr geehrter Herr Professor, ich sende Ihnen heute das V[iolon]-
c[el]l[o] Konzert, das ich druckfertig und zum Stimmen heraus-
schreiben bereit gemacht habe. Wenn Sie es angesehen haben,
möchte ich es dem Direktor Hertzka geben, um es ihm zum Verlag
anzubieten. Wenn Sie es aber günstiger finden, dass dies von der
I[nternationalen] M[usik] Ges[ellschaft] aus durch Sie, geschieht, so
wäre mir das auch sehr recht. Nur würde ich Sie in dem Fall bitten
Hertzka keine Auskunft über das Honorar zu geben, das ich von der
I[nternationalen] M[usik] G[esellschaft] bekomme. Denn Hertzka
drückt mich ohnedies stets sehr und wenn er hört, dass ich schon
etwas dafür bekommen habe (wenn auch nicht von ihm) dann fühlt
er sich dennoch für ihr Geld "solidarisch" mit Ihnen und wird mir
gar nichts oder sehr wenig dafür geben.
    Ich möchte gerne von ihm wenigstens eine halbwegs mög-
liche Summe zu bekommen und deswegen möchte ich zweierlei
gerne wissen:
I.   bin ich verpflichtet das bei der Universal-Edition zu ver-
      legen, oder kann ich es auch einem anderen Verleger
      geben?

The short cadenzas appear to me somewhat meager. But [it] is difficult to introduce something that short into the course of a movement so that it first makes a proper break, and then moves on again without interrupting the flow. With longer ones [cadenzas] this is easier, since one has room to extend oneself. If Casals has any requests, I shall consider them.

With highest esteem, I remain yours,
faithfully Arnold Schönberg

Ps I shall not answer Graf!

II.S-A.t.27

Arnold Schönberg Berlin-Zehlendorf Wannsee-Bahn
Machnower Chaussee, Villa Lepcke.   May 15, 1913

Esteemed Professor:
Today I send you the cello concerto, which I have ready for the press and for the copying of the parts. After you have a look at it I would like to give it to director Hertzka in order to offer it to him for publication. Should you consider it more appropriate that this be done by the International Music Society through you, this would also be all right with me. In this case, however, I would like to ask you not to give Hertzka any information about the honorarium I shall be receiving from the International Music Society. Hertzka **presses me very hard anyway,** and when he hears that I have already received something for it [i.e., continuo realization of the cello concerto], even though it is not from him, he will nevertheless feel "solidarity" with you concerning your money and give me nothing or only very little for it.

I would like to receive at least a halfway decent sum from him, and for this reason I would like to know two things:
I.   Am I under obligation to publish this with the Universal Edition, or can I also give it to another publisher?

II.   Wird Casals das Konzert spielen? Auch ausserhalb des
Festes?

Nun noch etwas: Es wäre mir sehr lieb, wenn ich das von
Ihnen mir zugesagte Honorar recht bald bekommen könnte. Ich
übersiedle nämlich am 25. Mai und da kann ich es sehr gut
brauchen.
Und: darf ich Sie bitten, das Honorar möglichst hoch
anzusetzen. Ich hatte doch recht viel Arbeit damit. Meinen Sie,
wären 500 Mark zu viel? Ich finde eigentlich nicht, denn wenn ich
Instrumentations Arbeiten habe, verdiene ich in der gleichen Zeit
leicht das Doppelte, ja noch mehr!! Aber ich hoffe die gleiche
Summe noch von Hertzka zu erhalten und da gienge es dann doch.
Ich habe alles in Allem fast vier Wochen daran gearbeitet. Wenn
Sie die Sache gesehen haben bitte ich zunächst noch nicht die
Stimmen ausschreiben zu lassen. Wie gesagt: vorher möchte ich
noch mit Hertzka einig werden. Und dann muss ich ja noch einiges
in Ordnung bringen, bis ich die Cadenzen von Casals zurückhabe
und die entgültig festgestellt sind.
Ich hoffe bald Ihre fr[eun]dl[iche] Antwort zu haben und
empfehle mich mit vorzüglicher Hochachtung
Ihr ergebener Arnold Schönberg

II.S-A.o.28

Arnold Schönberg
Südende, Berlinerstr. 17aI   31 / 5. 1913

Sehr geehrter Herr Professor, ich bin nicht Ihrer Meinung, dass ein
Honorar von 300 Kronen für meine Arbeit angemessen war und Ihr
Hinweis auf Monns vermutliches Honorar ist nicht nur deshalb
unzulässig, weil sich die Lebensverhältnisse inzwischen wohl sehr
geändert haben, sondern auch, weil ich selbst für derartige Arbeiten
stets mehr bekomme als für meine Kompositionen. Der Künstler
wird, weil er entbehrlicher ist als der Handwerker (das weil er ein
fertiges Werk anbringen müsste, während der Handwerker eine
angetragene Arbeit annimmt oder ablehnt), stets schlechter

II. Is Casals going to play the concerto? Will he also do so after the festival?

Now something else: It would be very nice for me if I could receive rather soon the payment we agreed upon. The reason is that I will be moving on May 25th and could really put it to good use.

Furthermore, may I beg that the payment be as high as possible? I had to put quite a lot of work into this. Do you think that 500 Marks would be too much? I do not really think so, because when I do orchestrations, I make easily twice as much as that (if not more) during the same amount of time!! But I also hope to receive the same amount from Hertzka, and so this would work out. All in all I worked almost four weeks on it. When you have seen the edition, I would like to ask you to not have the parts copied out yet. As I mentioned already, I would like to come to terms with Hertzka first. And then I still have some things to take care of before getting the cadenzas back from Casals and putting them into final form.

I do hope to receive your kind answer soon, and remain with highest esteem
                        Your devoted Arnold Schönberg

II.S-A.t.28

Arnold Schönberg
Südende, Berlinerstr. 17aI   May 31, 1913

Esteemed Professor:
I do not agree with you that the payment of 300 florins was in keeping with my labor, and your reference to the probable payment to Monn is inappropriate not only because living conditions have changed considerably since then, but also because I myself always receive more for such work than for my own compositions. Since an artist is more expendable than a workman (and that because the artist must bring about a completed work, while the craftsman may accept or decline a requested piece of work), his pay is always

beza[h]lt. Aber da wir kein Honorar verabredet hatten, wollte ich
nicht den Schein erwecken, als ob ich eine für mich günstige
Situation ausnütze und habe mich mit 300 Kr[onen] begnügt.
      Nun bitte ich Sie mir so bald wie möglich die Antwort
Casals zu senden. Vor der Aufführung möchte ich jedenfalls noch
einmal das Ganze genau revidieren. Denn ich will noch einige
Vortragsbezeichnungen nachtragen. Es ist jetzt meine Meinung,
dass man das noch viel genauer bezeichnen müsste.
      Auch werde ich für den Druck jedenfalls die tiefen Strei-
cher an einigen besonders dünnen Stellen weglassen. Ich bin zu
diesem Entschluss schon damals gekommen, als ich herausfand, dass
Monn selbst in der Klavierbearbeitung an gewissen Stellen die Bässe
schweigen lässt.
      Einstweilen bin ich mit ergebenen Grüssen
      Ihr Arnold Schönberg

II.S-A.o.29

                                    ? 1913 [in Adler's hand]

Sehr geehrter Herr Professor, ich habe jetzt etwas Zeit und könnte
zu den Continuos schauen. Bitte, könnten Sie mir möglichst bald
die Noten (hergerichtet mit Clavierzeilen) schicken!
      Dann: zur Fortsetzung hätte ich eventuell gerne etwas
Gesangsmusik, Arien, Duette, eventuell Kirchenmusik.
      Mit vorzüglicher Hochachtung
            Arnold Schönberg

inferior. But since we did not agree on the amount of payment beforehand, I did not wish to create the impression that I was taking advantage of a favorable situation, and have contented myself with 300 florins.

Now I would like to ask you to send me Casals' answer as soon as possible. In any case, before the performance I would like to review carefully the entire project, because I wish to add some performance indications. It is now my opinion that one should give much more precise indications.

At any rate, for this publication I also intend to leave out the lower strings in some especially thin passages. I had already arrived at this conclusion when I realized that Monn himself kept the basses silent at certain places in his keyboard version.

Meanwhile I remain with cordial regards,
Yours, Arnold Schönberg

II.S-A.t.29

? 1913 [in Adler's hand]
Esteemed Professor:
I have more time now to look at continuos. I would appreciate it if you could send me some music as soon as possible (with keyboard staves provided for)!

Following this, then, I would perhaps like some vocal pieces, i.e. arias, duets, possibly sacred music.

With high esteem
Arnold Schönberg

Notes

1. *Denkmäler der Tonkunst in Österreich* (DTOE), ed. Guido Adler. Gesellschaft zur Herausgabe der DTOE, Vienna.

2. The information concerning the purchase of the library and personal papers of Guido Adler is based on Mary Gail Means, *A Catalogue of Printed Books and Music in the Guido Adler Collection* (Master's Thesis, unpublished). University of Georgia, 1968, and the Reilly *Index* (see note 3).

3. Edward R. Reilly, *The Papers of Guido Adler at the University of Georgia: A Provisional Index* (1975, unpublished).

4. Edward R. Reilly, *Gustav Mahler and Guido Adler. Records of a Friendship.* Cambridge University Press, Cambridge, 1982. This book is based on Reilly's article which appeared in the July 1972 copy of *Musical Quarterly*. Before the publication of Reilly's expanded version in English (Cambridge, 1982, see above) this book was published in German: Edward R. Reilly, *Gustav Mahler und Guido Adler. Geschichte einer Freundschaft* (translated by Herta Singer-Blaukopf), Bibliothek der Internationalen Gustav Mahler Gesellschaft, Universal Edition. Vienna 1978.

5. Schoenberg's letters and cards to Adler are preserved in the Adler collection at the University of Georgia, and the letters of Adler directed to Schoenberg are in the Library of Congress.

6. *Denkmäler der Tonkunst in Österreich*, XIX Jahrgang, part II, vol. 39. Wiener Instrumentalmusik im XVIII Jahrhundert II, ed. Wilhelm Fischer. Artaria, Wien, and Breitkopf & Härtel, Leipzig, 1912.

7. Arnold Schoenberg, *Sämtliche Werke*, Abteilung VII. Series B, vol. 27, part 1, ed. Nikos Kokkinis. B. Schott's Söhne, Mainz; Universal Edition AG, Wien, 1977. Commentary and Critical Notes were published separately as vol. 27, part 2 in 1987.

8. Georg Matthias Monn (1717-1750) was a leading early classical composer. His basso-continuo exercises (with no explanations) suggest that he was also active as a teacher. Of his compositions only the sacred works include actual figures in the basso-continuo.

9. Karl Weigl (1881-1949) received the Ph.D in musicology under Guido Adler in 1903 from the University of Vienna. His composition teachers included Alexander von Zemlinsky, the only teacher of Arnold Schoenberg. From 1904-1906 Weigl served as rehearsal conductor under Mahler at the Vienna *Hofoper*. In 1918 he taught at the Vienna Conservatory, and from 1930 on Weigl served as a professor of music theory at the University of Vienna. After his emigration to the USA (1933) he remained active as a teacher and composer until his death in 1949. A composer of some repute, he was respected by Richard Strauss, Arnold Schoenberg, Pablo Casals and Bruno Walter.

10. The short-lived Association of Creative Musicians in Vienna (1904-1905) was founded in early 1904. Gustav Mahler served as honorary president, and among the members were Arnold Schoenberg, Alexander von Zemlinky, and Karl Weigl.

11. Wilhelm Fischer (1886-1962) studied musicology under Guido Adler at the University of Vienna, and graduated with a Ph.D in 1912. Because of his dissertation on G. M. Monn, Adler delegated Fischer to be the editor of DTOE, vol. 39, II (see note 6). Fischer served as an assistant to Adler (1912-1928) and started his academic career as an instructor at the University of Vienna.

12. Carl Prohaska (1869-1927) was a well respected Austrian composer in whom Brahms took an interest. After several other appointments he taught piano and theory at the conservatory of the *Gesellschaft der Musikfreunde* in Vienna, and was highly instru-

mental in the elevation of this institution to *Staatsakademie für Musik und darstellende Kunst*. Prohaska's letter, quoted here by permission, is preserved in the Adler Collection of the University of Georgia.

13. A.F. Hermann Kretzschmar (1848-1924), a German musicologist and conductor, received a Ph.D in musicology from the University of Leipzig (1871), studied and taught at the Leipzig Conservatory, and settled in Berlin (1904) as a professor at the university after several intervening academic appointments and engagements as opera conductor and director of choral societies. In 1909 he became director of the *Hochschule für Musik* in Berlin, succeeding Joachim. Kretzschmar was highly regarded as a musicologist; he was one of the founders of the *Neue Bach Gesellschaft*, and became the general editor of the *Denkmäler der Deutschen Tonkunst* in 1912.

14. Emil Hertzka (1869-1932), from 1907 on director of Universal Edition/Vienna. Under his leadership Universal Edition became the most important publisher of contemporary music.

15. Richard Heuberger (1854-1914) was an Austrian conductor, composer and critic. In 1878 he became director of the *Singakademie*, and in 1902 professor at the Academy of Music. Today he is best remembered for his operettas, especially *Der Opernball*.

16. Joseph Marx (1850-1914), a conservative Austrian composer (mainly art song), teacher and music critic. In 1914 he was appointed as a professor of theory at the Academy of Music, and he became director of this institution in 1922.

17. Siegfried Ochs (1858-1929), German choral conductor and composer, was educated at the Academy of Music at Berlin and became a protegé of Hans von Bülow. Compositions include a comic opera, two operettas and vocal music, and his interest in the music of J. S. Bach resulted in editions of the *St. Matthew Passion* and several cantatas.

18. See Chapter III.

19. The remaining portion of this letter and other reactions concerning Graf's negative review of Schoenberg's basso-continuo realizations in *Signale* (p. 283) will be discussed in Chapter VII, p. 289. The evolution of Schoenberg's cello cadenzas can be followed up in the letters of March 14, 1913; March 18, 1913; April 10, 1913; April 12, 1913; April 16, 1913; May 9, 1913; May 15, 1913 (see pp. 101, 107, 109, 111, 113, 115). It will be discussed in detail in Chapter III because it involves Pablo Casals' reactions.

20. George Szell (1897-1970). Of Hungarian birth, Szell grew up in Vienna, and after a distinguished conducting career in Europe, including an affiliation with Richard Strauss at the State Opera in Berlin, he was active as the chief conductor of the Cleveland Symphony until his death in 1970.

21. Josef V. von Wöss (1863-1943), an Austrian composer of mostly sacred music, was educated in Vienna and active in that city as conductor of the *Singakademie* (1899-1900), editor of *Musica Divina* (1913-1934), musical editor of Universal Edition (1908-1931), and from 1925 on as a member of the Commission for the Publication of the *Denkmäler*. In 1926 Wöss was promoted to professor.

22. For further discussions of Schoenberg's basso-continuo realizations and the *Tuma Manuscripts* see Chapter VII.

23. This is the abbreviation for *Verein Schaffender Tonkünstler in Wien*. See also the letter dated June 1, 1904 on p. 63.

24. Heinrich Rietsch (1860-1927) graduated with a law degree at the University of Vienna in 1883. While at the university he also pursued music as a minor with Hanslick and Adler. Further private studies enabled Rietsch to qualify as a lecturer in musicology (1895) at the University of Vienna, and in 1900 Rietsch succeeded Adler at the German University in Prague.

25. See note 23.

26. The Concert Society (Concert Verein) was a Viennese symphony orchestra.

27. This refers to Adler's intercession with the Rothschilds (letter dated October 27, 1904, p. 67).

28. This letter was written between 1903-1905 because Schoenberg lived at that address during this time.

29. Adler had requested excerpts from Schoenberg for his *Der Stil in der Music*; a passage from Schoenberg's *Pelleas und Melisande* can be found in Adler's book.

30. Oskar Fried (1871-1941) was a German composer and conductor. A friend of Mahler's, he performed all of Mahler's symphonies and also became interested in contemporary music. In 1934 Fried emigrated to Russia for an engagement as an opera conductor in Tbilisi.

31. Postal term, possibly parcel post, untranslatable.

32. Josef Labor (1842-1924), a student of Simon Sechter's, was a blind organist active in Vienna from 1868 on. Labor contributed basso-continuo realizations for the DTOE (compositions by Cesti, Biber, and Monn). He was, however, not a teacher of Schoenberg's as suggested by Eric Blom *(The New Grove Dictionary of Music and Musicians)* and Rudolf Quoika *(Die Musik in Geschichte und Gegenwart)*.

33. See also the letters of March 14, 1913 (p. 101); March 18, 1913 (p. 107); April 10, 1913 (p. 109); April 12, 1913 (p. 111); May 9, 1913 (p. 113); May 15, 1913 (p. 115); May 31, 1913 (p. 117); and Chapter III.

34. Emil Bezecny (1868-1930) was a Czech composer and musicologist. He studied at the University of Vienna with Guido Adler and served from 1896 on as professor of music at the German Music Academy in Prague.

35. See Chapter VII, p. 283.

36. Max Graf (1873-1958) graduated with a law degree, and after music studies with Hanslick and Bruckner he was granted a Ph.D in musicology from the University of Vienna (1896). He was a well-published author of several books and many articles, as well as numerous reviews of concerts. In 1938 Graf emigrated to the USA where he held several academic positions, but he returned to Vienna in 1947. Graf is best remembered as a notable music critic who supported modern composers.

37. Moritz Violin was a music theorist and pianist who grew up with Schoenberg.

38. See Chapter VII, p. 304, I, 3.
From here on references to the reprint of G. M. Monn's *Symphonia a Quattro in A Major 38.* (reprinted in Chapter VII, pp. 297-305) are given in square brackets with page and measure numbers. Graf's terminology, referring to the pagination of the DTOE, vol. 39, has been retained in order to make possible cross-references to his article in *Signale* (see Chapter VII, p. 283).

39. The Adler Collection at the University of Georgia includes a one-page shorthand draft of two letters. One of these could be identified as an outline of this letter. The other shorthand draft refers to two Schoenberg letters dated January 20th and 22nd respectively (no year), which are not known at present.

40. See endnote 38.

CHAPTER III

Pablo Casals - Guido Adler

Schoenberg's Continuo-Realization and Cadenzas for the
Violoncello Concerto in G Minor by Georg Matthias Monn

Pablo Casals (1876-1973), the most famous cellist of this
century, is considered by many to have been the greatest cellist of
all time. Born in Vendrell, Catalonia, he grew up in a musical
family, and his musical education was guided carefully by his
supportive parents. Because he was too young to pursue his earlier
studies away from home by himself, his mother and her younger
children went with him to Barcelona, Brussels, and Paris, at times
enduring great hardship. Casals' supporters and early sponsors
include Albeniz, the private secretary of the queen-regent of Spain,
Count de Morphy, Granados and many others. Quite by chance
Casals came accross Bach's solo suites for cello at the age of 13.
This was a milestone for him, and he devoted himself to this magnificent music throughout his entire life.[1]

As a performer Casals abhorred empty virtuosity, but he
revolutionized the techniques of bowing and fingering. His
analytical mind, brillant musicianship, and perceptiveness brought
about a unique style of performance whose sole and exclusive aim
was to serve the music. Casals' association with Alfred Cortot and
Jacques Thibaud (1905) in the performance of the piano trio
literature elevated the standards of this genre to an unprecedented
level, unequaled even today.

Casals' involvement in music was not restricted to his
instrument, for he was also an excellent conductor and a very
competent pianist. For that matter, he actually considered conducting to be the least restrictive, and therefore his preferred medium
of expression. In 1919 he took it upon himself to establish a
large symphony orchestra in Barcelona. For several years he served
as the chief conductor, molding this group of musicians into an
ensemble of international reputation through his patient and painstaking rehearsals; and since there were no other resources, he

126

financed the entire operation, salaries and all, out of his own pocket. With its growing reputation, this orchestra became more and more self-sufficient, but it was not until 1928 that it was completely self-supporting.

Casals was also concerned that concert attendance was out of reach for the working classes. With this in mind, he founded an organization entitled *Obrera Associacio de Concerts* (1925) which was run by its own members, published a journal, and admitted only members whose monthly income was below 500 pesetas. This association was immensely successful, and similar workers' associations sprang up all over Spain and were imitated in England.

The social concerns of Casals went far beyond the goals of these associations to disseminate music among the less affluent. When the Second Republic of Spain came into being in 1931, the independence of Catalonia within the framework of the Iberian Federation was celebrated during the same year with Beethoven's Ninth Symphony, conducted by Casals himself. During the ensuing Civil War, Casals pursued his international career, never appearing in Germany nor Italy, but continuing his work in Spain. After the fall of the Spanish Republic in 1939, Casals went into exile in France, taking residence in Prades, a region known as "French" Catalonia. His hopes that the restructuring of Europe after World War II would include at least some sanctions against Franco's Spain did not materialize. To express his disappointment, he published a letter in the *News Chronicle* on July 18, 1946,[2] entitled "Why Franco must go," and resolved for himself never to perform in public again in spite of numerous offers from everywhere. It was not until 1950 that he broke his silence, and his performances at the Bach Festival in Prades during that year ushered in another career culminating with his performance for the 13th anniversary of the United Nations in the General Assembly Hall (1958), and his appearance at the White House upon the invitation of President and Mrs. Kennedy in 1961.

As a composer Casals rather favored traditional styles which did not involve twentieth-century concepts. His oeuvre includes much sacred music, chamber music, and compositions with orchestra. His foremost work is the oratorio *El pesebre*, composed between 1943 and 1960, and performed all over the world in con-

nection with his peace campaign of 1962. Casals' indirect connection with Schoenberg predates by almost two decades his actual
correspondence with the composer. This early relationship can be
reconstructed from the Schoenberg-Adler correspondence (see
Chapter II), which engaged in the discussion of a matter of common
interest to Schoenberg, Adler, and Casals--the Cello Concerto in G
minor by Georg Matthias Monn (1717-1750), for which Schoenberg
had provided the figured-bass realizations and cadenzas.

The first reference to Schoenberg's cadenzas appeared in
Adler's letter to Schoenberg of March 9, 1913 (p. 97), in which he
informed Schoenberg of Casals' request for one or two cadenzas and
invited him, with the consent of Casals, to write cadenzas for the
Monn concerto. These cadenzas, as Adler informs us, were
intended for the first modern performance of this work by Casals at
the "historic" Vienna concert of November 19, 1913, in celebration
of the twentieth anniversary of the *Denkmäler der Tonkunst in Österreich*. Schoenberg responded enthusiastically with a letter dated
March 13, 1913 (p. 99), indicating that he had already considered
such a project himself. In the same letter Schoenberg also explored
the possibility of publishing the Monn cello concerto and his own
cadenzas separately from the *Denkmäler* series. A day later, on
March 14th (p. 101), Schoenberg made precise recommendations to
Adler as to where the cadenzas could be inserted, because Monn
himself had not made any provisions for cadenzas in the score.
Concerning the cadenza of the third movement, Schoenberg
attached to this letter a musical sketch of his alteration of Monn's
score in order to accommodate a cadenza (see Facsimile I on p.
103). The same letter also informs us that Schoenberg suggested
that such cadenzas should follow the preferences of performers
rather than historical concepts. With this Adler may have agreed
in principle, at least tacitly. It was this point of view which initiated
the indirect contact between Schoenberg and Casals, for Schoenberg
was quite willing to accommodate Casals' wishes in every regard.
In Adler's response of March 18, 1913 (p. 107) to Schoenberg's
letters of March 13th and 14th, he offered Schoenberg an honorarium for the cadenzas and answered his questions concerning a separate publication of the Monn concerto. From Schoenberg's next

letter to Adler on April 10, 1913 (p. 109) we learn about the first draft of a cadenza for the first movement, and the fact that he wished Adler to send the cadenza and his questions, numbered I through V, to Casals with a request for his response, preferably directly to Schoenberg. On April 12, 1913 (p. 111) Adler acknowledged receiving Schoenberg's cadenza, and informed Schoenberg that he considered it too long, since "a cadenza of the Mozart type was not yet customary at that time."

Concerning the cadenza for the third movement, Adler advised Schoenberg "to be content with a few notes," and in conclusion Adler told Schoenberg that he would wait for the second cadenza before forwarding all to Casals.

At this point Adler already may have had some misgivings about Schoenberg's cadenzas, since he left open the possibilty that Casals might not play the cadenzas in the concert of November 19th 1913 (letter of April 12, 1913, p. 111), but he also assured Schoenberg that he would receive the honorarium in any case, that the cadenzas would remain Schoenberg's property, and that they could be included in Schoenberg's separate publication of the concerto with Universal Edition.

Adler's next letter, of April 16, 1913 (p. 111), made references to Schoenberg's earlier remarks of April 10, 1913 (p. 109), which concerned the cadenza to be written for the third movement. He readily conceded to Schoenberg that "for a more elaborate cadenza for the third movement . . . the location and change of harmony you have chosen are correct and useable," but also suggested to him that "the virtuoso should be content to add a few notes to the second and third quarter notes, that is the A and f-sharp in m. 2, system 2 on p. 90 (second measure of Example 1 below). "I am of the opinion," continued Adler, "that an extended cadenza is not quite justifiable, either historically or artistically." It should be noted that the implementation of Adler's idea of adding only a short ornamental passage to the two notes singled out would not even have necessitated an alteration of Monn's score.[3]

In a letter of May 9, 1913 (p. 113), Schoenberg inquired if Adler had received the sketches of the cadenzas. At the same time Schoenberg also expressed his personal preference for longer cadenzas, and promised Adler that he would make the necessary performance indications in the cadenzas as soon as he heard whether or not Casals had accepted them.

Schoenberg sent the completed figured-bass realizations of
the cello concerto to Adler on May 15, 1913 (p. 115). From this
letter we also learn that Schoenberg had worked at the task for
about four weeks. Concerning the honorarium from the *Internationale Musik Gesellschaft* for the Cello concerto to be published in
the *Denkmäler* edition, Schoenberg tried to persuade Adler to set
the amount as high as possible, hopefully to DM 500. Furthermore,
Schoenberg asked Adler not to disclose this amount to Hertzka, the
director of Universal Edition, so that he would be able to extract
the same fee from him for the separate publication of this work.
Adler must have been somewhat annoyed, because--as Schoenberg
recounted at great length in his letter to Adler on May 31, 1913 (p.
117)--Adler had offered him only 300 florins, reminding Schoenberg
that Monn must not have fared much better back then. In conclusion, Schoenberg urged Adler to send him Casals' answers as soon
as possible because he had not heard from him as yet.

The autograph of Schoenberg's cadenzas for the Monn violoncello concerto in G minor was found in his estate by Rufer in
1957, and the cadenzas--two each for the first and third move-
ments--were published in 1977.[4]

The information on the Schoenberg cadenzas for the cello
concerto in G minor by Georg Matthias Monn found in the Adler -
Casals correspondence (Chapter II) allows for these conclusions
concerning the dates of composition: a draft of the longer cadenza
for the first movement originated between March 13 and April 10,
1913, that is, from the time when he accepted Adler's invitation to
write the cadenzas (p. 99) to the time when he sent the cadenzas to
Adler (p. 109). Adler's comments in his letter of April 12, 1913 (p.
111) confirm that Schoenberg had indeed sent him the longer cadenza for the first movement. From this and Adler's next letter of
April 16, 1913 (p. 111), we learn that Adler wanted shorter cadenzas. On May 9, 1913 (p. 113), Schoenberg informed Adler that he
had sent him the remaining cadenzas, and his comments concerning
the merits of the longer and shorter cadenzas strongly suggest that--
in accommodation of Adler's preferences--he had provided him
with both, the shorter and longer cadenzas.

Casals' first reference to Schoenberg's cadenzas is found in
his letter of July 2, 1913 (p. 139), in which he informed Adler that
it was impossible for him to use Schoenberg's cadenzas, and that he

rather wanted to write more idiomatic cadenzas himself. In response (undated letter, see p. 139) Adler assured Casals that he would be in agreement with his decision. On October 15, 1913 (p. 141) Casals expressed again to Adler that he regretted "that those of Schoenberg are impossible to play," that he had not yet written his own cadenzas, but that "they will be done in time."

Since the correspondence between Adler and Schoenberg ceased after Schoenberg's letter of May 31, 1913 (p. 117; the letter given on p. 119 is undated) there is no way to ascertain whether or not Casals' assessment of the cadenzas was ever conveyed to Schoenberg.

It is most unfortunate that only a draft (p. 139) of one of Adler's responses to Casals' earlier letters written between November 13, 1912 (p. 135) and April 16, 1914 (p. 141) has survived World War I. Casals himself recalled the circumstances concerning the loss of many of his personal effects, especially the letters, all of which he had stored in Paris:

> At the outbreak of the war, when I had given up my house at the Villa Molitor, I had packed many of my belongings in boxes and stored them in a small warehouse before leaving Paris. Now I went to collect them. I was dismayed at what I found. A scene of dreadful disorder! The boxes had been broken into--my books, musical works and correspondence were scattered all over the floor. Most of the correspondence was gone. Among it, scores of letters from dear friends and former collegues and acquaintances of mine--from Granados, Saint-Saëns, Richard Strauss, Julius Röntgen, Emanuel Moór and many others.
>
> These letters were very dear to me--voices that spoke of precious days and intimate thoughts we had shared--and I felt sickened at the idea of strange hands intruding among them. It was, I was given to understand, the work of the police. They had searched my belongings and taken whatever they desired. Of what I was suspected I still do

not know--perhaps my being a foreigner was
enough. In war time anything is possible. In the
hope of recovering my letters, I addressed several
communications to the French government authorities. Perhaps, I thought, my letters were stored
away in their official files. Perhaps they still are.
Not long ago a friend of mine tried to intervene
with the French writer André Malraux when he
was minister of culture under de Gaulle, to find
out if my letters were in the police files, but to no
avail. At any rate, I never heard from the authorities or saw my letters again. ...[5]

The remaining correspondence between Adler and Casals
is from the years 1926-1927 (p. 145, 147), 1931 (p. 147), and 1934
(p. 149). Some of Casals' letters to Adler from 1926-1927 must
have gotten lost at that time, for in a letter of October 20, 1926 (p.
145) Casals alluded to the fact that several of his letters to Adler
had remained unanswered, and he asked Adler for "a third time if
my proposal could be acceptable. If the answer is negative I would
ask you to please arrange that I may conduct an overture before the
Eighth Symphony." Casals did indeed conduct Beethoven's Eighth
Symphony in a concert in Vienna, given during the Beethoven
Centennial which had been organized during that year.[6]

Guido Adler, a highly respected member of the Jewish
community in Vienna and a major force in music and the arts, had
commanded such respect and position in public life, that he personally was never touched by the Nazis after Austria was annexed
by Germany.

Casal's letter of June 8, 1934 (p. 149) was written in response to Adler's request (lost) for help concerning his only son,
Hubert Joachim, a physician, to find employment and safety for his
family in Spain. The response to this letter has been preserved as
a hand-written draft from Adler dated June 15, 1934 (p. 149 and
Facsimile II, p. 150), and concludes with these sorrowful words:

"We shall remain friends for life and beyond in aeternum. The times are troubled, let us hope for the future. I do

hope to see you here very soon. My work and the care for the children help to keep my sanity."

III.C-A.o.1

13. Nov. 1912

Cher Monsieur Adler,

Votre mot m'a fait plaisir - nous nous rappelons de votre amabilité et de votre maison hospitalière! Hélas nous ne pouvons pas jouir de toutes les bonnes choses.

Nous sommes de passage ici - car nous arrivons maintenant de Prag[ue] et je pars tantôt pour Temesvar Hongrie - la prochaine fois ce sera malheuresement la même chose - j'arriverai à Wien le même jour du concert (22 Nov.) et je partirai après le concert pour Londres. Je vous donne ces ennuyeuses explications seulement pour que vous voy[i]ez que <u>nous sommes obligés</u> de nous priver du plaisir de vous voir!

Meilleurs compliments pour vous et Madame Adler de Madame Casals et de votre dévoué

Pablo Casals

III.C-A.o.2

23 Février 1913

Cher Monsieur Adler!

Entre deux trains j'ai été à Wien la semaine dernière trouvant parmi ma correspondence une communication téléphonique de vous m'annonçant votre visite pour le lendemain - n'ayant pas votre adresse en mémoire je n'ai pu vous avertir de mon départ ce que j'ai regretté infiniment - je suis heureux que votre mot me donne la possibilité de vous écrire pour m'excuser et pour vous remercier.

Je viens d'arriver d'une tournée en Hongrie et province Autriche. Je reste à Wien pour le concert d'après demain avec Madame Soldat et repars pour Prag[ue]. Je serai de retour le 28 et le concert du 1er mars - après cela mes devoirs dans ce pays seront finis pour cette saison.

Vous verrez par là qu'il [ne] m'en sera guère possible de vous faire une visite - ce qui serait mon grand plaisir mais je vous prierais de prendre un moment pour venir me voir et nous causerons de ce que vous voudrez notamment du Concerto de

III.C-A.t.1

November 13, 1912

Dear Mr. Adler,[7]

Your note gave me pleasure. We remember your kindness and your hospitality! Unfortunately, we cannot enjoy all good things.

We are only here in passing--because we have just arrived now from Prague and I am leaving in a little while for Temesvar, Hungary. The next time it will be unfortunately the same thing--I will arrive in Vienna the very day of the concert (22 Nov.) and I will leave after the concert for London. I give you these trivial explanations only so that you may see that we are obliged to be deprived of the pleasure of seeing you!

My best wishes for you and Madame Adler from Madame Casals and your devoted

Pablo Casals

III.C-A.t.2

February 23, 1913

Dear Mr. Adler,

Last week, between two trains, I was in Vienna and found among my correspondence a telephone communication from you announcing your visit the next day. Not having your address in memory I could not advise you that I was leaving, which I regretted immensely. I am happy to have your note because it gives me the possibility of writing you to excuse myself and also to thank you.

I just have arrived from a tour in Hungary and the Austrian province. I will remain in Vienna for the concert the day after tomorrow with Madame Soldat and then leave for Prague. I will return on the 28th and the concert the first of March; after that my duties in this country will be finished for this season.

By this you will see that it will hardly be possible for me to visit you--which would give me great pleasure, but I would ask that

Monn.

Je serai à la maison demain jusqu'à 2 heures et je vous prie de me faire avertir par téléphone l'heure à laquelle je dois vous attendre.

Veuillez présenter mes hommages respectueux à Mme. Adler et croyez à mes sentiments tout dévoués

Pablo Casals

III.C-A.o.3

20 Villa Molitor
Paris 17 Mars 1913

Cher Dr. Adler,

Je vous remercie de votre lettre et je note la date du 19 Nov. pour le concert de "Denkmäler." J'attends la Cadenza. Bon voyage et bon séjour en Italie et bonnes amitiés de nous deux.

Votre dévoué
Pablo Casals

III.C-A.o.4

20 Villa Molitor
Paris 10 Mai 1913

Cher Dr. Adler,

Puisque le 19 Nov. ne vous va pas, je vous propose une date en Février - si l'époque vous convient veuillez me dire quelques dates à choisir - J'attends les Cadenzas -

Bonnes amitiés
Pablo Casals

you take a moment to come and see me and we will talk about anything you wish, notably the Monn concerto.

I will be home tomorrow until two o'clock and I beg you to let me know by telephone the time that I should expect you.

Please convey my respects to Madame Adler and be assured of my devoted sentiments

Pablo Casals

III.C-A.t.3

20 Villa Molitor
Paris March 17, 1913

Dear Dr. Adler,

Thank you for your letter. I have taken note of the date of Nov. 19 for the "Denkmäler" concert. I am waiting for the cadenza. Have a good trip and a good stay in Italy, and my best regards from both of us.

Your devoted,
Pablo Casals

III.C-A.t.4

20 Villa Molitor
Paris May 10, 1913

Dear Dr. Adler,

Since the 19 of November is not good for you I propose a date in February--if this time period is convenient please give me a few dates to choose from. I am waiting for the cadenzas.

Best regards,
Pablo Casals

III.C-A.o.5

20 Villa Molitor
Paris 2 Juillet 1913

Cher Dr. Guido Adler,

A mon grand regret je dois vous dire que les Cadenzas de Schönberg sont d'une exécution peu possible malgré l'admiration que ce maître m'inspire. Je suis obligé de faire moi-même des cadenzas qui seront peut être insignifiantes mais qui auront je l'espère la condition d'être écrites avec quelque confort pour l'instrument.

Les quelques indications de nuances me conviennent parfaitement et les cadenzas viendront exactement à la même place (marqués au crayon). Je ferai l'envoi de la partition à Villa Waldessaum.

Je vous souhaite ainsi qu'à votre chère famille un bon été - mon adresse après le 15 Juillet est

Poste Restante
Vendrell
Prov. de Tarragona
Espagne

Mille bons souvenirs et amitié

Pablo Casals

III.A-C.o.1   [Adler's draft of a letter to Casals, no date]

Cher Monsieur Casals
ich stimme Ihnen vollkommen zu, dass Sie sich selbst Kadenzen schreiben wollen u[nd] sehe der ge[fälligen] Übersendung der Partitur (Partituren) nach Bad Aussee, Vild (St[eier]m[ark]) entgegen. Ihre Wünsche für den Sommer erwidere ich namens m[einer] Familie auf das Herzlichste u[nd] empfehle mich hochachtungsvoll Ihrer Frau Gemahlin.
Mit freundschaftlichen Grüssen von uns an Sie Beide
Ihr auf[richtig] erg[ebener]

III.C-A.t.5

20 Villa Molitor
Paris July 2, 1913

Dear Dr. Guido Adler,

With great regret I must tell you that the cadenzas of Schönberg have little possibility of execution in spite of the admiration that this master inspires in me. I am obliged to do myself the cadenzas, which will be insignificant perhaps, but which will have, I hope, the condition of being written with some comfort for the instrument.

The few indications of nuances suit me perfectly, and the cadenzas will come in the same place (marked in pencil). I will send the score to Villa Waldessaum.

I wish you and your family a good summer. My address after the 15th of July is

Poste Restante
Vendrell
Prov. de Tarragona
Espagne

With many good remembrances and best regards,
Pablo Casals

III.A-C.t.1

[Translation of Adler's draft of a letter to Casals, no date]

Dear Mr. Casals:

I agree completely with you, with your desire to write the cadenzas yourself, and I look forward to the shipment of the score (scores) to Bad Aussee, Vild (St[eier]m[ark]). My family and I return your wishes for the summer most cordially and please remember me to you wife.

With cordial regards from us to you both, your faithful

III.C-A.o.6

15 Oct. 1913

Cher Dr. Adler,

Un mot pour vous dire que la partition du Concerto de Monn vous à été envoyée au moment où je vous l'ai annoncé. Je suis étonné de savoir que vous ne l'avez jamais reçue - j'espère cependant que ce ne sera pas un malheur irréparable!

J'arriverai à Vienne le 19 matin et je compte pouvoir répéter soit le même matin soit l'après-midi - c'est comme vous voudrez. Les cadenzas ne sont pas encore faites - elles le seront au temps précis - je regrette que celles de Schönberg soient impossible[s] à jouer -

Milles bons souvenirs de votre dévoué

Pablo Casals

III.C-A.o.7

24. Oct 1913

Cher Dr. Adler,

C'est entendu je serai à la répétition du 19 à 10 h.1/2 - Malheureusement, mon temps étant tout ce qu'il y a de plus limité je ne pourrai ni assister à la reunion ni avoir le plaisir de passer quelques moments chez vous.

Mes hommages à Madame Adler et croyez à mes sentiments très dévoués

Pablo Casals

III.C-A.o.8

16 Avril 1914

Mon cher Dr. Guido Adler,

J'ai été bien surpris de recevoir votre mot avec la communication. Je vous remercie infiniment de votre intérêt et de votre aimable félicitation -

Permettez-moi de vous faire les suivantes questions:

III.C-A.t.6

October 15, 1913

Dear Dr. Adler.

Just a word to tell you that the score of the Monn Concerto was sent to you at the time I informed you of it. I am very surprised to learn that you never received it. I hope, however, that this will not be an irreparable misfortune!

I will arrive in Vienna the morning of the 19th, and I count on being able to rehearse either that same morning or in the afternoon--as you wish. The cadenzas are not yet done--they will be done on time--I regret that those of Schönberg are impossible to play.

Many good remembrances from your devoted

Pablo Casals

III.C-A.t.7

October 24, 1913

Dear Dr. Adler,

It is agreed that I will be at the rehearsal of the 19th at 10:30 a.m. Unfortunately since my time is most limited, I will not be able to attend the meeting nor have the pleasure of spending a few moments in your home.

My respects to Madame Adler, and accept my most devoted sentiments,

Pablo Casals

III.C-A.t.8

April 16, 1914

My dear Dr. Guido Adler,

I was very surprised to receive your note with the announcement. I thank you immensely for your interest and for your kind congratulations.

Please allow me to ask you the following questions:

1. Dois-je attendre la communication officielle du ministère des affaires étrangères ainsi que les insignes?
2. Je serais très heureux de savoir la signification de "Komtur"*kreuz*.
3. Cette décoration a-t-elle différents degrés? en ce cas à quel degré appartient celle qui m'est conférée?

J'espère cher Dr. Adler avoir le grand plaisir de vous voir à Vienne en Automne -

Vous avez sans doute reçu le faire part de mon mariage avec Miss Susan Metcalfe le 4 de ce mois à New York; j'espère que ma femme m'accompagnera à mon prochain voyage à Vienne et je serais bien heureux de vous faire faire connaissance -

Présentez, je vous prie[,] mes hommages à Madame Dr. Guido Adler et croyez-moi votre très sincèrement dévoué

Pablo Casals

P.D. Je resterai en Amérique jusqu'au 9 mai jour du départ pour Londres; mon adresse dans cette ville est: c/o Vert's Concert Agency, Cork St. London W.

III.C-DTÖ.o.1

16 Avril 1914

A la commission directrice de la Denkmäler der Tonkunst in Österreich

Tres honnorés Messieurs!

Je vous remercie de la communication que vous avez bien voulu m'envoyer pour m'annoncer l'honneur que sa Royale et Impériale Majesté Apostolique vient de me faire en me nommant Komturkreuz des Franz Joseph Ordens, auquel je suis très sensible et très reconnaissant.

Veuillez, honnorés Messieurs[,] agréer mes sentiments de haute considération

Pablo Casals

1. Should I wait for the official communication from the Ministry of Foreign Affairs as well as the insignia?
2. I would be happy to know the meaning of "*Komtur*" *kreuz.*
3. Does this decoration have different degrees? In this case,which one is the one that is being conferred on me?

Dear Dr. Adler, I hope to have the pleasure of seeing you in Vienna this autumn.

You have undoubtedly received the announcement of my marriage to Miss Susan Metcalfe on the 4th of this month in New York; I hope that my wife will accompany me on my next trip to Vienna and I will be very happy for you to meet each other.

May I ask you to offer my respects to Madame Guido Adler and consider me your sincerely devoted

Pablo Casals

P.S. I will remain in America until the 9th of May when I will leave for <u>London</u>; my address there is: c/o Vert's Concert Agency, Cork St., <u>London W.</u>

III.C-DTÖ.t.1

April 16, 1914

To the Directing Committee of the Denkmäler der Tonkunst in Österreich

Honorable Gentlemen!

I thank you for the communication you have kindly sent me announcing the honor that his Royal and Imperial Apostolic Majesty has conferred upon me, the Komturkreuz des Franz Joseph Ordens, for which I am touched and most grateful.

Please accept, honorable gentlemen, my sentiments of high esteem,

<u>Pablo Casals</u>

III.C-A.o.9

[NO DATE/LONDON]
from Dieudonne Hotel Limited

Très cher Monsieur Adler,
J'ai reçu votre précieux envoi - Le concerto sera mon travail d'été et s'il est prêt je le mettrai au programme d'un de mes concerts à Vienne l'automne prochain - quand à vos livres nous sommes en train de les lire moi, le Wagner et ma femme, Der Stil in der Musik et nous sommes, chacun de son côté, le plus intéressés, à sa lecture.
Croyez cher Monsieur Adler à nos sentiments les plus admiratifs et sympathiques

Pablo Casals

III.C-A.o.10

Barcelona 20 Oct. 1926
Diagonal 440

Mon cher Ami,
Qu'est-ce qui arrive avec mes lettres adressées à vous -
Il y a bien deux mois que Mons[ieur] Pena Secrétaire de mon orchestre vous a écrit en vous demandant de ma part de prolonger d'un jour le Festival Beethoven de façon que Mons[ieur] Weingartner puisse diriger tout un programme et moi de même -
Mons[ieur] Pena disait également que j'étais d'accord au sujet des autres concerts - A cette lettre je n'ai jamais eu de réponse. En plus, je vous ai écrit une lettre pour vous répéter ce qui avait été dit dans la lettre de Mons[ieur] Pena - à celle-ci point de réponse également.
Je viens donc vous demander une troisième fois si ma proposition pourrait être acceptée - dans le cas négatif je vous prierai de bien vouloir arranger pour que je puisse conduire une Ouverture avant la 8ème Symphonie -
Le Concerto de Monn a été mon travail de vacances et je crois l'avoir reconquis -
Mille bonnes amitiés avec les salutations affecteuses pour vous et Mad[ame] Adler de la part de ma femme

Votre dévoué
Pablo Casals

III.C-A.t.9

[No Date/London]
From Dieudonne Hotel Limited

Very dear Mr. Adler,

I received your precious package. The concerto will be my work for the summer, and if it is ready, I will put it in the program of one of my concerts in Vienna next fall. Regarding your books, we are in the midst of reading them, I the *Wagner*, and my wife *Der Stil in der Musik*, and we are, each one of us, most interested in the reading.

Please accept, Mr. Adler, our sentiments of highest admiration and sympathy

Pablo Casals

III.C-A.t.10

Barcelona October 20, 1926
Diagonal 440

My dear friend,

What is happening to my letters addressed to you? It has been already two months since Mr. Pena,[8] secretary of my orchestra, wrote to you asking you on my behalf to extend by one day the Beethoven festival so that Mr. Weingartner could conduct an entire program and I as well. Mr. Pena wrote also that I was in agreement concerning the other concerts. To this letter I never had a response. In addition I wrote another letter to repeat what had been said in Mr. Pena's letter. To this one there was no response either.

I am asking you now a third time if my proposal could be accepted. If the answer is negative, I would ask you to please arrange that I may conduct an overture before the Eighth Symphony.[9]

The Monn Concerto has been my work during my vacation and I believe I have reconquered it.

With my best regards and affectionate greetings to you from my wife

Your devoted
Pablo Casals

III.C-A.o.11

5 Avril 1927

Bristol Hotel

Mon cher Ami,
      Nous vous remercions de votre carte regrettant de ne pas vous avoir vu -
      Ainsi que je vous ai dit Dimanche dernier je n'avais aucune intention d'accepter quoique ce soit pour mes frais de séjour à Vienne mais dans la note de Knepler j'ai eu la surprise de voir une contribution à l'État d'une somme assez élévée sur mes concerts de Vienne -
      En ce cas je trouverais assez raisonable d'accepter votre offre et je vous propose de remettre à Knepler 1.500 Schillings que je me ferais avancer par lui demain matin à fin de pouvoir payer ma note d'Hôtel et frais nécessaires avant le départ.
      Je regrette de vous écrire sur ce sujet et avec mes félicitations renouvelées et en pensant à l'année prochaine je vous envoi ainsi que ma femme mes sentiments affectueux pour vous et Madame Adler -

Votre ami
Pablo Casals

N.B. La somme mentionnée représente les frais de quelques jours.

III.C-A.o.12

10 soir 1931

Mon cher ami
      Je n'ai pu vous avoir par téléphone. Comme je pars demain matin je vous envoi ce mot pour vous dire que je serai à Vienne en Mars et alors il faudra se voir.
      Le concert de ce soir a très bien marché - Je suis touché que malgré la crise qui se fait sentir partout les Viennois aient rempli la salle!
      Une bien affecteuse poignée de main de votre
Pablo Casals

III.C-A.t.11

April 5, 1927

Bristol Hotel

My dear friend,

    We thank you for your card regretting that we could not see you.

    As I told you last Sunday, I had no intention of accepting anything for the expenses of my stay in Vienna; but in the note from Knepler I was surprised to see a tax assessment by the state of a rather high sum on concerts in Vienna.

    In this case I would find it reasonable to accept your offer, and I propose to you to give Mr. Knepler 1,500 Schillings that he will advance to me tomorrow, so that I may pay my hotel bill and other necessary expenses before leaving.

    I regret having to write to you on this subject. With my renewed congratulations and thinking of next year, my wife and I send our affectionate sentiments to you and Mrs. Adler -

Your friend
Pablo Casals

N.B. The quoted sum represents the expenses for a few days.

III.C-A.t.12

10th evening, 1931

My dear friend,

    I could not reach you by telephone. Since I leave tomorrow morning, I am sending you this note to tell you that I will be in Vienna in March, and we will have to see each other then.

    The concert this evening went very well--I am touched that, in spite of the crisis that is felt everywhere, the Viennese filled the hall!

    A very affectionate handshake from your

Pablo Casals

III.C-A.o.13

8 Juin 1934

Mon cher Ami,

     J'ai reçu votre lettre et je me suis mis immédiatement en route avec le désir de satisfaire votre intention au sujet de votre fils -

     J'ai parlé d'abord avec mon médecin qui n'a pas été optimiste quant à la possibilité de l'entrée d'un étranger dans le Syndicat des Médecins - Malgré cela je me suis fait donner une introduction pour le Directeur de notre grand hôpital que j'ai pu voir - Je lui ai exposé le cas et il m'a dit l'absolue impossibilité de la chose. Ce Docteur à plusieurs reprises a voulu s'attacher des médecins allemands pour des certaines spécialités sans pouvoir y réussir, toujours à cause des lois syndicales -

     Je crois tout autre demarche inutile à moins que vous me demandiez d'insister - Pensez si j'aimerais vous servir -

Votre ami affectueux
Pablo Casals

III.A-C.o.2   [Adler's draft of a letter to Casals]

An Casals   15 . 6. 34

T[eurer] F[reund]!

     Innigen Dank fuer Ihre fr[eun]dl[iche] Bemühung u[nd] die gütige Absicht, wenn es nötig sein sollte, noch weitere Schritte zu unternehmen. Mein Sohn wird sich erlauben, Ihnen nächster Tage selbst zu danken u[nd] zu berichten. Seine Frau ist schwer erkrankt u[nd] somit muss sich seine Sorge ? ihr zuwenden.

     Zu der schönen fr[eun]d[l]ichen [Einladung ?] am Sonntag kann ich leider nicht kommen. Mein Schreiben an das Comité wird wo[h]l verlesen u[nd] Ihnen vorgelegt werden. Wir bleiben Freunde fürs Leben und darüber hinaus in aeternum. Die Zeiten sind trüb, hoffen wir für die Zukunft. Mich hält die Arbeit aufrecht und mein Sinnen für die Kinder.

     Mit ? herzlichem Dank umarmt Sie [?] - - - -

Sie hoffe ich bald wieder hier zu sehen

III.C-A.t.13

June 8, 1934

My dear friend.

I received your letter and I immediately went to work with the desire to satisfy your need regarding your son.

I first talked to my doctor, who was not optimistic about the possibility of a foreigner entering the Doctors' Union. In spite of that I got an introduction to the director of our big hospital, and I saw him. I explained the case to him, and he told me of the absolute impossibility of it. This doctor had several times tried to include German doctors for certain specialties but could not succeed, always because of the union laws.

I think that any other attempt is futile unless you ask me to insist. Just think how I would like to be of service to you.

Your affectionate friend
Pablo Casals

III.A-C.t.2   [Translation of Adler's draft of a letter to Casals]

To Casals   June 15, 1934

Dear friend!

My heartfelt thanks for your kind efforts and your good intentions to take further steps should it be necessary. Within the next few days, my son will take the liberty to thank you in person and to give you a report. His wife is seriously ill and he has to devote himself to her completely.

I will not be able to accept your kind invitation for Sunday. My letter to the committee will be read [at their meeting] and will then be presented to you. We shall remain friends for life and beyond in aeternum. These are troubled times; let us hope for a better future. I do hope to see you here very soon. My work and the care for the children help me to keep my sanity.

I embrace you with hearty thanks

I hope to see you here soon again

Facsimile II. Adler to Casals. Draft dated June 15, 1934.

Notes

1. J. Ma. Corredor, *Conversations with Casals*. New York: E.P. Dutton & Co., Inc., 1957, pp. 26-27.

2. For the full text of Casals' letter, see Lillian Littlehales, *Pablo Casals*. London: J.M. Dent, 1949, pp. 218-219.

3. See Chapter II, pp. 102 ff.

4. Arnold Schoenberg, *Instrumentalkonzerte nach Werken alter Meister*, ed. Nikos Kokkinis, Series B, vol. 27,1, pp. 67-72. Mainz: B. Schott & Sons; Vienna: Universal Edition AG., 1977. For further information on the concerto for violoncello in G minor by G. M. Monn, see Arnold Schoenberg, *Instrumentalkonzerte nach Werken alter Meister*, ed. Nikos Kokkinis, Series B, vol. 27, 2, pp. viii-xix and pp. 200-211. Mainz: Schott & Sons; Vienna: Universal Edition AG., 1987.

5. Albert E. Kahn, *Joys and Sorrows, Reflections by Pablo Casals*. New York: Simon and Schuster, 1970, pp. 150-151. Reprinted by permission.

6. J. Ma. Corredor, *Conversations with Casals*. New York: E. P. Dutton & Co., 1957, p. 83.

7. The French letters (pp. 134-149, 164-181) have been transcribed and translated by Marta Casals Istomin. All of Casals' letters are in cursive script, and since the French commonly omit accent marks in this script or indicate them only as a dot, they have been added in these transcriptions without further identification. Missing letters or words are added in square brackets. Casals' short letter to Adler of March 4, 1912 has been omitted here because it is of a purely social nature.

8. Joaquim Pena (1873-1944) was a highly influential music critic in Barcelona for over 50 years. His special interests were opera and art song; he translated all of Wagner's opera libretti into Catalan and introduced French and German solo song in Spain. Casals secured him as the first secretary of his orchestra in Barcelona. Pena used his personal resources to collect music books and scores and bequeathed his literary estate to the Bibliothek Central.

9. According to J.Ma. Corredor, *Conversations with Casals* (New York: E. P. Dutton & Co., 1957), p. 83, this concert took place in Vienna, with Casals conducting Beethoven's Eighth Symphony. This also establishes the year for this letter as 1927, the Centennial of Beethoven's birth.

CHAPTER IV

Arnold Schoenberg - Pablo Casals

Violoncello Concerto in D Major after Monn

In 1925 Schoenberg was appointed professor of music in Berlin in order to conduct the master class in composition, a post which had become vacant after the death of Ferrucio Busoni. The teaching contract required Schoenberg to be in Berlin for six months per year, thus allowing him to avoid the harsh winters of middle Germany which aggravated his respiratory problems. After an especially severe asthma attack and urgent recommendations of his physician to seek relief in a more moderate climate, the Schoenbergs went to Barcelona for the first time during the middle of October, 1931.

Schoenberg's connection with Barcelona had been established through Roberto Gerhard,[1] a Spanish composer who had been in touch with Schoenberg since 1923 and had become his student and a friend of the family in 1931. Upon his arrival in Barcelona Schoenberg was welcomed by Pablo Casals and his orchestra, and Schoenberg acknowledged this greeting with a very touching response on November 3, 1931 (p. 157). Schoenberg's letter of February 20, 1933 (p. 161) establishes that Schoenberg and Casals met for the first time in person in Barcelona between October 1931, and early January, 1932.

Gertrud Schoenberg's letter of February 17, 1932 (p. 157) on behalf of her husband refers to an invitation from Casals' orchestra to conduct a program of his own works.

Schoenberg's *Violoncello Concerto in D Major after Monn* came into being at the initiative of Casals. During the winter of 1931/32 Schoenberg responded enthusiastically (undated draft, p. 159) to Casals' request for a cello composition, suggesting several possibilities. This draft also includes some detailed suggestions concerning the *type* of piece, but refers only to transcriptions, or rather "re-interpretations" of compositions by J.S. Bach. In conclusion Schoenberg expresses his enthusiasm again, suggesting that "if I had a piece by Bach, I am not sure I wouldn't start out right away."

For reasons of his own, Schoenberg did not select a work by Bach after all, and decided on the harpsichord concerto in D Major by G. M. Monn[2] as the basis for this concerto. From Schoenberg's detailed letter of February 20, 1933 (p. 161), we learn about the new composition, the *Concerto for Violoncello and Orchestra after the Concerto per Clavicembalo by G. M. Monn in a Free Adaptation by Arnold Schoenberg.* Further information in this letter refers to the work itself, to the fact that Schoenberg wanted to dedicate the concerto to Casals, and that he also wanted to perform the work with Casals as the soloist and himself as the conductor. On February 25, 1933 (p. 165), Casals acknowledged Schoenberg's letter of February 20, asking him for the score and suggesting October of the same year as the possible date for a first performance. Casals' next letter (March 15; 1933, p. 167) confirms with compliments the receipt of the cello part and score. Casals, however, also expressed some reservations, for he considered Schoenberg's metronome indications for the first movement to be out of the question for the time being. Nevertheless he concluded his letter with the reassurance that "it is not for you to adapt to my means, but for me to try to reach yours. I will do my best to attain it."

Schoenberg's reaction to Casals' letter of March 15, 1933 (p. 167) is reflected in the opening of his letter of March 18, 1933 to Roberto Gerhard:

> Lieber Herr Gerhard, ich war jetzt längere Zeit damit beschäftigt, den Klavierauszug des Cello-Konzerts herzustellen und bin deshalb nicht dazu gekommen, Ihnen zu antworten. Nun habe ich den Auszug vor 3 Tagen an Casals geschickt und hoffe, dass Sie ihn auch bald ansehen werden. Können Sie dann Casals begleiten? Ich bekam heute von ihm einen ausserordentlich lieben Brief, worin er mir auch schreibt dass die Cellostimme ausserordentlich schwer ist, mich aber darüber beruhigt. Dieser Brief hatte sich mit einem gekreuzt, in welchem ich ihm sagte, dass die Cellostimme als

Skizze anzusehen ist, solange er irgend etwas daran
auszusetzen hat: Denn was ein Casals schwer
findet, das dürfte in Wahrheit nahezu unmöglich
sein. Ich werde ihm darüber auch noch schreiben;
aber in der Zwischenzeit könnten Sie ihm das
erzählen.

Dear Mr. Gerhard, I have been busy for some time
completing the piano reduction for the cello
concerto, and it is for this reason that I did not
have time to respond to your letter. Three days
ago I sent the piano reduction to Casals, and I
hope that you also will have a look at it soon.
Could you then accompany Casals? Today I received from him an extremely cordial letter in
which he wrote me that the cello part is extremely
difficult, but he put me at ease about it.   This
letter had crossed mine in which I told him that
the cello part should be considered as a draft as
long as he could find any fault with it: what a
person of the stature of Casals finds difficult must
be in truth almost insurmountable. I shall also
write him about this, but in the meantime you may
tell him of it.

In his letter of May 24, 1933 (p. 171), Schoenberg pressed
Casals for information concerning a possible date for the performance of the cello concerto, but Casals answered on July 22, 1933 (p.
173): "I can only say that I practice the Monn concerto constantly--I
have never worked as assiduously, which testifies to my admiration
for you. The difficulties will be surmounted, which is to say a lot,
but it is impossible to say *when* the work will be ready to be given
to the public."   On September 22, 1933 (p. 175), Schoenberg
pursued the matter further, telling Casals that on September 20th
he had been dismissed from the Academy of Music in Berlin, and
that "now, all of a sudden, I am obliged to do whatever I can do to
earn a living. I have to tell you that one of my greatest hopes was
to have a number of engagements as conductor playing this concerto with you and--perhaps--when it would be desirable, some

other of my original works."   More particularly, Schoenberg
implored Casals to consider a performance of the cello concerto for
the B.B.C. in London on November 29, 1933.   This date was
originally offered to Schoenberg for the performance of his *Concerto
for Violoncello and Orchestra after the Concerto per Clavicembalo by
G. M. Monn in a Free Adaptation by Arnold Schoenberg*, and when
his hope turned out to be unrealistic, Schoenberg offered a concerto
for string quartet.[3] Schoenberg explained then to Casals that he
was not able to complete this work because of the upheaval in his
life, that he would lose the engagement altogether, and with it a
substantial fee, which he could ill afford.   To influence Casals
further, Schoenberg concluded his letter thus: "My friend Roberto
Gerhard wrote me a letter two weeks ago in which he told me of a
private audition in your house, and that he heard you play the
concerto and was enchanted by your performance. He confessed to
me that he does not understand why you hesitate still about giving
a public performance." Casals responded to this letter on October
1, 1933 (p. 179) with great sympathy, but he declined Schoenberg's
request: "I am doubly upset by not being able to accept your
proposition--first of all because even though I am well along, I still
cannot give a public performance of the concerto, which you did me
the honor of dedicating to me, and then because my engagement for
next November has been abandoned by the B.B.C. of London
because they did not agree to my condition, and I have already
other commitments for November."

   According to his own recollections (p. 184), Casals had
worked for about two years on the concerto; but when he was ready
for a public performance, it did not work out because of the terms
of Schirmer, who had acquired the rights to this work in the meantime. On January 22, 1935 (p. 179), Schoenberg communicated
through Schirmer to Casals that he should disregard Schirmer's
requests and state his own terms.   Unfortunately, Casals never
performed this concerto in public.

   Because of their personal and artistic integrity, the mutual
admiration between Schoenberg and Casals remained very strong.
This is reflected in Casals' most cordial and appreciative letter of
July 25, 1950 (p. 181 and Facsimile III, p. 182), shortly before the
composer's death, in which Casals thanked Schoenberg for the book
(*Style and Idea*) he had sent him.

IV.S-C.o.1

Barcelona
Bajada de Briz 14
3. XI. 1931

Casals [in Adler's hand]

Sehr geehrte Herren,
    Sie haben die grosse Liebenswürdigkeit gehabt, mir, anlässlich meines der Gesundheit gewidmeten Aufenthaltes in Barcelona, eine Begrüssung zukommen lassen, die mir grosse Ehre bezeigt und grosse Freude bereitet.
    Denn ich weiss, dass ich das nicht der armseligen paar Noten willen verdiene, die ich der Öffentlichkeit übergeben habe, die sie mehr mit Widerwillen, als mit Dank empfangen hat, sofern sie überhaupt Lust hatte, davon Kentnis zu nehmen.
    Aber Ich darf mir wohl schmeicheln, dass Sie vielleicht die Haltung schätzen, die einzunehmen mein Charakter mich zwingt: dass ich nämlich immer und unentwegt zu meinem Werk stehe.
    Darf ich - Ihnen hierfür von ganzem Herzen dankend - sagen, dass solche Anerkennung auch den ehrt, der sie kundgibt: S i e nämlich, die Sie durch diese Ehrung - über alle ästhetischen Bedenken hinweg - einer moralischen Tatsache Aufmerksamkeit, rein geistige Aufmerksamkeit, erwiesen haben.
    Lassen Sie mich Ihnen nochmals herzlichst danken und seien Sie mit kollegialer Hochachtung begrüsst.   Ihr

[here follows in Schoenberg's hand:]
Antwort auf die Begrüssung der Catalonier (Casals etc.)

IV.GS-P.o.1

Barcelona, 17. 2. 32

An das Orquestra Pau Casals Secretaria
Herrn Joaquin Pena

Sehr geehrter Herr, im Namen meines Manns danke ich Ihnen bestens für Ihren sehr freundlichen Brief und [ich] soll Ihnen sa-

IV.S-C.t.1

Barcelona
Bajada de Briz 14
3. XI. 1931

Casals [in Adler's hand]

Esteemed Gentlemen:

You had the great kindness to extend to me in connection with my health-related sojourn in Barcelona a welcome which honors me greatly and gives me great pleasure.

I know, however, that I do not deserve such a welcome for the few paltry notes I rendered to a public which received them with aversion rather than with thanks--if indeed it saw fit to take notice of them at all.

But I do flatter myself that you may have appreciated the attitude which my character obliged me to take: that is to say that I always and unswervingly stand behind my work.

May I tell you--thanking you with all my heart--that such appreciation also honors him who extends it: namely *you*, as you through this honor--disregarding all aesthetic considerations--gave credence to morality, a spiritual fact.

Let me again thank you with all my heart, and accept with high esteem my regards   Yours

[in Schoenberg's hand:]
Answer to the Welcome of the Catalonians (Casals etc.)

IV.GS-P.t.1

Barcelona, 17. 2. 32

To the Orchestra Pau Casals, secretary
          Mr. Joaquin Pena[4]

Dear Sir, on behalf of my husband I want to thank you very much for the most kind letter, and to tell you that your kindness charmed him to such an extent that he will be pleased to content himself

gen, dass Ihn Ihre Liebenswürdigkeit sehr bestochen hat und er deshalb gern entschlossen ist sich mit dem vorgeschlagenen Honorar zu begnügen.

Als Termin zieht er den 3. April vor und wählt folgendes Programm:

Pelleas und Melisande   45-50 Minuten

Bach, Präludium und Fuge   30 Minuten
   Instrumentiert von Schönberg

Verklärte Nacht,   30 Minuten
   für Streichorchester,

Bitte das Material raschestens bei der Universal Edition zu bestellen!

Das Honorar bittet Sie mein Mann in Anbetracht der Kursschwankungen auf Mark 500.- zu stabilisieren.

Mit den herzlichsten und hochachtungsvollsten Grüssen von meinem Mann

IV.S-C.o.2

[Undated Draft of a letter by Schoenberg to Casals,
Winter 1932/1933]

Sie fragten mich gestern, ob ich denn nicht ein Violoncell-Stück schreiben würde. Ich antwortete Ihnen: ich habe oft daran gedacht und es x-mal vorgehabt. Ich hätte Ihnen mehr sagen können: ich hatte nämlich eben vorhin wieder daran gedacht, weil mir Ihr Spiel fabelhafte Lust dazu gemacht hatte; [und] weiter, welche Pläne ich habe.

Nun will ich es wirklich tun und möchte doch die kurze Zeit vor meiner Abreise noch benutzen, um - denn ich möchte das Stück für Sie schreiben und habe Ihnen bereits längst "Mass=genommen" - ein paar Ideen mit Ihnen zu besprechen. Ich will kurz einige andeuten:

with the remuneration you offered.

As a date he would prefer April 3rd, and he selected the following program:

Pelleas und Melisande	45-50 minutes
Bach, *Prelude and Fugue,* orchestrated by Schoenberg	30 minutes
Verklärte Nacht, for string	30 minutes

Please order the materials as soon as possible from Universal Edition.

Because of the current fluctuations, my husband asks you to stabilize the fee at 500.- marks.

With most cordial and respectful regards from my husband

IV.S-C.t.2

[Translation of undated draft of a letter by Schoenberg to Casals, Winter 1932/1933][5]

You asked me yesterday whether or not I would be willing to write a piece for violoncello. I told you then that I had thought about it often, and was often on the point of doing so. I could have told you something else, namely that I had thought about it just moments earlier because your playing created an enormous desire in me, and I could also have told you of my plans.

Now I really want to undertake it, and to make use of the short time before my departure to discuss a few ideas with you; for I would really like to write this piece for you, since I became aware of your ability long ago.

I indicate briefly some of the plans here:

1. Eine Phantasie über ein Bach-Stück (ein schönes Adagio
   oder Menuett [nicht zu entziffern] Gavotte oder d[er]gl[ei-
   chen]) eventuell in Variationenform; oder
2. Eine Klavier-Suite oder eine Trio-Sonate oder d[er]gl[eichen]
   cellomässig umdeuten.
3. Eine dieser Arbeiten entweder
   a) für Cello Solo oder
   b) " Cello mit Klavier oder
   c) " Cello mit Orchester

Ich kann mich nicht entscheiden ohne die Noten zu sehen. Wenn
ich [ein Stück ?] von Bach hätte [etc. ?], weiss ich nicht, ob ich
nicht gleich anfangen würde.

[in another hand: to Casals]

IV.S-C.o.3

Arnold Schönberg
Berlin W 50
Nürnberger-Platz 3
Tel.: B4, BAVARIA 4466

Sennor Don Pau Casals   20. II. 1933
Secretaria de lOrquestra
Institut Casals
Diagonal 440, pral 2.a̱
B A R C E L O N A

Lieber, hochverehrter Meister Casals
ich habe vor ungefähr 6 Wochen eine kleines Werk vollendet und
wol[l]te Ihnen auf verschiedenen Wegen davon Nachricht geben,
erfahre aber, dass sie noch immer nicht an Sie gelangt ist. Denn die
Londoner British Broadcasting Corporation (Radio) teilte mir mit,
dass sie erst in einigen Wochen ihr Programm fürs näch[s]te Jahr
machen und Ihnen deshalb noch keinen Vorschlag über die
Uraufführung dieses Werkes gemacht habe. Andererseits aber hat

1. A Fantasia based upon a piece by Bach (a beautiful Adagio, or Menuett, Gavotte etc.), possibly in the form of variations; or
2. to reinterpret a keyboard suite or trio-sonata idiomatically for cello.
3. One of the above, either
   a) for cello solo,
   b) for cello and piano, or
   c) for cello and orchestra.

I cannot decide on this without seeing [?] the music. If I had a piece by Bach, I'm not sure I wouldn't start out right away.[6]

[in another hand: to Casals]

IV.S-C.t.3

Arnold Schönberg
Berlin W50
Nürnberger-Platz 3
Tel.: B4, BAVARIA 4466

Sennor Don Pau Casals   20. II. 1933
Secretaria de l'Orquestra
Institut Casals
Diagonal 440, pral 2.a̲
B A R C E L O N A

My dear and most esteemed Maestro Casals:
         Approximately six weeks ago I completed a work and though I tried to inform you about it through various means, I now realize that this information did not get to you. Since the British Broadcasting Corporation has informed me that it will be several weeks before they make the decisions concerning their programs for the next year, they have therefore not yet made a proposal to you

eine Anfrage von R o s b a u d vom Frankfurter Radio Sie offenbar noch nicht erreicht, da Rosbaud keine Nachricht von Ihnen hat. Dagegen habe ich keine Nachricht von meinem Freunde und ehemaligen Schüler Gerhard, der aus unbekannten Gründen bisher nicht schreibt.

Zur Sache also: das Werk führt den Titel:
K o n z e r t für Violoncello und Orchester nach dem
Concerto per Clavicembalo von G.M. Monn
in freier Umgestaltung von Arnold Schoenberg.
Ich glaube, es ist ein s e h r brillantes Stück geworden. Jedenfalls habe ich mir wegen des K l a n g e s ganz besondere Mühe gegeben und bin sehr zufrieden damit. Das Stück ist in gewisser Hinsicht weniger soloistisch, als ein Konzert von Monn wäre; denn sehr oft ist die Funktion des Cellos etwa die eines Solisten in einer Kammermusik, durch dessen brillantes Spiel ein sehr schöner, interessanter Klang entsteht. Im Uebrigen war es meine Hauptsorge die Mängel des Handelstils (dem das Werk im Original angehört) zu beseitigen. Sowie Mozart es mit dem Messias von Handel getan hat, so habe auch ich hier ganze Hände voll Sequenzen (Rosalien, "Schusterflecke") entfernt und durch echte S u b s t a n z ersetzt. Dann habe ich mich bemüht, den andern Hauptmangel des Handelstils zu bekämpfen: dort ist nämlich das Thema immer beim ersten Auftreten am Besten und wird im Lauf des Stückes immer unbedeutender und geringer. Ich glaube, dass es mir gelungen ist, das Ganze etwa dem Stil Haydns zu nähern. In harmonischer Hinsicht gehe ich manchmal ein wenig (manchmal auf [auch] etwas mehr) über diesen Stil hinaus. Nirgends aber geht es wesentlich weiter, als Brahms, jedenfalls giebt es keine Dissonanzen, die nicht im Sinn der älteren Harmonielehre zu verstehen sind; und: nirgends ist es atonal!

Ich frage Sie nun, ob Sie Lust haben, die Partitur als E r s t e r zu sehen. Ich würde Ihnen nämlich, wenn es Ihnen gefällt und Sie Lust hätten es zu spielen, den Vorschlag machen, die ersten Aufführungen und auch sonst solche, die sich künstlerisch und materiell lohnen mit mir zu machen, mit mir als Dirigenten.

Ich habe dieses Stück bisher niemanden angeboten, da ich grösstes Gewicht darauf lege, mir das Vergnügen zu machen, mit Ihnen zu musizieren: ich habe zahlreiche Male gesehen, wie gut wir uns verständigen würden.

concerning the first performance of this work. On the other hand, Rosbaud's[7] inquiry from Radio Frankfurt seems not yet to have reached you, since Rosbaud has not heard from you. Also, I did not yet hear from my friend and former student Gerhard, who for unknown reasons does not write to me.

To come to the point: the composition is entitled
Concerto for Violoncello and Orchestra after the Concerto
per Clavicembalo by G.M. Monn
in a free adaptation by Arnold Schönberg.

I believe that it turned out to be an extremely brilliant piece. In any case, I took especially great pains with the sonority, and I am very satisfied with it. In certain respects this piece is less soloistic than a concerto by Monn would be, because very often the function of the cello is rather that of a soloist in chamber music, through whose brilliant performance a very beautiful and interesting sound is achieved. For the rest it was my main concern to do away with the deficiencies of the Handel style, which was also a characteristic of the original composition. As Mozart did with Handel's Messiah (Rosalien, "Schusterflecke"), I removed whole handfuls of sequences and replaced them with true substance. Then I also took the trouble to deal with the other main fault of the Handel style, which is that the theme is always best at its first appearance, but becomes more insignificant and trivial in the course of the piece. I believe that, on the whole, I succeeded in moving it closer to the style of, say, Haydn. Regarding harmony, at times I go a little beyond that style (on occasion more than a little perhaps). But never is this carried any further than Brahms, nor are there any dissonances which would be incomprehensible in the light of the older concepts of harmony; and nowhere is it atonal!

I ask you now if you would be interested in being the very first person to see the score? Because, if you wish to do so and if you would be interested in performing it, I would like to propose to you to do the first performance and also other performances which would be artistically as well as financially worthwhile for me, that is, with myself as conductor.

As yet I have offered this piece to *nobody* because it is very important to me to have the pleasure of making music with you: I have realized many times how well we would understand each other.

Dagegen, hat sich der Cellist Mainardi, der durch einen Bekannten, ohne mein Wissen von dem Stück erfahren hat, an mich gewendet. Aber ich habe ihm bisher nicht geantwortet, weil ich Ihnen das Vorrecht wahren wollte.

Es wäre mir sehr lieb, wenn ich von Ihnen womöglich innerhalb 8 Tagen eine Antwort bekommen könnte. Dann sende ich sofort die Partitur und die Cellostimme.

Ich würde mich sehr, sehr freuen, wenn wir uns hierbei finden konnte [könnten]. Denn seit ich das Vergnügen hatte, Sie in Barcelona persönlich kennen zu lernen, freue ich mich sehr auf ein Wiedersehen mit Ihnen und wenn es dabei zu gemeinsamem Musizieren käme, so wäre das wirklich sehr schön!

Ich hoffe recht bald von Ihnen Nachricht zu haben und bin in grösster Hochachtung, mit vielen aufrichtigen Grüssen,

Ihr ergebener   Arnold Schönberg

IV.C-S.o.1

<u>Diagonal 440</u>
Barcelone   25 Février 1933

Cher Ami et admiré Maître,

Je suis enchanté de votre lettre - notre ami, votre élève Gerhard, m'a, il y a quelques jours, donné la bonne nouvelle de votre version pour violoncelle du Concerto pour Clavicembalo de Monn.

Je n'ai pas besoin de vous dire que je suis extrêmement intéressé à cette oeuvre que je vous prie de m'envoyer à fin de la mettre en étude pour l'exécuter la saison prochaine -

Si vous venez en Octobre à Barcelone nous pourrons en donner la première audition et j'espère que d'autres suivront après-

Je me rends compte du style de cette oeuvre et je tâcherais de bien l'assimiler - quant à votre version je ne doute de son importance - en somme je me réjouis énormément.

Je vous envoie tous mes voeux pour votre santé. Quel dommage que vous n'ayiez pu faire un séjour d'hiver à Barcelone cette fois-ci. Votre présence honnorera toujours notre pays.

Votre tout dévoué   Pablo Casals

On the other hand, the cellist Mainardi, who heard about this composition without my knowledge from an acquaintance, has contacted me. But as yet I have not answered him because I wanted to preserve this privilege for yourself.

I would be most pleased if I could possibly receive an answer from you within eight days. Then I would send you promptly the score and the cello part.

I would be very, very glad if we could work together with this. Since I have had the pleasure of meeting you personally in Barcelona, I have looked forward to meeting you again; and if this were to result in music-making together, how wonderful it would be!

I hope to hear from you quite soon, and remain with highest esteem and many sincere regards,

faithfully yours,[8]
Arnold Schönberg

IV.C-S.t.1

<u>Diagonal 440</u>
Barcelona   February 25, 1933

Dear friend and admired master,

I am delighted by your letter--our friend, your student Gerhard, a few days ago gave me the good news about your violoncello version of the Concerto for Harpsichord by Monn.

I don't have to tell you that I am extremely interested in this work, and I ask you to please send it to me so that I can study it to play it next season.

If you come to Barcelona next October we can give a first performance, and I hope that others will follow afterward.

I am aware of the style of this work and I will try to assimilate it well. As for your version I don't doubt its importance--in short, I am enormously delighted.

I send you all my good wishes for your health. What a pity that you could not come for a winter visit to Barcelona. Your presence will always honor our country.

Your very devoted
Pablo Casals

IV.S-C.o.4

Lieber hochverehrter Herr Casals, vielen Dank für Ihren so liebenswürdigen Brief. Ich bin sehr glücklich, dass dieses Stück mir die lange erwünschte Gelegenheit geben wird, mit Ihnen zu musizieren! Es wird schön werden!

In der Eile sende ich Ihnen hier eine Photographische Partitur (mit der Lupe kann man alles lesen) und in einem separaten Brief die Cello-Stimme. Ich selbst arbeite augenblicklich an einem Klavier Auszug. Sobald dieser fertig ist - in 8-12 Tagen - sende ich ihn an Sie. - Darf ich Sie bitten, mir den Empfang der Stimme und der Partitur gleich mitzuteilen.

In der Eile grüsse ich Sie von ganzem Herzen und bin Ihr herzlichst ergebener Arnold Schönberg

1932

Arnold Schönberg
6 Berlin W 50
Nürnberger Platz 3
Tel. B4 Bavaria 4466

IV.C-S.o.2

15 Mars 1933

Cher Maître et Ami,

J'ai reçu la partie de violoncelle et quelques jours plus tard la partition du Concerto que j'admire comme tout ce qui vient de vous.

Malgré que je suis en plein travail de mes partitions (les répétitions d'orchestre doivent bientôt commencer) je n'ai pu résister de regarder avec le violoncelle ce Concerto. Laissez-moi vous dire que je suis très intéressé par votre traitement de l'instrument que vous connaissez théoriquement à merveille. Je ferai ce qui me soit possible pour approfondir et dominer cette nouvelle thècnique mais ---!! Combien de temps il me faudra je ne le sais pas. Il s'agit d'énormes difficultés à vaincre - à tel point que l'Allegro à ♩ = 112 du premier mouvement me paraît maintenant hors de question si l'on tient compte de la figuration et de l'écriture violoncellestique.

IV.S-C.t.4

Dear and most esteemed Mr. Casals:

Many thanks for your kind letter. I am very glad that this composition will afford me the desired opportunity to make music with you! It will be wonderful!

In haste I send you now a photographic copy of the full score (with a magnifying glass it is possible to read everything) and in a separate letter the cello part. I myself am working on a piano reduction at the moment. As soon as it is completed--in eight to twelve days--I shall send it to you.[9] May I ask you to acknowledge the receipt of the part and the full score at your earliest convenience.

In haste I greet you most sincerely, and I remain sincerely your faithful   Arnold Schönberg

1932

Arnold Schönberg
6 Berlin W 50
Nürnberger Platz 3
Tel. B4 Bavaria 4466

IV.C-S.t.2

March 15, 1933

Dear Master and Friend,

I received the cello part and a few days later the score of the concerto which I admire as everything that comes from you.

In spite of the fact that I am hard at work on my scores (the orchestral rehearsals will start soon) I could not resist looking at this concerto from the cellistic point of view. Let me tell you that I am very interested in the way you treat the instrument, which you know marvellously from the theoretical point of view. I will do my best to understand and master this new technique, but ---!! How long it will take me, I don't know. It is a question of overcoming enormous difficulties to such a point that the Allegro at $\downarrow$ = 112 of the first movement seems to me now out of the question, if one considers the figurations and the cellistic writing.

Que ceci ne vous contrarie pas trop. Je vous admire en grand que vous êtes - ce n'est pas à vous à vous adapter à mes moyens mais bien à moi à tâcher d'atteindre les vôtres. Je ferai tout pour y arriver

Votre dévoué
Pablo Casals

IV.S-C.o.5

16. III. 1933

Arnold Schönberg
Berlin W50
Nürnberger Platz 3
Tel. B4 BAVARIA 4466

Herrn Pablo Casals
Barcelona, Diagonal 440
Secretaria del'Orquestra Casals

Lieber, hochvereehrter Freund und Meister,
    vor Allem nochmals meinen herzlichsten Dank für Ihren so lieben Brief. Ich freue mich sehr auf das gemeinsame Musizieren!
    Vor ungefähr 8 Tagen habe ich Ihnen eine photographische Verkleinerung der Partitur (die grosse wird zur Materialienherstellung gebraucht) und die Cello-Stimme geschickt und vor 2 Tagen den Klavierauszug, den ich selbst gemacht habe. Heute sende ich Ihnen beiliegend eine Liste von Fehlern, die ich in der Partitur gefunden habe und eine (Nr. 5 und 6.) die sich auf die ausgeschriebene Cellostimme bezieht.
    Ich weiss nicht, ob ich schon erwähnt habe, dass ich die Cello-Stimme solange, als Entwurf, als Skizze ansehe, als Sie der Meinung sind, dass etwas nicht gut klinge, oder nicht gut liege: Selbstverständlich will ich hier alles solange ändern, bis wir ganz einig sind. Aber darüber hinaus beabsichtige ich bei der Herausgabe auch noch Erleichterungen anzubringen, damit auch jüngere Cellisten, Lernende und Amateure es spielen können. Ich bin aber sehr neugierig auf Ihr Urteil über den Cello Part. Nun hoffe ich hierüber und über den Empfang der Noten recht bald von Ihnen

May this not trouble you too much. I admire you greatly as you are. It is not for you to adapt to my means, but for me to try to reach yours. I will do my best to attain it.

Your devoted
Pablo Casals

IV.S-C.t.5

16. III. 1933

Arnold Schönberg
Berlin W 50
Nürnberger Platz 3
Tel. B4 BAVARIA 4466

Mr. Pablo Casals
Barcelona, Diagonal 440
Secretaria del'Orquestra Casals

My dear honored friend and maestro:
First of all my most cordial thanks for your so very kind letter. I look forward very much to our music making together!
About eight days ago I sent you a photographic reduction of the score (the big one is being used for the production of the performance materials) as well as the cello part, and two days ago the piano reduction which I made myself. Attached to this I send you today a list of mistakes that I found in the score and one (No. 5 and 6) which refers to the written-out cello part.
I do not remember whether I mentioned before that I consider the cello part to be a sketch or draft just as long as you may be of the opinion that something may not sound good or lie well, and it is understood that I will make any alteration whatsoever until we are in complete agreement. In addition to this I intended to add some simplifications for the publication so that younger cellists, students and amateurs may be able to play it. I am, however, very curious about your opinion of the cello part. I do hope now to hear from you quite soon about this and your having received the music. And let me again remind you: this score will

Antwort zu bekommen. Denn, um das gleich zu sagen: die Partitur
wird, wenn Ihnen das Stück zusagt, I h n e n g e w i d m e t sein!
     Mit vielen herzlichsten und hochachtungsvollen Grüssen,
bin ich Ihr Arnold Schönberg

IV.C-S.o.3   27 Mars 1933

Institut Musical Casals
Barcelona
Diagonal 440, Pral. Telefon 6-1408

Cher Maître at Ami,
     Je vous ai envoyé la partition photographique, que j'espère
vous avez reçue, l'étude de laquelle m'a énormément intéressé.
     Quant à la partie de violoncelle manuscrite je la garde pour
mon travail, cependant si vous en avez besoin je vous l'enverrai
après en avoir fait une copie. D'après la feuille indiquant les fautes
ou omissions j'ai corrigé la partie solo.
     J'ai dédié au Concerto tout le temps que mes occupations
m'ont laissé libre - les répétitions de mes concerts d'orchestre
commençant aujourd'hui je me verrai privé de continuer l'étude de
l'instrument puisque l'orchestre me prend tout le temps et forces.
     Soyez assuré que je donnerai toutes mes possibilités à fin
de réussir à m'assimiler l'oeuvre en tant que musique et technique
de l'instrument.
     Salutations très cordiales de votre devoué et admirateur
                         Pablo Casals

IV.S-C.o.6

Arnold Schönberg   24. V. 1933
P a r i s
Hotel Regina

Lieber, sehr verehrter Meister Casals,

be dedicated to *you* if it meets your favor!
With many cordial and respectful regards, I remain yours
Arnold Schönberg

IV.C-S.t.3

Institut Musical Casals
Barcelona
Diagonal 440, Pral. Telefon 6-1408   March 27, 1933

Dear Master and Friend:
I sent you the photocopy of the score that I hope you have
received, the study of which has interested me enormously.
Regarding the manuscript of the cello part, I am keeping
it for my work, but if you need it I will send it to you after making
a copy of it. I have corrected the solo part according to the list
indicating the mistakes and omissions.
I have dedicated to this concerto all the time that my
occupations have permitted. With rehearsals for my orchestral
concerts beginning today, I will be deprived of continuing my
practice of the instrument since the orchestra takes all my time and
energies.
Please be assured that I will do everything possible in order
to assimilate this work both in music and in instrumental technique.
Most cordial greetings from your devoted and admiring
Pablo Casals

IV.S-C.t.6

May 24, 1933

Arnold Schönberg
P a r i s
Hotel Regina

My dear and very esteemed Maestro Casals:

ich bin seit acht Tagen in Paris und las vor zwei Tagen, dass Sie auch hier waren. Wie schade, dass ich das nicht rechtzeitig erfahren habe, um Sie zu sehen!

Ich schwankte, ob ich meinen Urlaub in Spanien oder in Frankreich verbringen soll. Ich habe hier noch eine Reihe "geschäftlicher" Angelegenheiten zu betreiben. Deren Erledigung kann sich noch 14 Tage hinziehn. Aber voraussichtlich werde ich dann noch ein- oder zweimal hier sein müssen und da schrecke ich vor den hohen Kosten der Reise ein bischen zurück (da ja heute manche Dinge, auf die man früher rechnen konnte, unsicher worden sind).

Ledliglich aus diesem Grunde möchte ich gerne wissen, wie es sich mit der Aufführung des Violoncell-Konzertes steht und ob Sie mir nicht jetzt bereits sagen könnten (so dass ich fix damit rechnen kann), ob und welche Konzerte in Spanien und anderswo ich mit Ihnen zusammen in diesem Jahre werde machen können und welche Honorare hiefür geboten werden.

Es wäre für mich schon eine wesentliche Entscheidung, wenn es auch nur vier oder fünf Konzerte wären, die einstweilen sicher sind und mir meine Kosten decken.

Ich hoffe recht bald Ihre freundliche Antwort zu haben, weil ich mich über meinen weiteren Aufenthalt innerhalb zehn Tagen gerne entscheiden möchte.

Ich freue mich ausserordentlich, Sie recht bald zu sehen und wenn wir wirklich nach S. Sebastian kommen, werden wir sicher einen sehr schönen Sommer mit Ihnen verbringen. Darum grüsse ich Sie schon heute mit aller Herzlichkeit,

Ihr ergebener Arnold Schönberg

IV.C-S.o.4

Orquestra Pau Casals
Barcelona
Secretaria:
Diagonal 440, Pral. Telefon 73975   22 Juillet 1933

Cher Maître et Ami,

En répondant à votre bonne lettre je puis vous dire seule-

I have been in Paris for a week, and two days ago I read that you also were here. What a pity that I did not learn about this earlier so that I could see you!

I am undecided as to whether I shall spend my vacation in Spain or in France. Here I have yet to take care of a couple of "business" matters. To conclude these may well take another fourteen days. But it is also likely that I will have to be here another time or two, and I am somewhat weary of the high cost of travel; many things one could count on earlier have become uncertain today.

It is solely for this reason that I would like to know of the performance status of the Violoncello Concerto, whether you can tell me now (so that I can make plans) concerning any concerts you and I could do together this year in Spain and elsewhere, and what sort of honorarium would be offered for them.

It really would be an important thing for me if there would be even only four or five concerts which--for the present--would be guaranteed and would cover my expenses.

I do look forward to your kind and prompt reply since I would like to come to a decision within ten days concerning my further stay.

I am extremely glad to be able to see you very soon, and if we really come to S. Sebastian, we will certainly have a wonderful summer with you. Thus I send you today my most cordial regards.

Sincerely yours, Arnold Schönberg

IV.C-S.t.4

Orquestra Pau Casals
Barcelona
Secretaria:
Diagonal 440, Pral. Telefon 73975   July 22, 1933

Dear Master and friend,
        In answer to your good letter, I can only say that I practice

ment que je travaille le Concerto de Monn sans cesse - jamais je n'ai fait un travail aussi assidu et ceci pour vous té-moigner mon admiration. Les difficultés seront vaincues et c'est beaucoup dire. Impossible cependant de fixer <u>quant</u> l'oeuvre sera prête pour la donner au public. Je vous tiendrai au courant de mes progrès que j'espère seront rapides.

　　En vous souhaitant un été de repos et aussi de bon travail
　　je me dis votre tout dévoué
　　Pablo Casals

VI.S-C.o.7

ARNOLD SCHOENBERG   22. IX. 1933
VILLA STRESA
AVENUE RAPP
ARCACHON (GIRONDE)

Mr. Pau Casals
Diagonal 440
Secretaria de l'Orchestra Casals
Barcelona

Cher ami et grand maître
　　malheureusement je suis forcé de vous demander, s'il vous serait possible de jouer la première audition du Concert pour Violoncell[e], que je vous ai dédié, avec moi à Londres déjà le 29 XI. 1933 au Broadcasting. J'ai dit: malheureusement et ça est, dans cet[te] cohérence, presque ridicule; parce que, en verité, je serais heureux, si c'était possible: de donner une première audition avec un maître sans pareil, que vous. Mais ce quiest "malheureusement", c'est la cause, qui me force de vous demander, de jouer cet oeuvre à un temps, qui ne vous vonvienne pas, peut-être! Cette cause, bref dit, est: Hier j'ai reçu une lettre de l'académie des arts où, vous savez donc, j'ai été "Chef d'une classe de composition musicale". J'ai été; parce-que dépuis cette lettre, je ne le suis plus. On m'a donné mon congé, hier, le 20 IX, et on a fixé, que je recevrai le premier octobre mon cachet mensuel pour la dernière fois!! Tout

the Monn concerto constantly--I have never worked so assiduously, which testifies to my admiration for you. The difficulties will be overcome, which is saying a lot. Impossible however to say *when* the work will be ready to be given to the public. I will keep you informed of my progress, which I hope will be speedy.

I wish you a summer of rest , and also one of good work.

I remain very devotedly,

Pablo Casals

IV.S-C.t.7

ARNOLD SCHOENBERG   22. IX. 1933
VILLA STRESA
AVENUE RAPP
ARCACHON (GIRONDE)

M. Pau Casals
Diagonal 440
Secretaria de l'Orchestra Casals
Barcelona

Dear friend and grand maestro,

Unfortunately, I am forced to ask you if it would be possible for you to play the first performance of the Concerto for Violoncello that I have dedicated to you in London, already on the 29th of November, 1933, at the Broadcasting. I have said "unfortunately," and that is, in this sense, almost ridiculous, because in reality I would be happy if it were possible: to give a first performance with a master without parallel as you are. But what is "unfortunately" is the cause that forces me to ask you to play this work, at a time which is perhaps not convenient to you. The reason, briefly, is: Yesterday I received a letter from the Arts Academy at which, as you know, I was the "Director of a class in composition". I was, because after this letter, I no longer am. I was dismissed yesterday the 20th of September, and it has been determined that I will receive on October 1 my monthly payment for

à coup, sans le moindre avertissement ++) on à anéanti mon contract, qui, sans cette violation, m'aurait laissé un delai de deux années établir une nouvelle vie dans l'étranger.

Mais maintenant, soudain, je suis contraint, de faire tout ce que je peux faire, pour gagner de l'argent. Et, il me faut vous dire, qu'une de mes plus grandes espérances, fut, d'avoir une certaine quantité d'engagements, comme chef d'orchestre, exécutant avec vous ce concert et - peut-être - quand il soit désiré, aussi quelques [-unes] de mes oeuvres originales.

J'espère que vous me comprenez, sans qu'il me faut encore faire beaucoup d'explications: je perderai cet engagement, parce que Broadcasting ne peut pas remettre ce concert à un autre jour. D'abord j'ai espéré de jouer déja à cette date le concert de Violoncell[e] avec vous; et comme ce n'était pas possible j'ai proposé un concert pour Streichquartett. Mais malheureusement, causé par ces troubles-ci, je ne l'ai pu achever, que ces jours là et il ne fut plus possible d'envoyer les parts solistes au Kolisch-Quartett. En conséquence, le Kolisch-Quartett ne pourra pas commencer d'étudier ce concert, que dans le moi[s] de Novembre et c'est trop tard pour parvenir à une exécution, qu'à la fin du mois de décembre.

C'est pourquoi j'ai proposé au Broadcasting d'exécuter le 'Cello-Konzert".

Cher ami, donnez moi, s.v.p. votre réponse au retour du courrier. Le temps presse et c'était une grande perte pour moi, si le Broadcasting retirerait son invitation, parce que je perdrais un assez grand cachet.

Mon ami Robert Gerhard m'a écrit une lettre, il y a quinze jours, dans laquelle il me fait savoir d'une audition privée chez vous, où il vous a entendu, jouer le concert et qu'il eusse été enchanté de votre exécution et me confesse, qu'il ne comprenne pas encore pourquoi vous hésitez encore, d'en donner une audition publique.

++) Je vous prie de ne pas publier ces faits; parce que le gouvernment venge (comme a montré le cas de Einstein) et en mon cas ce seraient mes parents qui sont encore en Allemagne, et qui pourraient leur servir comme otages!

the last time!! All of a sudden, without the slightest warning
++) my contract has been voided, which, without this violation
would have given me two years to establish a new life abroad.

But now, all of a sudden, I am obliged to do whatever I can
to earn money. I have to tell you that one of my greatest hopes was
to have a number of engagements as conductor playing this
concerto with you and--perhaps--when one so desired some other of
my original works.

I hope that you understand me, without my having to give
you many explanations: I will lose this engagement, because
Broadcasting cannot move the concert to another date. First of all
I had hoped to play the Concerto for Violoncello with you already
by this date; and when that was not possible, I proposed a concerto
for String Quartet. But unfortunately, because of these troubles, I
could not finish it, and it was not possible to send the parts to the
Kolisch Quartet. Consequently, the Kolisch Quartet will not be
able to study the work until November and it is too late to have a
performance any sooner than the end of December.

This is why I proposed to Broadcasting to perform the
'Cello-Konzert."

Dear friend, please give me a response by return mail.
Time is pressing and it would be a great loss for me if the Broadcasting withdrew its invitation, because I would also lose a substantial fee.

My friend Robert Gerhard wrote me a letter fifteen days
ago, in which he told me of a private hearing at your house, where
he heard you play the concerto and was enchanted by your performance, and he confessed to me that he does not understand why you
still hesitate to give a public performance.
This--in truth--has encouraged me to beg you to accept this date.

++) I beg you not to publish these facts because the govern-
       ment takes revenge (as the case of Einstein has shown),
       and in my case, it would be my parents, who are still in
       Germany, who could serve as hostages!

       Ceci - en Verité - m'a encouragé de vous prier d'accepter
cette date.

       Espérant, de recevoir bientôt une réponse favorable, je suis
avec beaucoup des salutations les plus cordiales et respectueuses
    votre dévoué
    Arnold Schönberg

IV.C-S.o.5

S. Salvador   1 Oct. 1933

Cher Maître et Ami,
       Votre lettre m'a beaucoup impressionné. Je regrette tant
ce que vous dites de votre situation après la décision du gouverne-
ment Allemand à votre sujet et je comprends votre désir d'une acti-
vité artistique qui vous permettrait de faire face aux préséntes
difficultés.

       Je suis doublement contrarié de ne pouvoir accepter votre
proposition - d'abord parce que, quoi que très avancé je ne puis pas
encore donner au public et moins par Radio le Concerto que vous
m'avez fait l'honneur de me dédier. En suite à cause de mon engagement prévu pour Novembre prochain et abandon[n]é par la
B.B.C. de Londres ne pouvant celle agréer mes conditions et de
mon côté ayant disposé de mon temps pour Novembre.

       Croyez cher maître que j'en suis désolé.

       En attendent une occasion que je désire favorable je me dis
votre très sincèrement dévoué
    Pablo Casals

III.S-C.o.8

Arnold Schoenberg
5860 Canyon Cove
Hollywood, California
Tel. Hempstead 1095   Janvier, le 22, 1935

Cher maître,
       je crains que la lettre de la "G. Schirmer Inc." vous a causé

Waiting to receive a favorable answer soon, I am with many
most respectful and cordial greetings
your devoted
                Arnold Schoenberg

V.C-S.t.5

S. Salvador   October 1, 1933

Dear Master and Friend
        Your letter has greatly upset me. I regret very much what
you say about your situation after the decision of the German
government regarding you, and I understand your desire for an
artistic activity that would help you face the present difficulties.
        I am doubly frustrated by not being able to accept your
proposition - first of all because even though I am well along, I still
cannot perform in public and even less on the radio the concerto
which you did me the honor of dedicating to me. And then because
my engagement for next November has been abandoned by the
B.B.C. of London because they did not agree to my conditions--and
because I myself already have other commitments for November.
        Believe me dear friend that I am sorry. Waiting for an
occasion which I hope will be favorable,
        I am your very sincerely devoted
                Pablo Casals

IV.S-C.t.8

Arnold Schoenberg
5860 Canyon Cove
Hollywood, California
Tel. Hempstead 1095   January 22, 1935

Dear Maestro,
        I fear that the letter of G. Schirmer Inc., has caused you

quelque surprise par les conditions, qu'on vous a nommé[es] et, parce-que ceux-là ne prennent pas regard de la situation financielle en Espagne. C'est pourquoi j'ai demandé [à] la maison, respectif son président, Mr. Carl Engel, cet excellent musicien et homme de science, de vous livrer les parts et les droits d'exécution de mon "Concert pour Violoncell[e]" à des conditions offertes par vous-même.

Veuillez donc, cher maître, s'il vous plaît, nommer ce montant, qui vous convient et soyez assuré que les sentiments de la maison de Schirmer à l'égard d'une éxécution par vous correspondent parfaitement avec les miens.

Je serais très heureux d'entendre que vous jouez cette pièce et en plus de vous entendre moi-même. Et je voudrais bien savoir comme vous vous portez et recevoir quelque fois une ligne de vous à ce subjet.

Agréez cher maître l'expression de la plus haute considération et les meilleures salutations, de vôtre
Arnold Schoenberg

IV.C-S.o.6

25 Juillet 1950

Cher Maître,

Vous me faites un grand honneur en m'envoyant votre livre. Je me réjouis infiniment de sa lecture, sûr d'y trouver l'élévation de pensée qui est la vôtre. Déjà en le feuilletant je trouve dans le chapître "Gustav Mahler" de si belles choses!

Merci - et avec mes fervents voeux pour votre santé et bien-être je vous prie d'agréer, cher maître l'expression de mes sentiments affectueusement reconnaissants

Pau Casals
1, Route du Canigou
PRADES
(P.O.)

some surprise, by the conditions that have been quoted to you, because they do not take into account the financial situation in Spain. This is why I have asked this firm and its president Mr. Engel, that excellent musician and man of learning, to send to you the parts and the rights of performance of my concerto for Violoncello at conditions offered by you.

So please, dear master, name the figure that suits you and be sure that the sentiments of the house of Schirmer in regard to a performance by you correspond perfectly to mine.

I would be very happy to hear that you are playing this piece and in addition to hear you myself.

I would like to know how you are and to receive a word from you sometime regarding this subject.

Please receive the expression of my highest regard and best wishes from your

Arnold Schoenberg

IV.C-S.t.6

July 25, 1950

Dear Master:

You do me a great honor by sending me your book. I infinitely enjoy reading it, sure to find in it the loftiness of thought that is yours. Leafing through it I find in the chapter "Gustav Mahler" such beautiful things!

Thank you, and with my fervent wishes for your health and well-being, I ask you to accept, dear master, my most affectionately grateful sentiments.

Pau Casals
1, Route du Canigou
PRADES
(P.O.)

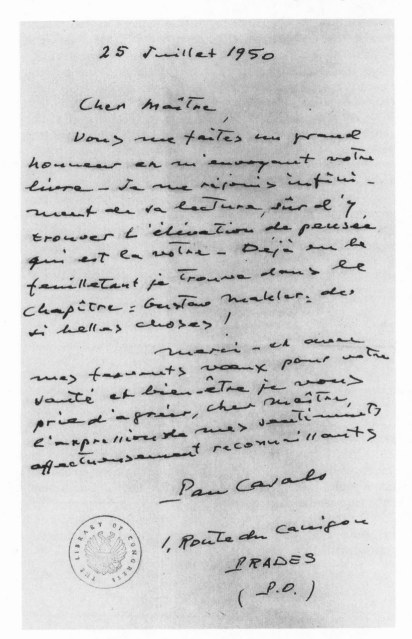

Facsimile III. Casals to Schoenberg. Dated July 25, 1950

[From: *Conversations with Casals*, J.Ma. Corredor, trans. from the French by André Mangeot. E.P. Dutton & Co., Inc: New York, 1957, pp. 169-171].[10]

Did you know Schönberg well?

Yes, I was in touch with him, I followed his evolution and, through conversations I had with him I know what his anxieties and aspirations were. I know where he stands, and when I hear that he and some modern composers are put together in the same category I say: No, there is a mistake. In Schönberg we have a man who deliberately chose the path of research with complete sincerity towards himself. Some people thought that, because he was successful, he allowed himself to write insignificant works in the belief that they would naturally be applauded by people who were unable to understand his compositions, but wanted to look as if they did.

Schönberg was not like that: he had musical genius and he revered all composers who deserved it. (What would some of the iconoclasts of our time say if they had heard him say, as I have, how well he understood and admired even a composer like Donizetti?)

With the prophetic instinct of his race and his profound devotion to music he wished to explore unknown spheres, like atonality, with the object of finding out what could be done with it. His attitude was one of self-sacrifice--it consisted of putting on one side the "known" methods (in which he excelled) in order to penetrate into the "unknown". His goal was not to break with the past, but to increase the treasures of music with the new possibilities produced by his researches.

What was he like as a person?

Oh, delightful! Very simple, full of charm and possessing a brilliant intelligence.

You have played a 'Cello Concerto of his?

Not in public. I'll explain to you what happened. On the occasion of a musical festival in Vienna, Schönberg had found a

Figured Bass of an unpublished Concerto by G. M. Monn (a
remarkable and unknown composer of the XVII century). Schoenberg's work on it was masterly, and I played this concerto a good
many times, especially in Vienna where it was given its first performance. Then Schönberg discovered another work of Monn from
which he borrowed the themes, and made a 'Cello Concerto of it
after he had added a good deal himself. He sent it to me with a
dedication and I thought that it was a highly interesting work. I
worked on it for some two years; just as I was on the point of
playing the Concerto, the music publishers, Schirmer of New York,
who had acquired the rights of the work, told me that I would have
to pay one hundred dollars for each performance. I said I did not
agree, and on hearing my answer they reduced it to fifty dollars.
This haggling made me feel so sick that I said I would have nothing
to do with it. (Schönberg, having heard of this, wrote me a letter
in which he begged me not to accept Schirmer's terms.)

Feuermann played this Concerto for the first time, and in
spite of the remarkable performance he gave, the work had no
success at all. I never heard any more about this Concerto except
when a 'cellist called Bartsch played it on Paris Radio. It is a pity
that it has not become known, as I think it is a masterly work.

What did you think of Schönberg's innovations?

By and large I think that some of his ideas will help in the
normal (but not purely cerebral) development of music. But, on the
other hand, I think that some of his innovations will prove fruitless.
I remember one day in Vienna when Schönberg talked to me of his
plans. In spite of all his enthusiasm, I could not escape the vision
of the abyss which was opening beneath his feet!

*I have read that some of the former pupils of Schönberg and
Alban Berg said: "The twelve-tone system cannot form a
school. It is only a valueless doctrine in itself, in which
Schönberg has experimented on his own account, and when
passing it on to his pupils he always warned them against
taking it too seriously."*

Of course, it is natural to find pupils following the teachings of their master, even taking it too seriously. They cannot all have as much talent as Schoenberg had, nor his great sincerity when experimenting. And have we not seen already how ridiculous some people can be when they are afraid of looking old-fashioned?

Our compatriot Roberto Gerhard, when he came back to Barcelona after a stay in Vienna, had been so influenced by the innovations of Schoenberg that he wrote exclusively in that style. He managed to express his talent, but it became sterile since (as I think) any music which is not expressive has no reason to exist. I told him, "You are walking in a maze and you must do everything to get out of it." Later on, Gerhard changed his way of writing, but in his latest works, which are of a different kind as far as structure and style are concerned, one can detect the mark of Schoenberg. I feel sure that this period under Schönberg, and the experience he had through it, have been useful to him. Any kind of new ideas are profitable to those who have something to say.

Notes

1. Roberto Gerhard (1896-1970), a Cataloni composer, studied with Granados from 1915 to 1916 and Pedrell from 1915 to 1922. In 1923 Gerhard went to Vienna to study with Schoenberg, and after the completion of his studies with Schoenberg in Berlin (1928) he returned to Spain. In 1939 Gerhard emigrated to England and settled in Cambridge. Later in life he achieved an international reputation as a composer, scholar and teacher.

2. Schoenberg's basso-continuo realization for this harpsichord concerto was published in the *Denkmäler der Tonkunst in Österreich*. See also note 6 of Chapter II.

3. Arnold Schoenberg, *Concerto for String Quartet and Orchestra in B-flat Major after the Concerto Grosso Opus 6 Nr. 7 by G. F. Handel*, in Arnold Schoenberg, *Instrumentalkonzerte nach Werken alter Meister, Sämtliche Werke*, Abteilung VII, Reihe B, vol. 27, edited by Nikos Kokkinis. Mainz: B. Schott & Sons; Vienna: Universal Edition AG, 1976, pp. 101-220.

4. See Chapter III, note 8.

5. Given the fact that Schoenberg made reference to the composition of his violoncello concerto in D Major as to ca. six weeks before the date of his letter of February 20, 1933 (p. 161), Schoenberg's undated letter above must have been written after the middle of October 1932, but no later than early January 1933.

6. For another English translation see Erwin Stein, *Arnold Schoenberg Letters*. London: Faber & Faber, 1964, 1955.

7. Hans Rosbaud (1895-1962) was an Austrian conductor who had a special interest in contemporary music. He served as the conductor of the radio symphony orchestras in Frankfurt am Main and Baden-Baden, and as the director of the Munich Konzertverein. In 1957 Rosbaud conducted the first staged performance of Schoenberg's *Moses und Aron* in Zurich.

8. For another English translation, see Stein, *Letters*. London: Faber & Faber, 1964, pp. 171-172.

9. Since Schoenberg made the piano reduction between March 7th and March 11th, 1933, Schoenberg's own date [1932] given at the end of his letter is erroneous, and this letter was actually written in early March. See Arnold Schoenberg, *Instrumentalkonzerte nach Werken alter Meister*, Abteilung VII; Bearbeitungen Series B, vol, 27, 2. The score of the D Major concerto is published in *Sämtliche Werke*, Abteilung VII, Series A, vol. 27, ed. Nikos Kokkinis. Mainz: B. Schott's Söhne; Vienna: Universal Edition AG, 1976, pp. 3-99.

10. From *Conversations with Casals* by J.M. Corredor, trans. by André Mangeot. Copyright (c) 1956, renewed 1984 by E.P. Dutton. Reprinted by permission of Penguin Books USA Inc.

CHAPTER V

Arnold Schoenberg - Emanuel Feuermann

Schoenberg's Violoncello Concerto in D Major
New Projects for Violoncello

Emanuel Feuermann (1902-1942), the Austrian cellist, studied with Julius Klengel in 1918. He began his teaching career in Leipzig, and from 1929 to 1933 he taught at the Academy of Music in Berlin. Feuermann's first performance in the United States took place under Bruno Walter in 1935. In 1938 Feuermann and his family emigrated to the U.S., and in 1941 he joined the faculty of the Curtis Institute of Music in Philadelphia. Throughout his career Feuermann was associated with the greatest musicians of the time for solo and chamber music performances; he made recordings with Paul Hindemith, Szymon Goldberg, Artur Rubinstein, Arturo Toscanini, Rudolf Serkin, Jascha Heifetz, Leopold Stokowski, Gerald Moore, William Primrose, Leon Barzin, Sir Thomas Beecham and many others.[1]

Schoenberg and Feuermann knew each other from the time when they both were teaching at the Academy of Music in Berlin. Feuermann was terminated for the same reason as Schoenberg; a letter of March 27, 1933 informed him of the "non-renewal" of his teaching contract, and on April 8 he was given a leave of absence for the remainder of his contract.[2]

A first performance of the *Violoncello Concerto in D Major* with Casals as the preferred soloist did not materialize (see Chapter IV, p. 179), and during this time Schoenberg explored several other possibilities for the publication[3] and performance[4] of this work. Feuermann, accompanied by Walter Goehr,[5] performed it privately in Schoenberg's presence, in Paris in 1933. The concerto had its first public performance on November 7, 1935 with the B.B.C. orchestra in London, with Feuermann as soloist and Sir Thomas Beecham conducting.[6] It is not possible to ascertain whether or not Feuermann had to abide by Schoenberg's terms for this performance as specified in the composer's letter of February

187

23, 1934 (p. 199). The concert seems to have been a success, but the performance was not received as well by the music critics of the *Times* and *Daily Telegraph*:

> ... Later Herr Emanuel Feuermann gave the first performance of what was announced as a Concerto for Violoncello and Orchestra by Arnold Schoenberg, and there was naturally some curiosity to know how Schoenberg's latest harmonic theories could be applied to the *cantilena* of a solo stringed instrument. The piece, however, has nothing to do with the latest harmonic theories. It is a curiosity in its own way, but its way is quite different from the way of atonality.
>
> Schoenberg, it seems, has long been interested in the forgotten works of Georg Matthias Monn (1717-1750). Riemann's Lexicon records that he edited a violoncello concerto by Monn twenty years ago. His method in this case is to take another concerto by Monn and to elaborate it with his own improvisations for the solo instrument and up-to-date orchestration. Of course it is possible that we may hear later that it contains no actual Monn, but only what Monn might have written had he had a mind to. It does not much matter. The principal theme of the first movement is practically what Monn's English contemporary Arne did write as the beginning of "Rule, Britannia". The whole thing seems rather affected and silly, for the violoncello part is so awkwardly written that even Herr Feuermann could get very little effect from it. After the interval the performance was concluded with Dvorak's Symphony in G.
>
> [*The Times*, 8 Nov., 1935][7]

> ... The novelty of the evening was a violoncello concerto by Arnold Schoenberg - a quasi original

work, for it is a transcription of an old harpsichord concerto by G. M. Monn, who flourished at Vienna in Bach's age. This turned out to be Schoenberg's "Pulcinella", or perhaps his "Rhapsody in Blue". A quaint production.

What can Schoenberg be thinking of? He, as keen an intelligence as there is in the whole contemporary world of art, was surely not born to be funny. He jests with dee-ficulty. Rude noises on the trumpet surely date from the day before yesterday. Many a lesser man would have made a merrier rag.

But perhaps the concerto was not meant to be funny. What is the clue? - Perversity, cynicism? The Schoenbergians must tell us. Clearly it is a case for psychological criticism. Anyhow, as a squib or an epigram, the composition was long. The audience applauded with warmth - principally, perhaps, as a tribute to the elegant demeanour of the soloist, Emanuel Feuermann, unflinching under thumbscrew and rack. ...

[*The Daily Telegraph*, 8 Nov., 1935][8]

On December 19, 1938 (p. 201) Schoenberg approached Feuermann concerning the composition of one or more cello concerti based on the viola da gamba sonatas or other compositions by J.S. Bach, offering Feuermann the performance and publication rights for a fee. Feuermann responded enthusiastically on January 1, 1939 (p. 203), but told the composer that he would be unable to raise the money, and that he would like to take up the matter personally with Schoenberg in connection with his concert in Hollywood on January 19th. In his enthusiasm Schoenberg had already started to work on this project before he received Feuermann's reply; the opening fragment of the orchestration of Bach's *Sonata for Viola da Gamba and Harpsichord in G Major* (BWV 1027) is dated January 3, 1939 by the composer:

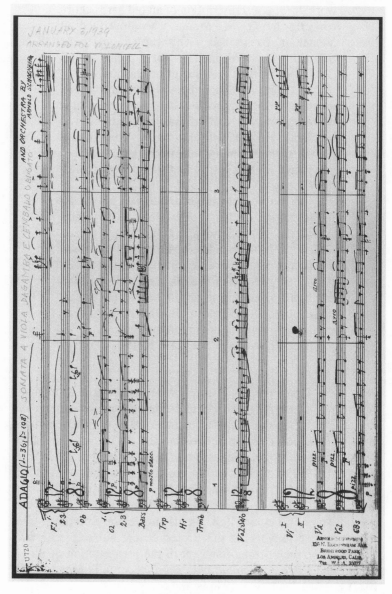

Facsimile IV.
The Opening Measures of Schoenberg's Cello Concerto, based on
J.S. Bach's Sonata for Viola da Gamba in G Major, [BWV 1027]

Facsimile IV, continued

One wonders whether or not Schoenberg's sketch of only five measures, fully orchestrated with dynamic and articulation markings, could have been part of the fair copy of a longer manuscript, of which the rest has been lost. For some composers this would be the only possible conclusion. However, Schoenberg's compositions, like Mozart's, were created and completed in the composer's mind and needed only to be written down. As Rufer observed in his article "Hommage à Schoenberg," which precedes the correspondence in this volume, Schoenberg did not orchestrate in retrospect; for him tone color, rhythm, melody, and harmony were rather a simultaneous part of musical inspiration. See Chapter I, p. 19.

Schoenberg's personal copy of vol. IX of the *Bach-Gesamt-ausgabe*[9] evidences the great care with which he approached such a task; his corrections in the verbal introductory section and in the music itself document the extent to which the composer had studied the entire volume.

The opening movement of Bach's *Sonata for Viola da Gamba and Harpsichord in G Major*, p. 175 in Schoenberg's Bach volume has the metronome marking: $\boldsymbol{.} = 36$ ($\flat = 108$), and Schoenberg's comments, in green pencil, between the two keyboard parts, afford us some insight as to what Schoenberg's rational for the metronome indications may have been:

12/8 are 15.5 seconds, this can only be sustained by an organ. On my piano, even with a forte attack, the tone dies out completely at the 12th eighth note (!) and the continuation sounds dried-up, just as if after a rest. Could the Bebung [on the clavichord] keep the tone alive longer? How was the long note sustained on the harpsichord?

Schoenberg's most important comment on this sonata refers to m. 242 of the third movement, and is found in the right-hand margin of p. 187 (see Facsimile V on p. 194 below):

Here we now have conclusive evidence that the

"long" grace note is nonsense--a position I have
always maintained. Were it so, as is commonly
believed, and as Ph. E. Bach seems to suggest,
then there would be parallel fifths between cello
and keyboard:

Here one would have to argue that the grace note
be played as an upbeat (2)

because (3) also results in parallel fifths:

Schoenberg then comes to this conclusion (left-hand corner of
p. 187, on Facsimile V, p. 194):   "It was probably left to the 'intelligence' of the performer, thus the confusion."[10]

Facsimile V.
Page 187 from Schoenberg's Personal Copy of the
Old Bach-Gesamtausgabe, vol IX.

Here Schoenberg demonstrates clearly how he arrived at the most appropriate interpretation of a particular grace note (see Facsimile V on p. 194, m. 242). With his unfailing musical instinct he did not follow the rather rigidly applied rules of performance practice which reigned supreme then (and are still adhered to by many today). Rather he was guided by the musical context, an approach which has been vindicated by modern musicological research. Frederick Neumann acknowledges this flexibility as stylistically correct, recognizing that grace notes (Vorschläge) could be prebeat, onbeat, short, long, or even overlong. For Bach, however, Neumann considered the overlong interpretation the exception:

> . . . As far as the *Vorschläge* are concerned, his use appears to have ranged approximately as indicated . . . from the anticipated "grace note" to an appoggiatura that can take from short binary notes (8th-notes and less frequently quarter-notes) up to about half their value. What is labeled in the tabulation [not given here] as "overlong" designs, such as one-half of a long binary note (half-note or more) or two-thirds of a ternary note, was generally not intended. Exceptions always occur, but they must have been rare. The "overlong" interpretations were mostly later developments brought to the fore by the *galant* style. Musical evidence will confirm their inappropriateness for Bach's music.[11]

In his letter of December 19, 1938 to Feuermann (p. 201) Schoenberg also reveals some details of the compositional approach he intended to take. Schoenberg indicated that he would leave the three original voices by Bach unaltered, but possibly add--at least for certain parts of the *Originalstimme* (solo gamba part)--a more brilliant alternate version for the solo cello, and possibly one or several cadenzas (ad libitum) if appropriate places could be found for them.

Concerning the orchestration Schoenberg suggested that the orchestra should be small [!], utilizing at most double, or perhaps only single woodwinds, two French horns, two trumpets, one or two trombones, and in the case of the brass possibly less.

In his sketch of the five opening measures of J.S. Bach's *Sonata for Viola da Gamba and Harpsichord* (BWV 1027), Schoenberg settled for three flutes, one oboe, three clarinets, and one bassoon; one trumpet, French horn, and trombone; and strings (see Facsimile IV, p. 190). Compared with the *Violoncello Concerto in D Major* (in free adaptation after Monn) which features a very large orchestra (including a big percussion section), Schoenberg's sketch of the opening measures of Bach's gamba sonata can be considered much closer to chamber music.

In the Schoenberg sketch the three original Bach parts are utilized as follows:

a. Bach's gamba part has been transferred literally to the solo cello, including the original articulation and bowing. The only noticable difference is that Schoenberg converted Bach's grace notes, shown in the original as eighth notes, into sixteenth notes, with a diagonal slash, indicating that he definitely wanted these grace notes to be of the short type and played before the beat. Given the fact that the context is that of a slow movement, Bach's indication, "Adagio" in compound meter, is to be interpreted as "Andante" in today's terms. Present-day performance practice would not be in agreement with Schoenberg's recommendation, but rather opt for onbeat and longer graces.

b. The highest voice in the Bach sonata (right hand of the harpsichord) is introduced by Schoenberg transposed one octave up by the first flute and joined in m. 2 by the oboe at the original pitch. In m. 4, when the motion of the solo cello comes to an end with a high sustained note (the cello part starting in m. 4 is the transposed equivalent of the first three measures stated by Schoenberg in flute 1 and oboe), the upper woodwinds revert to free accompaniment figuration in a discreet pianissimo, with some soft punctuating notes in the brass section.

c. Of particular interest is Schoenberg's treatment of Bach's bass line (left hand of the harpsichord), which, in Schoenberg's version, is shared between the lower strings (bass, cello, viola) and the bassoon, the latter of which moves freely when the lower strings have Bach's original pitches. In the first measure, for example, the first four notes (pizzicato-bass an octave lower and bassoon, marked "molto staccato" on the original pitch) are overlapped with the next four notes given to the cello and viola (also pizzicato). The third flute in m. 1 anticipates Bach's syncopated rhythm, introduced in the middle of m. 2, emphasizing this effect with additional *fp* indications. This subtle rhythmic treatment by Schoenberg counterbalances the lighter second and fourth beats of the bass line as referred to above, creating much variety. For the same reason, the double bass omits the sixteenth notes on the second beat of m. 2. For the next two measures (mm. 2-3) the lower strings (bass, cello, viola) govern the bass line, with the bassoon doubling the bass in m. 2, but continuing freely in m. 3, and the same reinterpretation of the bass line is maintained for the rest of Schoenberg's fragment.

Schoenberg also added dynamics to his adaptation. It is quite remarkable that he provided no dynamic indications in the strings except for the general 'piano' markings in m. 1 and m. 4, but gave very explicit indications for the winds, using many crescendo and decrescendo signs, frequently even on single notes. Some of these crescendo indications occur between unemphasized and accented eighth notes, and this attests to Schoenberg's desire to avoid an emphasis on downbeats in order to keep the music flowing.

The notes added by Schoenberg are either doublings in unison or octaves between the winds and strings for color, additional chord tones which are clearly implied by Bach's basso-continuo, or very subtle melodic and rhythmic embellishments.

The first of Schoenberg's letters to Feuermann (February 23, 1934, p. 199) also exists in an almost full-length literal draft in Schoenberg's own hand. Both of Schoenberg's letters to Feuermann (February 23, 1934 and December 19, 1938, pp. 199 and 201 respectively) are reproduced here from the composer's own carbon copies because the originals have been lost.

V.S-F.o.1

Herrn Emanuel Feuermann   23. Februar 1934
per Adr. M. Stern
30, Rue Raffet
Paris

Lieber Herr Feuermann, ich traf dieser Tage in Chicago zufällig
Piatigorsky, den ich nicht kannte, der sich mir vorstellte und mich
wegen meines Cellokonzertes fragte. Er wusste nicht von unseren
Probrn und ich sagte auch nichts davon, sondern nur von Casals.
Er machte mir aber einen anscheinend ganz praktischen Vorschlag:
ich sollte nicht einem Einzelnen das Aufführungsrecht geben,
sondern mehreren (4,5,8,10 etc.), dann kann keiner beleidigt sein.

　　Nun ist die Sache die: Ich habe mit einem einzigen Agenten
Verbindung und der ist nicht sehr geschickt (wie hätte ich sonst
Verbindung mit ihm ?!). Er erklärt es für unwahrscheinlich, dass
er eine genügende Anzahl von Orchesterengagements für einen
Cellisten heute finden könne, obwohl er Sie für den Ersten der
jüngeren Cellisten-Generation hält. Ich kann natürlicherweise nicht
kontrollieren, ob die überall vorgeschobene "Depression" daran
schuld ist: aber in der Tat muss ich zugestehen, dass anscheinend
heute niemand das Risiko eines Reklamefeldzuges tragen will und
ohne einen solchen ist das Publikum nicht in die Konzertsäle zu
bringen (auch mit ihm nicht: alle Orchester sind notleidend
geworden). Ich sehe also keine Aussicht, Sie für mich nach
Amerika zu bringen: so gerne ich das um meinetwillen getan hätte.
Und deshalb bin ich auf folgenden Ausweg, eine Variante des
Vorschlags Piatigorsky's, gekommen.

　　Ich würde Ihnen stillschweigend die Uraufführung und
eventuell auch einen Vorrang bezüglich weiterer 4-5 Konzerte unter
folgenden Bedingungen für   E U R O P A   zu überlassen:
Stillschweigend heisst, das[s] wir es niemanden sagen oder auch nur
andeuten; aber wir werden so handeln. Wenn Sie mir innerhalb
sechs Wochen plus 2 mal 10 Posttage das ist also bis zum 30. April
als äussersten Termin fünf Engagements nennen, welche (ich
reflektiere nicht darauf zu dirigieren; das käme zu teuer!) bereit
sind als Materialgebühr an mich je cirka 30-50 Dollar, zusammen
aber wenigstens ungefähr 200 Dollar zu bezahlen, so würde ich für
Sie ein Material anfertigen lassen und es Ihnen für die nötige Zeit

V.S-F.t.1

Mr. Emanuel Feuermann   February 23, 1934
c/o M. Stern
30 Rue Raffet
Paris

Dear Mr. Feuermann:
        Recently in Chicago, I happened to meet Piatigorsky whom
I did not know, and who introduced himself to me and asked me
about my cello concerto. He did not know anything about our
rehearsals and I also did not tell him anything about them, but only
about Casals. However, he presented me, it seems to me, a rather
practical proposition: I should not grant the performance rights to
one, but to several (4,5,8,10 etc.), then nobody can be insulted.
        Now the situation is this: I am associated with just one
agent who is not very skillful (how could I have been connected
with him otherwise!?). He considers it to be improbable that, at
present, he could find a sufficient number of orchestra engagements for a young cellist, even though he considers you as the
foremost among the generation of the younger cellists. Naturally,
I cannot verify whether or not the "depression" cited everywhere is
the cause of this: but indeed I must concede that apparently nobody
today is willing to take on the risk of an advertising campaign, and
without it the public cannot be brought into the concert halls (not
even with him [the agent]: all orchestras are in distress). Thus I do
not see any prospect of bringing you to America as much as I would
have liked to for my sake. And, for that reason, I came up with the
following idea, based on Piatigorsky's suggestion:
        I would grant you <u>tacitly</u> the premiere performance and
possibly an option for 4-5 more concerts in E u r o p e under the
following conditions: tacitly means that we shall deal with it thus:
if within six weeks plus twice ten postal days, that is until April 30th
as the absolute deadline, you come up with five engagements, which
would include the provision to pay to me as a fee for the material
about $ 30-50, or at least $ 200 or so altogether, I would be willing
to have the material produced for you and to leave it with you for
the time necessary.   If you think, however, that you can obtain
further performances in the near future, I would be pleased to let
you have the material for a season for a lump sum. Perhaps make

überlassen. Wenn Sie aber meinen, weitere Aufführungen in der
nächsten Zeit erzielen zu können, so bin ich gerne bereit, Ihnen das
Material gegen einen Pauschalbetrag für eine Saison zu überlassen.
Machen Sie mir eventuell einen annehmbaren Vorschlag. Ich würde
mich verpflichten--sofern Sie darauf reflektieren, keine Aufführungen vor 30. April zu vergeben, d[as] h[eisst] also, bevor Sie
mir nicht geantwortet haben wie oben bestimmt. Es tut mir leid,
dass hier einstweilen nichts zu machen ist, aber ich glaube, die hiesigen Agenten degenerieren bereits: ich finde sie eben so engstirnig,
wie die europäischen.

Lassen Sie mich bald Antwort von Ihnen hören und grüssen
Sie Madame Stren [Stern] herzlichst von mir.

Schreiben Sie mir, wie es Ihnen geht.

Herzlichste Grüsse, Ihr

V.S-F.o.2

Herrn Emanuel Feuermann   19. XII. 1938
c/o G. Schirmer, Inc.
Music Publishers
3 East, 43rd Street
New York City

Lieber Herr Feuermann:

Ich beabsichtige eine oder mehrere der Cellosonaten mit
Clavicembalo von Bach (aus dem "Neunten Jahrgang" der Bachgesellschaft bei Breitkopf and Härtel fü[r] Cello und Orchester zu
arrangieren. Es kommen hiefür in ersten Linie selbstverständlich
die von Bach lebst [selbst] für Viola di Gamba arrangierten in
Betracht, aber ich würde gegebenenfalls auch irgend eines der anderen Stücke aus diesem Band machen, wenn die geeigneter wären./

Mein Plan ist, die Solostimmen unverändert zu lassen.
Aber ich habe auch daran gedacht, nebst der Originalstimme eine
mehr brillante Fassung (wenigstens teilweise) beifügen. Auch denke
ich daran, wenn sich ein geeigneter Platz findet eine oder mehrere
Kadenzen einzustreuen (ad libitum natürlich).

Das Orchestra soll klein sein, höchstens 2-faches Holz
(vielleicht sogar nur einfaches, 2 Hörner, 2 Trompeten, 1 oder 2

me a proposition which is acceptable to me. I would be obliged, provided that you are interested, not to grant rights for performances before April 30th, that is not until you have answered me, as outlined above. I am sorry that for the present nothing can be done here, but I believe that the local agents are already degenerating; I do find them just as narrow-minded as the European ones.

Let me hear your answer from you soon, and give my best regards to Madame Stern.

Do write me how you are.   Sincerely yours,

V.S-F.t.2

Mr. Emanuel Feuermann   December 19, 1938
c/o Schirmer, Inc.
Music Publishers
3 East, 43rd Street
New York City

Dear Mr. Feuermann:

I intend to arrange one or several of the cello sonatas by Bach (from the "Ninth Jahrgang" of the *Bach-Gesellschaft* by Breitkopf and Haertel) for cello and orchestra. Principally the ones arranged by Bach himself for viola da gamba are to be taken into consideration, but I would possibly also do one of the other pieces from this volume if they are more suitable.

It is my plan to leave the solo voice unchanged. But I also thought to add a more brilliant version (at least in part) besides the original part. Also, I am contemplating interspersing one or several cadenzas (ad libitum, of course).

The orchestra shall be small, at the most double woodwinds (perhaps also only one of each), two horns, two trumpets, one or two trombones, perhaps even fewer of these.

Posaunen, vielleicht aber da auch weniger[)].

Ich frage Sie nun, ob Sie sich für einen solchen Plan inter-
sieren. Ich frage Sie als Ersten, obwohl Sie ja meinen Monn
garnicht mehr spielen, aber weil Sie ihn wirklich ausserordentlich
gut gespielt haben.

Es kommen folgende Fragen in Betracht: Wollen Sie eine
solche Bearbeitung erwerben? Das heisst: a) ganz ankaufen, mit
allen Rechten, inclusive Verlags- und Aufführungsrecht: oder
b) lediglich das alleinige Aufführungsrecht fuer eine festzusetzende
Anzahl von Jahren, nach Ablauf welcher ich erst berechtigt bin, es
drucken zu lassen: oder c) dass Sie mir das Recht lassen, es zu
publizieren und beliebig aufuehren zu lassen und nur die
Urauffuehrung erwerben und das Recht es lebenslaenglich ohne
Bezahlung (Auffuehrungsgebuehren etc) aufzufuehren.

Sagen Sie mir Ihre Meinung und machen Sie mir ein
generoeses Angebot (nicht nach dem Prinzip "was kostet bei Ihnen
gar kein Hund?") auf das ich ohne weiteres eingehen kann.

Bitte antworten Sie bald, denn ich moechte bald anfangen.

Wie geht es Ihnen und Ihrer Frau?

Herzliche Grüsse von uns allen

Ihr

V.F-S.o.1

EMANUEL FEUERMANN   Den 1. Januar 1939

100 Pelham Road
New Rochelle, N.Y.

Herrn Arnold Schoenberg
116 North Rockingham Avenue
Brentwood Park
Los Angeles, Cal.

Mein sehr verehrter Herr Schoenberg:
        Ich habe Ihren Brief vom 19. Dezember mit grosser Freude

I do ask you now whether or not you would be interested in such a plan. You are the first one I ask, even though you do not perform my Monn anymore, because you played it really extraordinarily well.

There are two questions to be considered: would you like to acquire such an arrangement? That means a) to purchase it outright, with all rights, including publication and performance; or b) only the exclusive performing rights for a number of years to be determined, only after the expiration of which I would be entitled to have it printed; or c) that you acquire only the premiere performance and the right to perform it for life without any fees (performance fees), leaving to me the publication rights and the right to have it performed freely.

Do tell me your opinion and make me a generous offer which I cannot refuse (not according to the principle "What is your price now for no dog?").

Please, do answer me soon because I would like to begin soon.

How are you and your wife?

Cordial regards from all of us, Your

V.F-S.t.1

EMANUEL FEUERMANN   January 1, 1939
100 Pelham Road
New Rochelle, N.Y.

Mr. Arnold Schoenberg
116 North Rockingham Avenue
Brentwood Park
Los Angeles, Cal.

My very esteemed Mr. Schoenberg:
I read your letter of December 19th with great pleasure,

gelesen und bin begeistert von Ihrer Idee, uns Cellisten ein Bach-Konzert zu verschaffen. Ich finde Ihre Idee wunderschön und werde sehr dankbar sein wenn es so weit ist.

Auf Ihre Vorschläge in puncto Aufführungsrechte usw. kann ich leider nicht eingehen. Der Grund ist rein finanzieller Art; durch meine verschiedenen Verpflichtungen jetzt ist es mir tatsächlich unmöglich. Der zweite Grund ist, dass durch den Wegfall von Deutschland die Anzahl der Orchester-Konzerte und damit die Möglichkeit, ein solches Konzert zu spielen, sehr vermindert ist.

Was ich glaube, versprechen zu können, ist eine ziemliche Anzahl von Aufführungen in Amerika, England und Holland.

Ich wäre sehr traurig, wenn das dumme Geld auch in diesem Falle einen Strich durch die Rechnung machen würde.

Im übrigen spiele ich am 19. Januar in der ach so geliebten Kraft Hour in Hollywood, und ich denke, ich hole mir Ihre Antwort persönlich.

Mit vielen herzlichen Grüssen an Sie und Ihre Gattin und den allerbesten Glückwünschen zum Jahreswechsel bin ich

in alter Verehrung
Ihr Emanuel Feuermann

V.S-M.o.1

ARNOLD SCHOENBERG
  HOTEL REGINA
PLACE DES PYRAMIDES
P A R I S

Mr. Joseph Malkin   10. X. 1933
Malkin Conservatory
299 Beacon Street
Boston Massachusetts

Sehr geehrter Herr Malkin:
        Wir vertelegraphierten eine Menge Geld und verständigen uns doch nicht über manches Wichtige. Da es nun gewiss ist, dass

and I am enthusiastic about your idea to create a Bach Concerto for us cellists. I find your idea wonderful and I will be most grateful when it becomes a reality.

Unfortunately, I cannot consider your proposals concerning performance rights, etc. The reason is purely financial; because of my various commitments it is really impossible for me at present. The other reason is that, because of the unavailability of Germany, the number of orchestral concerts, and with it the possibility of performing such a concerto, is quite reduced.

What I believe I can promise is a considerable number of performances in America, England and Holland.

It would be very unfortunate if in this case, too, wretched money were to throw a wrench in the works.

By the way, I play on January 19th in the oh-so-beloved Kraft Hour in Hollywood, and I think I will get your answer in person.

With many cordial regards to you and your wife and the very best wishes for the New Year, I remain

in old faithfulness,   Your   Emanuel Feuermann

V.S-M.t.1

ARNOLD SCHOENBERG
  HOTEL REGINA
PLACE DES PYRAMIDES
   P A R I S

Mr. Joseph Malkin
Malkin Conservatory
299 Beacon Street
Boston, Massachusetts   October 10, 1933

Esteemed Mr. Malkin:

We spent a lot of money telegraphing each other, yet we did not come to an agreement concerning some important matters.

ich mit I l e de F r a n c e am 25.X. reise (nämlich: ich, meine Frau und mein 17-Monate altes Kind) so schreibe ich einen Brief und hoffe, dass er Sie sicher vor meiner Ankunft, vielleicht aber noch vor meiner Abreise erreicht. Ile de France gibt meine[r] Frau und der Tochter 30% Nachlass und mir 50 (fünfzig), so dass ich für die Reisebillets zu bezahlen haben werde 220 + 110 -99 + 110 d[as] i[st] 440 - 99 = 341 Dollar. Hie[r]zu kommen noch einige kleinere Beträäge, die Sie gewiss besser wissen, als ich und die Trinkgelder. Was ich für Gepaäck und sonstiges ausgeben muss, ist mir unbekannt. Ich werde jedenfalls nicht unter 500 Dollar benötigen, weil ich ja aus Deutschland, wie Ihnen bekannt sein wird, nicht mehr als 200 Mark per Erwachsenen herausbekommen kann, welche Summe in diesem Nonat schon behoben wurde. Es ist nictzunmöglich, dass ich den Reisevorschuss nicht hätte in Anspruch nehmen müssen, da drei verschiedene Angebote in der letzten Zeit and mich herangetreten waren. Aber ich bezweifle, dass all das noch vor der Abreise erledigt werden kann.

Warum ich am 25. erst fahre, hat vor Allem diesen letzteren Grund: ich [hätte] gerne noch einiges hier abgeschlossen. Denn die Frage, ob es besser ist, sich Fehlendes noch hier, oder erst in Amerika anzuschaffen, ist keineswegs geklärt. Aber ausserdem liegt noch ein sehr wichtiger Grund vor: Sie haben vergessen, dass ich bis anfangs September nichts von Ihnen gehört hatte und selbstverständlich gar nicht mehr an Boston gedacht hatte, sondern alles für ein Verbleiben in Paris disponiert hatte. Nun haben Sie mir aber erst E n d e September definitiv gesagt, dass Sie mich erwarten und nun soll ich in wenigen Tagen alle eingegangenen Verpflichtungen so lösen, dass mir kein Schade daraus erwächst! Hier ist nun, neben einer Anzahl kleinerer und grösserer Engagements der unangenehmste Fall der zweier Londoner Konzerte in der dortigen Broadcasting Corp[poration], wo ich am 24.XI Pierrot Lunaire und das Klavierseptett (Suite) op. 28, aber am 29. das neues Konzert für Streichquartett und Orchester (freie Transcription nach einem Concerto grosso von Händel) zur Uraufführung hätte bringen sollen. Die Broadcasting Corp[oration] scheint nunsehr beleidigt über meine Absagen zu sein und deshalb wollte ich ein (Casals gewidmetes) Konzert für Cello u[nd] Orch[ester] nach einem Klavierkonzert von Monn (1740), da Casals mit dem Studium noch nicht fertig ist, mit Emanuel F e u e r- m a n n (der es fabelhaft spielt) als Ersatz für das zweite Konzert

Since it is certain now that I shall depart on October 25th on the Ile de France (that is me, my wife and my 17-month-old child), I write you a letter in the hope that it may reach you for sure before my arrival, perhaps even before my departure. The Ile de France is giving my wife and daughter a 30% and me a 50% (fifty) discount so that I will have to pay for the tickets 220 + 110 - 99 + 110, that is 440 - 99 = $ 341. Still to be added are several smaller amounts which, I am certain, you are more aware of than I, and the tips. What I will have to pay for luggage and miscellaneous, I do not know. Certainly, I shall need no less than $ 500, because--as you may know--I will not be able to take out of Germany more than DM 200 per adult, the amount of which was already withdrawn this month. It is possible that I will not be obliged to use the travel advance because I had three different offers lately. Yet I doubt that I will be in a position to take advantage of them before my departure.

The reason why I am not leaving before the 25th is mainly that I would like to take care of several matters over here. It is not at all clear whether or not it would be better to acquire certain necessary items here or later in America. Furthermore, there is another very important reason. You have forgotten that I had not heard anything from you until the beginning of September. Obviously, I did not think about Boston anymore, but arranged everything to settle in Paris. But now that you have told me definitely only at the end of September that you expect me, I am supposed to undo in a few days all the commitments I made without any disadvantage resulting for me! Among them--besides a number of lesser and greater engagements--the most unpleasant situation arose concerning the two London concerts with the local Broadcasting Corporation, for whom I was obliged to perform Pierrot Lunaire and the Piano Septet (Suite) op. 28 on November 24th, and then to present on the 29th the premiere performance of the new Concerto for String Quartet and Orchestra (my transcription after a concerto grosso by Handel). Now the Broadcasting Corporation seems to be very insulted because of my cancellations, and it is for this reason that I wanted to offer them instead for the second concert in London a concerto for cello and orchestra (dedicated to Casals) after a harpsichord concerto by Monn (1740) with Emanuel F e u- e r m a n n (who plays it fabulously), because Casals is not quite ready for it. It is for this reason that I agreed not to leave until the

in London anbieten. Deshalb habe ich mich bereit erklärt erst am
25. zu fahren, wobei ich bloss um vier Tage später ankomme, als
wenn ich mit Degrasse gefahren wäre. Bis heute habe ich keine
Antwort von dem Agenten, der diesen Vorschlag gemacht hat und
glaube also, dass nichts mehr werden wird. Aber da ich bei Ile de
France nicht nach Southampton fahren muss, wie bei Majestic und
nicht neun Tage unterwegs bin, wie bei Degrasse, bin ich sehr
zufrieden mit dieser Lösung.

Ich hoffe, Sie haben mein gestriges Telegramm, in welchem
ich Sie ersuchte: "Erforderliches" zu überweisen, dahinverstanden,
dass es sich auch um die Einreisebewilligung [handelte] und nicht
bloss um die Fahrkarten und den Reisevorschuss respektive, wenn
ich die Karten h i e r bezahlen soll (oder tun Sie es lieber in
Boston selbst?)! [sondern] den ganzen Reisevorschuss. Ich nehme
an, dass ich bis dahin auch die Benachrichtigung von der Bank, bei
welcher Sie die Garantie erlegen wollen, erhalten habe.

Werden wir uns in New York aufhalten müssen oder kön-
nen wir gleich nach Boston weiterreisen? Im ersteren Fall bitte ich
Sie für uns nicht nur in Boston, sondern auch eben in New York
Unterkunft zu wählen.

Findet der Empfang in New York oder in Boston statt?
Wo werde ich interviuewt werden?

Kann das nicht in der Narcose oder wenistens mit Lokal-
anästhesie geschehen?

Ich bin sehr neugierig, wie es schliesslich werden wird, ob
scih viele Schüler gemeldet haben und wie es mit Konzerten sein
wird.

Ich freue mich sehr Sie bald kennen zu lernen und kann
Ihnen mit Vergnügen sagen, dass ich mir das Allerbeste verspreche.

Mit herzlichsten Grüssen,
Ihr   Arnold Schoenberg

25th, whereby I would arrive only four days later than if I had taken the Degrasse. As yet I have not received a response from the agent who made this suggestion, and I believe, therefore, that it will not work out. But since I do not have to go to Southampton for the Ile de France as I would have to for the Majestic, and since I will not be at sea for nine days as with the Degrasse, I am very pleased with this solution.

I do hope that you understood my cable of yesterday in which I requested you to transfer the necessary funds, insofar as they would also have to take care of the entry visa and not just the tickets and the travel advance respectively if I am expected to pay for the tickets *here*, but the full travel advance (or would you prefer to take care of it in Boston yourself)? I assume that by then I will have also received a notification from the bank at which you will have posted the security deposit.

Will we have to stay over in New York, or can we travel to Boston directly? In the first case I would like to ask you to provide for us accommodations not only in Boston but also in New York.

Will the reception take place in New York or Boston?

Where will I be interviewed? Would it not be possible to do this with full, or at least local anaesthetic?

I am very curious as to how it all will turn out in the end, if many students enrolled, and how it will be as far as concerts are concerned.

I am very pleased to meet you soon, and I can tell you with pleasure that I have the highest expectations.

Most sincerely yours,
Arnold Schoenberg

New York Times[12]
February 20, 1938

'CELLO CONCERTO HAS ITS PREMIERE

The Schoenberg-Monn Work is Given for the First Time here by Feuermann

Boccherini Music Played

Leon Barzin Leads National Orchestra Association in Support of Soloist

A special feature of the concert given by Emanuel Feuermann, the Austrian 'cellist, and the National Orchestral Association, under Leon Barzin yesterday afternoon in Carnegie Hall was the Schoenberg-Monn concerto, which received what is believed to be the New York premiere. The rest of this second program of the series being presented by Mr. Feuermann and the orchestra consisted of the Schumann concerto, the Boccherini concerto in B-flat major and Tschaikovsky's "Rococo Variations."

The Schoenberg-Monn concerto published in 1913[13] was first played in America by Mr. Feuermann in Los Angeles in 1936 under Otto Klemperer. It consists of an elaborate transcription by Arnold Schoenberg of a clavicembalo concerto written in 1746 by Georg Matthias Monn, an Austrian composer. The solo part allotted the 'cello proved exorbitant in its technical demands and [is] highly elaborated. As for the orchestral support, although seldom deviating from the traditional type harmonically, its complicated scoring for large orchestra, with frequent resorting to celeste, glockenspiel, muted trumpet, xylophone, harp and percussion effects, gave a modern and strange tang to the interesting music.

The consummate ease with which Mr. Feuermann delivered this fiendishly difficult show-piece was amazing. His accomplishment here as in the three other works presented, reached the acme of cello playing in all respects. Nothing more memorable has been heard this season from any soloist than the rendition granted to the adagio of the Boccherini concerto, with its ravishingly warm and sensitive tone, deep poetic feeling and [?] classic outline. The orchestra provided careful support at all times.

N.A.

New York Herald Tribune[14]
Sunday, February 20, 1938

Barzin Directs Second Concert of 'Cello Series

Schoenberg's Concerto After Monn's for Clavicembalo

Gets First Hearing

Feuermann is the Soloist

Boccherini, Schumann and
Tschaikovsky Also Played

By Jerome D. Bohm

The second concert in the series covering 'cello literature being given by the National Orchestral Association, with Leon Barzin directing, assisted by Emanuel Feuermann, 'cellist, took place in Carnegie Hall yesterday afternoon. Four works were played. One of them, Schoenberg's concerto after the concerto for clavicembalo, composed in 1746 by the Austrian composer, Georg Matthias Monn, had not been heard here before. The remaining three were Boccherini's concerto in B flat, Op. 34; Schumann's concerto in A minor, op. 129; and the Rococo Variations by Tschaikovsky.

Schoenberg's treatment of Monn's classic subject matter is most extraordinary. He has made use of all the resources of the modern orchestra, with special attention to the percussion instruments, to which, in addition to the usual tympani, he has called in the glockenspiel, celesta, xylophone, triangle, cymbals, bass drum, snare drum and tambourine to lend piquancy to his instrumentation. Not content with the unusual effects obtainable with this combination, he has introduced muted instruments and other bizzarre effects, stylistically indefensible in a work with eighteenth century roots, but often intriguing in themselves.

The composer has, for the most part, retained the basically diatonic harmonies of the period, but has not refrained from employing a chromaticism which recalls the Reger of the Hiller variations and a tonal coloring which occasionally suggests Mahler. The work bristles with enormous technical intricacies which Mr. Feuermann tossed off with the greatest nonchalance; Mr. Barzin and the orchestra provided a well coordinated and carefully adjusted accompaniment.

[The remainder of the review is omitted because it discusses only the other works on the program. For excerpts of the two reviews of the premiere performance of Schoenberg's Cello Concerto in D Major on November 7, 1935 in London, see p. 188 and 189].

Notes

1. Seymor W. Itzkoff, *Emanuel Feuermann, Virtuoso*. University of Alabama Press, 1979, pp. 235-245.

2. Ibid., p. 124.

3. Schoenberg's letter to Emil Hertzka of Universal Edition, dated January 8, 1933.

4. Schoenberg's letter to Feuermann, dated February 23, 1934, p. 199.

5. Walter Goehr (1903-1960) was a German-born composer who studied until 1933 with Schoenberg in Berlin. Later Goehr emigrated to England were he became instrumental in the dissemination of Schoenberg's music.
   Goehr's activities in Great Britain included positions as musical director with the Columbia Gramophone Company, and appointments as conductor, including one with the B.B.C. Theatre Orchestra.

In Arnold Schoenberg, *Sämtliche Werke*, Abteilung VII, Reihe B, Band 27, Teil 2, Mainz/Wien: Schott/Universal Edition, 1987, footnote 11 on p. XV, Nikos Kokkinis gives 'Rudolf' as the given name, but he must have meant Schoenberg's student Walter Goehr.

6. Ibid., pp. XIV-XV; XX-XXI.

7. *The Times*, London. Quoted by permission.

8. *The Daily Telegraph*, London. Quoted by permission.

9. Johann Sebastian Bach, *Bach-Gesamtausgabe*. Bachgesellschaft zu Leipzig, ed. Breitkopf & Härtel, 46 Jahrgänge, 1851-1899, vol. IX.

10. For the original German text, consult Facsimile V on p. 194.

11. Frederick Neumann, *Ornamentation in Baroque and Post-Baroque Music. With Special Emphasis in J. S. Bach.* Princeton University Press, 1978, pp. 124 ff. Quoted by permission.

12. Copyright (c) 1935 / 38 / 48 by The New York Times Company. Reprinted by permission.

13. The date refers incorrectly to Schoenberg's basso-continuo realization of Monn's 'cello concerto G minor which had its first modern performance in Vienna on November 19, 1913 with Casals as soloist.
Schoenberg's 'cello concerto in D Major is based on Monn's harpsichord concerto D Major of 1746, and was written by Schoenberg in 1932.

14. I. H. T. Corporation. Reprinted by permission.

CHAPTER VI

Arnold Schoenberg - Olin Downes

Suite in G of 1934--Variations for Orchestra op. 31--
The Schoenberg-Downes Controversy about Mahler--
Schoenberg and Copland

Olin Downes (1886-1955), the eminent American music critic, was educated in Boston and at the National Conservatory of Music in New York. He embarked on his career of music criticism at the *Boston Post* (1906-1924), and was then active as the music critic at the *New York Times* from 1924 to 1955. Other appointments included guest lectureships at Harvard University and Boston University.

In 1965 the University of Georgia acquired the personal papers of Olin Downes, including approximately fifty thousand letters. Many of these were between Downes and major figures of the arts at the time, including other critics, performers, and composers, most notably Arnold Schoenberg.

So far only four letters (three by Schoenberg, one by Downes) of the Schoenberg-Downes correspondence have been published unabbreviated.[1] Stein restricted himself to the Schoenberg letters themselves, omitting the responses of those to whom these letters were directed. One of these Schoenberg letters (p. 241), included in the volume *Olin Downes on Music*, is given here together with Downes' response (p. 245).[2] For the rest, there are occasional quotes or summaries from Schoenberg's letters, or references to them in the biographies on the composer. Like the Adler, Casals, and Feuermann correspondence (Chapters II, III, IV and V in this book), Schoenberg's letters to Downes are complemented here with the responses, and--in addition--some of the more important reviews in the *New York Times* or *New York Herald Tribune* referred to in the letters.

The extant correspondence occurred between 1935 (draft) and 1949, and includes eight letters or cables by Schoenberg, eight responses by Olin Downes, and three very revealing Schoenberg drafts of letters to Downes that were never sent.[3]

The points of discussion between Schoenberg and Downes include the circumstances and reactions to the *Suite in G for Strings* of 1934 (no opus number) on pp. 217, 221 and 226; the revival of their old disagreements on Schoenberg's *Variations for Orchestra, op. 31* (pp. 218, 230); Schoenberg's reaction to a radio quiz on Wagner (p. 236); about Toscanini (Facsimile VI, p. 234); an exchange concerning permission to use the Hollywood Bowl for political speeches (p. 237); the famous "Mahler Controversy" (p. 241); and another controversy between Schoenberg and Copland (p. 261).

The *Suite Written in the Old Style for String Orchestra* of 1934--Schoenberg's first tonal composition since the early 1900s-- generated a great deal of discussion by friends and foes alike. In an undated handwritten draft of a letter to Olin Downes (p. 217), Schoenberg himself gave a detailed account of the story of this work, telling us that the suite was written with American school or college orchestras in mind, in order "to enlarge their repertoire and especially to lead them to a better understanding for modern music and the very different tasks which it puts to the player." As it turned out, the composition was too difficult for such orchestras, "and so it came that I agreed with the publisher's wishes to let it at first be a normal concert work and only later develop its original purpose." Downes' preview and two reviews of the *Suite in G* (pp. 221, 226, 228) are unusual in that they dealt with it in an almost insulting and certainly quite personal manner. Going far beyond the usual boundaries of reviews, Downes then embarked on an extensive discussion of the principles of atonality, referring to Schoenberg's *Variations for Orchestra, op. 31*. In Schoenberg's personal copy of that preview from which the reprint in this book was taken (p. 221), he underlined the passages which were of special concern to him. In his draft to Downes, Schoenberg (p. 217) first congratulated him on his brilliant style and his "astonishing knowledge about the subject." Then Schoenberg dismissed Downes' little jokes in a very restrained and cordial manner, and took issue with his understanding of atonality as well as his concepts concerning phrases of irregular length.

Another of Schoenberg's letters to Downes also exists only as a draft (p. 230), dated November 8, 1938, which, according to Schoenberg's handwritten German comment added to the letter, was never sent: "I did not send this letter because I became already aware of its futility while writing it. Notwithstanding I wrote the one copied on the back (p. 231), which, after all should be as embarrassing as the former, but would permit him the pitiable retreat he deserves." Perhaps it should be pointed out here that Schoenberg himself is incorrect in his draft of November 8, 1938 (p. 230) concerning the length of the theme in his *Variations for Orchestra, op. 31*, mm. 34-57, for the theme is not 32 measures long as he says in his draft, but consists of only 24 measures.

Political considerations are the topic of another exchange (p. 237), and for further clarifications of his political ethics Schoenberg referred Adler to his short essay "On Artists and Collaboration" (p. 240).

And then there is the famous Mahler controversy (p. 241). In his collection of Schoenberg's letters, Stein included Schoenberg's two letters concerning Mahler[4] (the first undated, the other of December 21, 1948 (p. 248), which are based on Schoenberg's personal carbon copies, now in the Library of Congress (the signed original letters are in the Olin Downes Collection at the University of Georgia). The argument cannot really be fully understood without Downes' letters of December 3, 1948 and December 31, 1948 respectively (p. 245 and p. 251). It is for this reason that Downes' letters and also his review of November 12, 1948 in the *New York Times* (p. 253), which first led Schoenberg to the reaction in his undated letter (p. 241), have been reprinted here. To round off the picture and in fairness to Downes, comments pro and con published in the *New York Times* (November 21, 1948) have also been included (p. 254). The exchange is further complicated by a mixup of Downes' letters to Schoenberg and Mitropoulos. From Schoenberg's letter of December 10, 1948 (p. 247) and a cable which Downes sent to Schoenberg on December 13, 1948 (p. 248), we learn that Schoenberg read the letter intended for Mitropoulos before realizing that it was not directed to him. He returned the letter to Downes with a request for the letter intended for him (December 3, 1948, see p. 245). Downes obliged and sent a copy of this letter, now dated December 16, 1948 to Schoenberg who, in the meantime had received the original letter of December 3, 1948 directly from Mitropoulos with a cover letter dated December 9, 1948 (p. 247). This is perhaps the explanation for the fact that both identical letters, signed by Downes, but with different dates, came into Schoenberg's possession. It should also be noted that the later of the letters is not the carbon copy of the former because of the different dates, different position of the text on the page, and one variation in spelling (Carl Maria von Weber versus Karl Maria von Weber).

Finally, there are two handwritten drafts of letters to Downes. In the first of these, a draft (dated 8-22-1949) of his own speech on the occasion of his 75th birthday (for the printed version of his speech see p. 260), Schoenberg took issue with the advances of the twelve-tone concept in Europe and also with the lack of interest for his work in the United States: "Thanks to the attitude of most American conductors and under the leadership of Toscanini, Koussevitzki and Walter, suppression of my work soon began with the effect that a number of performances of my works sunk to an extremely low point" (p. 260). Schoenberg continues to inform us there that "A year ago I had counted in Europe alone about one hundred performances of my work." Schoenberg's reference to Hitler's powerful Propaganda Minister Dr. Josef Goebbels is astonishing: "even so that Mr. Goebbels himself in his *Der Angriff* (a political newspaper) reprimanded me for leaving Germany." According to Schoenberg his twelve-tone technique was not supressed by the Nazis, for, "on the contrary it was compared to the idea of *Der Führer* (Hitler) by the German composer Paul von Klenau[5] who composed operas in this style."

VI.S-D.o.1   [undated draft written in response to Downes'
                          article of October 13, 1935 in the *New York Times*]

Dear Mr. Downes, a friend sent me your article "New Suite by Arnold Schoenberg" (see p. 221 below) an[d] I am very glad to have the opportunity to tell you, how much I enjoyed it. It is not only very brillantly written, but shows too an astonishing knowledge about the subjects of my [?]. And when I consider that it is already two years, that I had the pleasure to meet you and to give you some explanations about this so-called "method", and when

I further consider, how poor my English was at this time (over in comparison with the little capacity, I possess at present) I can congratulate you very heartly.

I understand very well that you do not mean it in earnest, as your nice little joke in the beginning of your article make believe, that I am now in the least influenced by the spirit of Hollywood. I came to these city because I was seriously sick and I restored indeed here my health. Also I am convinced you do not believe that I intend to leave my former musical creed. Perhaps you know already that I am . . . [working on ?] a violin concerto in the 12 tone technic. But, although I know that to write a work "Im alten Stile" as many of my predecessors did (even Bach wrote his English and French Suites, which are doubtless understandable in a similar meaning) would be sufficient to justify this my attempt. But-- confidentially, and please do not publish it, I shall tell you the story of this opus. Mr. Martin Bernstein a music professor of the New York Uni[versity] whom I had met in Chautauqua told me and in such a nice and interesting manner of his own doings with students orchestras and of the general aims of all the other orchestras of this kind, that I found, it would not only be a good work, but a necessary one, to do something for the sake of these youths to enlarge their repertoire and especially to lead them to a better understanding for modern music and the very different tasks w[h]ich she puts to the player. And so I promised him to write something for him and already the next day noted a number of sketches.

Now unfortunately musicians whom I showed the work when it was finished found it too difficult for pupils, but liked the music very much. (I can not object to that because I did my best, and like it too.) And so it came that I agreed with the publishers wishes to let it at first be a normal concert work and only later develop its original purpose.

Meanwhile you listened to it and I hope you find yourself, that this work doesn't need an excuse and that, if I should have had intentions like Ernest Bloch, I had not to regret it. Because I had indeed much pleasure during the composing and I could see myself how much my knowledge is based on the masters and how much I developed it from my own and how many ways, still unused, I could show to composers, who hate "atonality[.]"

Now speaking of your very interesting analysis of my Varia- tions for Orchestra, I want to tell you, that a certain number of esthetical or compositional concerns, which you find problematical, or even baseless or wrong, seem in my opinion not only very well to be resolved and explained, but I myself have already been able to do it. At first to the concept of atonality. Already in the first edition (1911) of my "Harmonielehre" I stated: that atonality is a wrong expression, which never could be used in musical belongings. Atonal is a table, a ship, a pair of sissers etc, but their extra [?] is always a relationship between tones, at least from one to the other. But atonality would indicate the perfect absence of any tonal relation between, and it is obvious that this is impossible. Therefore: a table is atonal, but tones possess always tonal relation. Therefore I said in my Harmonielehre, it might perhaps be a kind of tonality, not known, not discovered, not described [?] up to the present.   I believe, this point of view eliminates some of the problems. And it does so especially in connection with your very brillant statement, that the reappearance of the notes of the theme in every variation is constituting a tangible substitution for tonality. Of course, themes of the "basic set" and its transformation is founded on the intention to substitute the formal and unifying effect of the key. And as this is the foremost principle of this method you will understand, that I am glad to find your explanation perfectly conformable with my own theories. On the other hand I do not believe that the simple use of one or more tonal chords can be called tonality, because it can never have its result. The effect of tonality is based on the more or less complicated use of the relations of the different degrees (roots) to the tonal center, to the basic root. [I think my "Suite" gives an example of extended tonality, similar to that of my former works (Kammersymphonie etc)].

Now I arrive to the point, where you blame the "unconventional length of the four sections" of the theme of the "Variations." [At this point Schoenberg had entered the word Counterpoint in the left-hand margin]. Now I have at first to state, that this irregularity of the length of formal parts is one of the characteristics of all my writing. I would almost suppose that the capacity to write this way be an inborn one, if I did not know, that I owe it at least partly to my education, to the influence of these two masters: Mozart and Brahms who were my foremost models during the greatest part of my existence as a musician. By the way, Brahms not only showed himself structures of an irregularity like that, but he even asked younger composer to study these forms and referred to

Mozart and Haydn. I myself gave once in Germany a lecture about Brahms in which I mentioned many very characteristical examples of that kind, among them the one of Mozart, which no pupil of mine during thirty years could escape:

Menuett from the Str. Quartett in B-flat [K. 458][6]

Certainly I myself have develop[ed] this kind of phrasing which by Mozart I called: "barock" until a degree, which corresponds to a concept of "rhythmical prose" or even right-away "prose." And you will perhaps agree, that besides the quasi "quasi verified" style of music, which approaches to dance forms, their could be written a musical prose. And I am certainly not the first who writes it and not the only one. Because the form of "introduction" is if not direct "prose" so at least very related to it.

Now, although this letter is already unduly extended, one more, but fortunately, a simple question, and a short answer. Although the aspect of my s[c]ores seems to be alike counterpoint, and although the use of vertical and horizontal inversions origins from the counterpuntal methods, I do not believe that my style has to be called a counterpuntal-one. Firstly I find already in the counterpuntal style inversions have for themselves no counterpointal meaning but only one of motivical utilization. Therefore, (2ndly) you find it also used in homophonical compositions. 3rdly it is here too only the manner in which the "basic set" is turned to avoid monotony and to produce under the oppositions of the unifying intervall relations different themes. But besides these negative facts I have the positive feeling, that there can be stated a new style of structure, vertically and horizontally. I am at present not able to describe this style in a scientific manner and not even could give it [a] name. Perhaps I shall know it in a few years, but the fact seems to me to be doubtless. Certainly there are places where I write real counterpuntal combinations. But a new style does not mean, that no connection is to be found with former styles. By that reason we find in Mozart and Haydn and Beethoven very often parts of a counterpuntal retrospective aspect. By this circumstance we can better realize the manner of the development of the styles.

Now, finally, I want only to express the feeling, that it might be very useful if critics and composers would converse and discuss as often as possible such matters. I should have done it very often if it were not so seldom that critics understand as much of these questions, as you do, but utter their judgement in such a respectful manner, as you do too. And now I am very anxious to learn your reaction to my opinions and I will very much appreciate your answer.

With heartiest greetings
I am yours truly

New York Times
October 13, 1935[7]
NEW SUITE BY ARNOLD SCHOENBERG

Composition in Old Style for String Orchestra to
Be Played by Philharmonic-Symphony--The Atonalist's Progress

By Olin Downes

Only one thing more fantastical than the thought of Arnold Schönberg in Hollywood is possible, and that thing has happened. Since arriving[8] there about a year ago Schönberg has composed in a melodic manner and in recognizable keys. That is what Hollywood has done to Schönberg. We may now expect atonal fugues by Shirley Temple.

The work in question is Schönberg's Suite for String Orchestra, which Mr. Klemperer will give [its] first New York per-

formances at the Philharmonic-Symphony concerts of this week
[Thursday and Friday, October 17th and 18th, 1935]. He introduced this suite to the public last spring at a concert given by
the Los Angeles Philharmonic Orchestra. It has five movements,
and is written in classic forms, overture, adagio, gavotte, minuet and
gigue.

Outwardly the suite is in some degree the return of an
ultra-modernist to the past. Are we then to assume that Schönberg
has abandoned atonality and the Schrecklichkeit [horrors] of the
twelve-tone scale? Hardly! The suite bears probably the same
relation to other scores of Schönberg's mature period that Ernest
Bloch's "Concerto Grosso" bears to his orchestral tone poems. In
the "Concerto Grosso" Bloch makes momentary excursion into
classic forms, proving that when he chooses to do so he can write
masterfully in this vein. There is little doubt that Schönberg
composed his suite with similar purpose.

Schönberg or no Schönberg, what is the future of atonality?

Atonality is a much abused and misunderstood term. The
etymological implications of the word are clear. Atonality means
the negation of tonality. It denies any harmonic relationships
between tones or keys, and it dismisses the key system of the past.
The scale systems perfected in the late centuries by the Western
World are so designed that their intervals, when they move, tend to
gravitate toward certain sonorous centres. Atonality denies these
centers of tonal gravity. Each one of the twelve tones of the
chromatic scale may be arbitrarily grouped and move in any
direction, undeterred by such things as the "fifth," "third" or other
relations hitherto accepted as fundamental.

"By this means, the predominance of the dominant-tonic of
the older system is extinguished and now laws have to be discovered
empirically." We quote the "Dictionary of Modern Music and Musicians." But the word "atonality," in the definition of the more staid
and longer established dictionary founded by Sir George Grove, "is
not of much use for purposes of exact description, because it logi-
cally includes modal, neo-modal and all kinds of arbitrary melodic
or harmonic dialects, even to the degree of complete chromatization." This is the "degree of complete chromatization" proposed
by Schoenberg in his late scores and identified by the term, "twelve-
tone scale," of which the composer once spoke as "composition on
a basis of twelve tones related only mutually." The composer can

proceed as one of our most enterprising atonalists did when Mr. Toscanini performed his symphony. At the last rehearsal, it is said, the master of the baton hesitated, and finally begged the composer for just one chord, just one common, ordinary, garden variety of triad with which to end the piece. Finally, according to the tale, the composer assented. Whatever happened in the rehearsal room, one thing is known: the symphony did end, after long and labyrinthin [?] atonal developments, with a major chord which had the most shocking effect. Every one was unnerved.

Pure atonality is much rarer than is generally realized. The story about the four authors, of as many different nationalities, who were engaged each to write on the same subject, comes here to mind. The ordained subject was the elephant. The German wrote "Introduction in twelve volumes to a study of the elephant"; the Frenchman two volumes, entitled "L'Elephant et l'amour." "Elephants I have shot," wrote the Englishman. It was left to the Russian with the vexed and tormented Dostoievskian soul to advance the most devastating question: "The elephant: does he exist?"

We ask about atonality what the Russian asked about the elephant. Does it exist? Can it exist and constitute music?

People use the word atonality when they mean other things. It is confounded, for example, with polytonality and polyharmony, which are basically different practices. These are in fact logical modern extensions of old principles of counterpoint. Strife as well as concord between the voice parts of composition is the life of counterpoint. Contrapuntal "note against note" becomes chord against chord, even key against key. But it is obvious that this conflict within a harmonic unity is only effective because of the presence of tonal boundaries. Dispense entirely with the boundaries and you have no unit. The dimensions of music are not merely linear, they are sonorous. You cannot provide them by writing intricate lines of notes on a piece of paper. That is geometry, not music.

The apostle of pure atonalism has actually abandoned the basic principles of his professed art. As long as you maintain in composition tonal centers you may be bold as you please, and may pile discord upon discord. If you have creative power and the true instinct of music, the next generation, if not this one, will accept your sounds. Everybody knows that sonorities unacceptable to one generation may be taken as a matter of course by the next. The language of music changes very rapidly. And still there must be a limit of freedom, which is always conditional upon the existence of order. That limit, in music is surely reached when relations consequent upon <u>tonality</u> are <u>abolished</u>.

The manner in which the ideas of Schönberg have evolved as he considered these problems is very interesting. The successive steps of the prophet of atonalism would take too long to chronicle here, but a representative score of his late period is indication of the light in which the question of tonality has appeared to him. The score referred to is the set of orchestral variations, Op. 31, which created a riot at the Berlin premiere in 1928, and were performed in this city in October 1929 by Stokowski and the Philadelphia Orchestra.

These variations are built upon a completely chromatic theme, which, dodging every implication of atonality, may be accepted as a typical Schönbergian thesis. The theme is in four sections, unconventional in length. <u>Sections one and three are five measures long, sections two and four, seven.</u> The fact that Schönberg here discarded <u>one convention of phrase length only to fall into another, less natural and of his own making, need not here detain us. The first five measures</u> contain every note of the twelve-tone scale. The theme is in the form of a palindrome. That is to say, the third section of five measures is the first section read backward--"cancrizans"--and the fourth section of seven measures is the second section, in similar reverse order. From this whole <u>arbitrary</u> arrangement of tones various equally <u>arbitrary</u> "groups" or "series" of figures are made and treated in various inversions and reverses, and inversions of the reverses, and all the rest of the Schönberg trickery, with the result of a veritable <u>Chinese puzzle of contrapuntal calculation</u>. It is a perfectly amazing invention, one that might, from the <u>standpoint of sheer geometrics</u>, reward years of examination. It ends with a nightmare of a fugue, and in that fugue, sometimes as a figure, sometimes as a harmony, the tones B-A-C-H.

But now as to the atonality of it. Ostensibly this music is perfectly keyless. The theme annihilates key, or seems to. The variations are the adventure of an atonalist afloat in a heaven of his own creation, where the earth-bound tonalities of mortal man are not. There, you would say, the Schönbergian spirit might wander

free and triumphant. But it is not quite so. Something echoes from
below, as the basic C mutters against B harmonies at the end of
Strauss's "Zarathustra." It is the notes of the theme itself which
encumber [hindern], or better, serve to anchor the flight of our
iconoclast [Bilderstürmer]. The position of this theme can be called
a dead give-away. In the midst of atonality, in every variation, the
theme, inverted or otherwise, is kept rigidly upon the same notes of
the scale. It appears, of course, in different octaves, but always on
the same notes, constituting at least a tangible substitution for
tonality.

Hence the theme, a figment [fühlbare Erdichtung] of the
twelve-tone, tonic-less scale, provides a tonal centre for the counterpoint as inescapable as the thematic centre of the Bach C minor
passacaglia. That the experiment works as well as Bach's is not
claimed. What is obvious is the admission of the need of something
to give the music a harmonic point of departure [Ausgangspunkt],
and the flat confession of the impossibility of musical procedure
without a centre.

Schönberg can of course say that these variations represent
only one of his experiments, though they are directly in line with
the procedure of his twelve-tone opera, "Von Heute auf Morgen,"
his third string quartet, Op. 30, and other works of that "period."
He might with complete sincerity say that he never meant to dispense with the conception of tonality, but only to practice it in new
and emancipated ways of his own.

The probabilities are that atonality will prove to exist as a
musical value only when it is not atonality in the strict sense of the
word, but an extension and intensification of long-accepted
principles of tonality as well as counterpoint. What the atonalist
has done is to extend our musical horizon and sharpen the tools of
the composer. Up to that point he is an indispensable element of
musical progress. Beyond it his product is likely to wither and
decay through lack of real meaning. It now appears that having
essayed to upset an old rule he has developed devices which merely
conduce to its wider application--that he has fortified the very thing
he was attacking, giving it added richness and power.

New York Times[9]
October 18, 1935

SCHOENBERG SUITE IN PREMIERE HERE
Played by the Philharmonic Symphony Orchestra at Carnegie Hall

TWO MOVEMENTS PLEASE

On the Program With Wagner's 'Lohengrin' Prelude and
Tschaikovsky Symphony

By Olin Downes

If ever arid intellectualism and emptiness were put on the
spot and exposed for the useless things that they are, this occurred
at the Philharmonic-Symphony concert directed by Otto Klemperer
last night in Carnegie Hall when Arnold Schoenberg's new "Suite
for String Orchestra" was given its first New York performance.
The music, which professes to be in the classic vein, and which is a
return by Schoenberg from the method of atonality to the intervals
and harmonic relations of the established scales, was mercilessly
exposed in its paucity. For it was preceded by the miracle of
Wagner's "Lohengrin" Prelude and followed by the sensuous song
and the throbbing humanity of Tschaikovsky's Fifth Symphony. In
this environment the Schoenberg music was mercilessly revealed, a
pale monument to lifeless theory.

One had expected more of this music. The suite was
evidently intended by Schoenberg as an excursion into classic
territory, in the simpler and more melodic vein. Possibly because
of the color and the cerulean transparency of the Wagner music
which had preceded, the opening measures had a particularly
depressing effect upon the ear. They are thickly and muddily
written. The thematic material, plausibly diatonic, is commonplace. There is affectation of the old sturdy manner, and thereafter
mordant counterpoint. But it is an empty and unbeautiful exhibi-
tion. A fatigued person might thus make a show of gymnastics.
One! Two! Three! Four! Up go the arms and down the legs. It
is hollow; it is "ersatz." Ersatz music, music on and of paper!

Two movements more agreeable than the others, and therefore a pleasant surprise to the audience, were the Gavotte and Gigue. The Gavotte is lively and plausibly fashioned, with a pseudo Viennese flavor and a drone bass accompaniment in the middle part. The Gigue starts out with a four-note figure and makes use of a sort of hunting motive in 12-8 time, as many old gigues did. And it doesn't cost a cent more, either. The net effect of this music would have been self-condemnatory, even if it had not come between the fertile and creative expressions of Wagner and Tschaikovsky.

If they served to emphasize the artificiality of Schoenberg, Schoenberg served to heighten the effect of their beauty, potency and feeling. We hear the Lohengrin Prelude so often that we forget is is one of the miracles of all music. None but Wagner could have done it, and Wagner only did it once. Among his sublime pages it remains entirely unique, spun out of the invisible stuff of the spirit, and of a special radiance that is without compare in orchestral literature. The listener is spellbound by interweaving themes which follow a special law of organic development, while a nimbus of orchestral sonorities envelop the theme as a luminous mist might envelop and protect from impious eyes the Grail. Here is one of the incredible demonstrations of Wagner's power of transmuting a poetical image into tone. And they say music has no association with ideas outside itself! What of this image of descent and return of the Grail to the skies?

The performance of Schoenberg's suite was very painstaking and comprehending. Undoubtedly it said everything that was to be said for the composition. For Wagner's Prelude a more glamorous edgeless tone, and subtler blending of choirs, would have served, though the interpretation was devout and dramatic. The performance of Tschaikovsky's symphony, of course, exited the audience. But Tschaikovsky deserved better from Mr. Klemperer, who more than once was unduly hasty, noisy, frenetic, tearing passion to tatters. For this is more than sound and fury, or mere Russian hysteria. The finale alone, the one majestic and victorious gesture to be discovered in Tschaikovsky's symphonic music, has a grandeur and a wild triumph at moments suggestive of Beethoven. Now and again there was a fine plasticity, poetry and irresistible emotional sweep, required by the music. Then Mr. Klemperer, victim of his own dramatic temperament, would fly off the track, with disaster to the proportions of the symphony.

New York Herald Tribune[10]
October 18. 1935

New Music By Arnold Schoenberg
Given Last Night at the Philharmonic Concert

By Lawrence Gilman

3.123th concert of the Philharmonic Symphony Society
of New York, Otto Klemperer conductor, at Carnegie Hall.

PROGRAM

1. Wagner   Prelude to "Lohengrin"

2. Schönberg   Suite for String Orchestra

     I. Largo-Allegro
     II. Adagio
     III. Minuet
     IV. Gavotte
     V. Gigue

(First time in New York)

INTERMISSION

3. Tchaikovsky   Symphony No. 5 in E minor, op. 64
(Reprinted from yesterday's late editions)

The hero of Thursday night's Philharmonic-Symphony concert was no less a personage than the eminent Arnold Schönberg, once of Vienna and Berlin, now of Hollywood, U.S.A. Herr Schönberg has for years, as we all know, held an undisputed pre-eminence as the most menacing of the ultra-modernist composers. Godfearing conservative musicians have pictured him shudderingly to themselves as a maniacal wrecker of the tonal hearth and home, dragging the lyric Muse by her sacred braids to some destination of unimaginable horror.

But that was in the old, so far-off days, before Herr Schönberg left the Fatherland and came to Boston, New York, Hollywood, and other debilitating centers. Something has happened to
Herr Schönberg. What it was remains a mystery, at least to this
deponent. But the results are plain, and the interference is
unescapable. Some Hollywood Delilah must have shorn his locks;
for this Samson of the twelve-tone scale, this once horrific atonalist
who had made even the mighty Richard Strauss sound like Ethel-
bert Nevin--this insuperable champion of the New Era has become
a harmless composer of salon music, the Nevin of today, apt at
pretty tunes and harmless harmonies, edged nostalgically with a
little red pepper and a dash of dissonant Tabasco.

The facts appear to be that Herr Schönberg, for some reason that is not quite clear, composed last winter at Hollywood what
he referred to as "a school suite," a suite for strings in five movements, using certain of the old dance forms dear to the classic
masters--a Minuet, Gavotte, Gigue, etc. Mr. Klemperer played the
Suite last May at a concert of the Los Angeles Philharmonic Orchestra in the composer's presence, and Thursday night he disclosed
it to New York.

We had been told that Schönberg had reformed, had taken
the diatonic pledge, sworn off Atonalism and the Twelve-Note
Scale, and had determined to compose in the manner sanctified by
those ancients who had struggled along for centuries without benefit
of Atonality. It was said that Schönberg had decided to go straight,
to write discernible, coherent tunes, even to palter with ideas.

But perhaps it wasn't so simple as Herr Schönberg thought
it was going to be. He has doffed the elaborate costume of atonality, has removed the makeup of the professional modernist; but
there seems to be hardly anything underneath--no profile, scarcely
a countenance, obviously not a brain. If there could be anything
drearier than Schönberg in his elaborate makeup as a prophet of
the tonal future, uttering solemnly vacuous nonsense, it is Schönberg stripped of his pretensions, trying to generate and organize a
pattern of musical ideas.

For there is nothing there--nothing but emptiness and ste-
rility, savored by an occasional reminiscence of "Oh Promise Me,"
and some rather pretty tunes that Mr. Gershwin would have
chucked impatiently into Porgy's ashcan.

Mr. Klemperer played the Suite Thursday night as if he believed in it. All things are possible.

VI.S-D.o.2

Arnold Schoenberg
116 North Rockingham Avenue
Brentwood Park
Los Angeles, Calif.
Telephone: W.L.A. 35077

Mr. Olin Downes
The New York Times
New York   November 8, 1938

Dear Mr. Downes:
        It is now the second time that I see you call my "Varia-
tions for Orchestra" in a variation of the title I gave it: "Variations
upon the theme of B-A-C-H."
        I am sure this change has been applied by you on the basis
of a very profound study of my score (which flatters me very much),
a study as profound as to discover a secret of which even not the
author himself was conscious.
        I thank you very much for this great achievemnet. But the
discrepancy between my own title (which is based on the seemingly
wrong idea that the 32 measures [see p. 216 and the letter below]
which I call "THEME" are a theme of my own) and your homemade
title seems dangerous to either me or you. Sometimes there might
come a knowing person and realize the difference.   Accordingly I
would suggest, you ask the publisher to change the title in harmony
with you[r] research so that the future historian does not need to
study the score himself to find out who was wrong.
        Yours very truly

Here follows the following handwritten note in German:
        Ich habe diesen Brief nicht abgesendet, da mir schon wäh-

rend des Schreibens seine Zwecklosigkeit klar wurde. Dagegen habe ich den auf der Rückseite kopierten geschrieben [next letter, below], der schliesslich ebenso beschämend sein sollte, wie dieser, ihm aber den kläglichen Rückzug erlaubt, den er verdient.[11]

VI.S-D.o.3

Arnold Schoenberg
116 North Rockingham Avenue
Brentwood Park
Los Angeles, Calif.
Telephone W.L.A. 35077

Mr. Olin Downes
New York Times
New York City   November 8, 1938

My dear Mr. Downes:

I see in the New York Times from October 30, 1938 that you call my "Variations for Orchestra" eroneously "Variations upon the theme B-A-C-H."[12]
This error might have been provoked by the quotation of these four tones on several places. But I consider as the theme of these variations the measures 34 to 57 incl[usive] on pages 7 and 8.
If I should explain why I used these quotations I had to say: I saw suddenly the possibility and did it (perhaps one will call it "Sentimental") with pleasure as "Hommage à Bach:" Perhaps an excuse for such a procedure might be found in Beethovens "Diabelli-Variations," when he quotes from Don Juan "Keine Ruh bei Tag und Nacht," or by Mozarts quatation of a contemporary opera-melody in Don Juan (later replaced by a quatation from Figaro). Of course my quotation is not as humorous as both these before-mentioned. But again I have an excuse: I believe I have woven it in rather thouroughly.
I hope this might interest you.
I am with sincere greetings
                    yours very truly Arnold Schoenberg

VI.D-S.o.1

New York Times
Times Square

Mr. Arnold Schoenberg
116 Rockmore Avenue
Brentwood Park
Los Angeles, California   November 14, 1938

Dear Mr. Schoenberg:
        I want to thank you very much for the correction of my misstatement in the Sunday article on the Variations. This was a slip of the pen, as I remember them so clearly, and I remember some years ago being called upon to analyze in some exactitude your actual theme. I shall take occasion to correct this error, which I regret having made.
        I hope that working in California is proving interesting for you, and that there is some spiritual encouragement as well as, no doubt, some undeserved penalties in your having changed your home from Europe to America. I fancy, however, that you do feel the obligation which is upon us all these days - and a most heavy and disheartening one it is - to fight against the catastrophic series of evils that are now falling upon humanity, and each of us joins as best we may in our individual efforts toward repelling these evils and endeavoring in some way to construct, as they say at the New York World's Fair, a better "World of Tomorrow."

        With best wishes, I am
                Very sincerely yours,   Olin Downes

VI.S-D.o.4

TOSCANINI

Dear Mr Downes

I would like to have this suggestion printed in [the] New York Times:

As lovers of serious music seemingly are not capable of liking symphonic programs in sum[m]ertime, would it not be a good idea to allow serving of beer frankfurters and cigarettes during Toscaninis popular concerts over NBC? Too bad only that such service can not be extended to the listeners of the broadcast.

Arnold Schoenberg

August 27, 1944

nicht abgesendet
[not sent]

TOSCANINI

Dear Mr Downes

I would like to have this suggestion printed in New York Times:

As lovers of serious music seemingly are not capable of liking symphonic programs in summertime, would it not be a good idea to allow serving of beer, frankfurters and cigarets during Toscanini's popular concerts over N BC.² Too bad

Facsimile VI.
Schoenberg to Downes Concerning
Toscanini. Draft dated August 27, 1944

only that such service
can not be extended
to the listeners of the
broddcast.

Arnold Schoenberg

August 27
1944

nicht abgesendet

Facsimile VI, continued

VI.S-D.o.5

ARNOLD SCHOENBERG
115 N. ROCKINGHAM AVENUE
LOS ANGELES, 24, CALIFORNIA

Mr. Olin Down[e]s
Music Editor
New York Times
New York, N.Y.   March 31, 1946

Dear Mr. Down[e]s:

Last Saturday I heard (unfortunately partly only) a discussion of some problems of the opera in which beside you, Mr. Deems Taylor, Mr S. Spaeth and a gentleman whose name I could not understand, participated.

In the course of this discussion one of the gentlemen made a statement which surprised me tremendiously: That Hans Richter should have had "a hand" in the orchestration of some of Richard Wagner)s scores.

I never heard a thing like that and I can not believe it at once. Every one who knows the elaborate art of Wagners organization of his scores will doubt this contention. Such features can not be imitated. They are the achievement of the one man who could invent them. Of course, one can imitate the sound and some others of the external qualities and effects. But only one who is able of inventing a style of his own could write things of this perfection-but this man does not need imitating somebody else'[s] style.

You would oblige me if you would be kind enough to tell me upon which real facts this statementwas based, which was not repudiated by one of the participants.

May I mention that Grove says that Richter copied the score of the Meistersinger and that of the Ttetralogie.

Thank you,
I am sincerely, yours

VI.D-S.o.2

The New York Times
Times Square, New York 18, N.Y.
Lackawanna 4-1000

April 15, 1946

Dear Mr. Schoenberg:
    I respect you very greatly indeed for your immediate protest against something that you believe to be a parody of the masterly art of Richard Wagner when a member of our Quiz panel suggested that somebody else had a hand in the orchestration of his scores. This Quiz, being a purely spontaneous conversation, I only recall that someone made that suggestion, but I thought that the rest of us corrected it. Such a statement, of course, is preposterous. I remember being surprised at it when it was made, but I thought, I repeat, that we set it straight.
    The Quiz is now over for the season. Next winter, if it is continued, and I have its chairmanship, I shall suggest that we carry over from week to week such important letters as yours, which either confirm or criticize our statements, so that a matter like that will not be left hanging in the air in a way to create any confusion in the public mind.

    Thanking and esteeming you for your protest, I am
    Sincerely yours,   Olin Downes

Mr. Arnold Schoenberg
116 N. Rockingham Avenue
Los Angeles 24 Cal.

VI.D-S.o.3

WESTERN UNION
ARNOLD SCHONBERG
116 NORTH RICKINGHAM   AVE WEST LOSA=

May 13, 1947

STRONGLY URGE YOU SEND STATEMENT PROTESTING

ACTION OF HOLLYWOOD BOWL AUTHORITIES IN RE-
FUSING BOWL FOR HENRY WALLACE MAY 19TH MEET-
ING ON GROUNDS THAT BOWL IS DEDICATED TO
CULTURE. CONTROVERSIAL PUBLIC FIGURES INCLUD-
ING THOMAS E. DEWEY, WENDELL WILLKIE, CHARLES
LINDBERG, CLAUDE PEPPER, HAVE IN THE PAST SPOKEN
THERE. IT IS OBVIOUS THAT CULTURE HAS NO MEAN-
ING APART FROM THE CONCEPT OF FREE SPEECH.
DENIAL OF WALLACE'S RIGHT TO USE PUBLIC FACILI-
TIES TO EXPRESS HIS POINT OF VIEW IS ONLY A STEP
FROM THE DENIAL OF MUSICIAN'S RIGHT TO BE HEARD
BECAUSE AUTHORITIES DISAPPROVE OF HIS IDEAS.
PLEASE WIRE STATEMENTS TO GEORGE PEPPER, PCA,
1515 CROSS ROADS OF THE WORLD, HOLLYWOOD,
CALIFORNIA=

OLIN DOWNES.

VI.S-D.o.6

Arnold Schoenberg
116 N. Rockingham Avenue
Los Angeles, Calif. - 24
Phone ARizona 35077

Mr. Olin Downes,
New York Times,
New York, N.Y.   May 14, 1947

Dear Mr. Downes:
        I agree completely with you in condemning the blunder of
the Hollywood Bowl Authorities to deny the Bowl to Mr. Wallace.
It seems to me to constitute a violation of the concept of free
speech.
        But you have probably read my article in Modern Music
Magazine on collaboraters [p. 240] and will understand that I am

not inclined to mix in political affairs. I am too busy, I am too tired, I am not well enough to indulge in fights to which I could not attend with the full weight of my (former) temperament.

Thank you anyway for inviting me.

With cordial greetings,
Sincerely yours,
           Arnold Schoenberg

VI.D-S.o.4

Mr. Arnold Schoenberg
116 N. Rockingham Avenue
Los Angeles 24, California.   May 21 1947

Dear Mr. Schoenberg:

I appreciate your letter of May 14th very much. I had not read your article in the Modern Music Magazine on collaborators, and I shall make haste to do so. But I can well understand why you feel that you have other things to do now than to mingle in political matters. I think in this you are perfectly right, and I wish you every happiness that the artist has when he is doing his own creative work. That for him is the all-important thing, regardless of the world he lives in. If this creative activity and his political convictions and his physical energy go hand in hand, it is well and good, and even highly desirable. But certainly, and particularly at this stage of your very significant career, the thing for you is continued creation, regardless of politics, or even, shall we say - critics!

With warm regards, I am,
sincerely yours,
Olin Downes

On Artists And Collaboration[13]
A Symposium

A DANGEROUS GAME---Arnold Schönberg

There are a great many categories of collaborators in Germany and in the conquered countries. One must distinguish between the many who have been forced and those who have voluntarily collaborated. There are, besides, others who simply "missed the bus," who would have preferred to emigrate rather than to bow to dictates, if it had not become too late for them. And there are those whose stupid egotism led them to believe that evil could happen only to others while they themselves would be spared. Some did only what they were ordered to do, others functioned as agitators, prosecuting those who did not conform to the prescribed style, and based on their conduct on the theoretical party line.

With the thought in mind that the captain in *Carmen* is not intended to represent a coward but simply a man who yields to the argument of the guns which confront him, only those should be authorized to blame the forced collaborator who have themselves proved fearless before the menace of the concentration camp and of torture. People like that of course also exist.

Curiously, few realize that politics, a nice topic to talk about, is a rather dangerous game into which one should enter only if he is aware that his life and that of his opponent are at stake and if he is willing to pay for his conviction - even that price.

Artists generally deal with this problem as thoughtlessly as if it were merely a controversy on artistic matters; just as if they were discussing merely "art for art's sake" as contrasted with "objectivity in art." Even in such arguments a participant's life may be at stake. I wonder whether Richard Wagner knew that he would be living in exile for so many years as an outlaw when, because of artistic corruption, he participated in setting the Dresden Hoftheater on fire.

On the other hand, very few of those who emigrated can ask to be honored for their political or artistic straightforwardness. Most of them had no other chance of being spared, either because of their race, or that of their matrimonial partner. Many had been politically implicated and others came under the ban of "Kultur-Bolschewismus." There are probably not many who emigrated voluntarily; and even among such "real" emigrés there are some who tried hard to come to an agreement with the powers only to give up in the end.

Yet despite the fact that little personal merit attaches to the inability of many to swim with the official current (*Gleichschaltung*), there is this to be said for them; they all had to abandon their homes, their positions, their countries, their friends, their business, their fortune. They all had to go abroad, try to start life anew, and generally at a much lower level of living, of influence, of esteem; many even to change their occupation and to suffer humiliation.

There may be not merit in all that; still if those who had to do it could do it - why should not others also have preferred to preserve their honesty, their integrity, their character, by taking upon themselves of their own free will the suffering of an emigré, like those who had no other way?

That would have been of some merit!

I am inclined to say:

Those who here acted like politicians are politicians and should be treated in the same manner in which politicians are treated.

Those who did not so act should escape punishment.

But considering the low mental and moral standard of artists in general, I would say:

Treat them like immature children.

Call them fools and let them escape.

VI.S-D.o.7   [written before December 12, 1948]

TO MR. OLIN DOWNES, MUSIC EDITOR OF NEW YORK TIMES NEW YORK[14]

Dear Mr. Downes:

You end your review[15] on Mitropolous' performance of

Gustav Mahler's Seventh Symphony with the words: "Chacun à son goût".

This seems to me a great mistake, because if once, for instance, all of you "chacun's" who are so proud of your personal "goût" would vote for or against a work, one could perhaps make an advance poll, predicting the result of this voting. This true opinion of the majority might decide the destiny of the work of a master, right or wrong; it would include, at least, instead of the "goût" of only one single "chacun", various opinions; and everybody would understand that in the average which it presents there are included positives and negatives, pros and cons of various grades.

Unfortunately you are so few in whose hands the destiny of a work is laid and your authority has been bestowed upon you by people who are too modest to do this job themselves. They deem that you understand much more from music than they. But they do not expect that you are so much at variance with other, and even important, musicians, who possess greater authority, based upon their personal achievements, upon studies and upon being recognized by a multitude of even greater authorities.

If I who would not dare always to depend upon my personal gusto, if I would look around for support of my judgement, I would in first line think of Richard Strauss, who spoke once to me about Mahler with great appreciation and with a respect derived from his own self-respect. "Only one who deserves respect himself is capable of respecting another man," I have once written. But nothing can surpass the enthusiasm of Anton von Webern, Alban Berg, Franz Schmidt, and many other Viennese composers about Mahler's Symphonies. And why do you forget Mitropolous' enthusiasm?

One who is able to study a score needs not depend upon his personal taste. He would see all these strokes of genius which never are to be found in lesser masters. He would discover them on every page of this work, in every measure, in every succession of tones and harmonies.

But all of you have the habit of criticizing a work only when it is performed, and then after one single hearing you pronounce your sentence of life and death, regardless of all experience your trade has gone through when history turned to the absolute contrary of your judgement.

I assume you have, two or more decades ago, written in an unfriendly manner about Mahler and now you are afraid to deviate from your primary judgement. Why? You are not so old that you should not dare changing your mind. I am at least ten to twenty years older than you. I can assure you that I am still ready to change my opinions, to learn something new, to accept the contrary and to digest it, the contrary of all I have believed in my whole life-- if it is capable of convincing me. If it is truly great it is capable.

No courageous man would hesitate to do this.

I ascribe your favorable review of my Five Orchestra Pieces to the same resistance against a revision of your former attitude toward a composition. I assume, similarly to the case of Mahler, that you have two or more decades ago already written about these pieces, but in a favorable manner--as it was the tendency among young men at that time. Tell me: why should an honorable man be afraid of changing his mind at the time of greater maturity? Must he remain forever the slave of his time of immaturity?

I am afraid many people, who read both these reviews a-bout Mahler and me, will say: One who writes as unfoundedly about Mahler will certainly also be wrong about Schoenberg. Accordingly, I must either be ashamed to please you, or it will cease to be favorable to me.

As I have said before: if you would study the orchestra score you could not overlook the beauty of this writing. Such beauty is only given to men who deserve it because of all their other merits. You should not call me a mystic--though I am proud to be one--because this statement is based on experience. I have seen so many scores, and I could tell at one glance how good the composition is.

Even the piano score of Mahler's Symphony would have revealed much of its beauty.

In the piano concerto of a French composer you were able to discover a charming popular French folksong. Why would you not discover such qualities in Mahler's Symphonies? You seem to consider the use of a popular melody as an asset. I say it is a liability. It is a sign that he was not able to contribute one of his own; therefore he must borrow other peoples' property.

If you only had noticed a few of these wonderful melodies. I do not know whether your enthusiasm would h[a]ve reached up to Webern's (my dear old friend), who could play and sing it many times and would never stop admiring it:

First this accompanying figure of the Clarinet

Then after the Horn, the Oboe

Then this continuation:

Or this melody in the last movement:

    In these melodiestthe creative power cannot be ignored.
A master of this degree needs not borrow from other people--he
splendidly spends from his own riches.
    I am cordially yours truly Arnold Schoenberg[16]

Arnold Schoenberg
116 N. Rockingham Avenue
Los Angeles 24, Calif.
Phone - ARizona 3-5077

VI.D-S.o.5

205 West 57th Street
New York 19, N.Y.

Mr Arnold Schoenberg,
116 N. Rockingham Avenue
Los Angeles 24, California.   December 3, 1948

Dear Mr. Schoenberg:
        I have read with interest and appreciation your letter con-
cerning my review of Mitropoulos' recent performance of Mahler's
Seventh Symphony. You say some interesting things which it is a
pleasure to read. I must add, however, in frankness, that some of
your remarks appear to me to be illogical.
        I entirely disagree with you that your sentiment about "Cha-
con à son goût" is "a great mistake." It simply means that in reviewing a work I express my convinced opinion, but that everyone
else who listens is entirely <u>entitled to his</u> [and cannot write about
it]¹⁷ own opinions and his own tastes in the matter. It also means
that while I am frank to say as I did say and as I completely believe
that this symphony of Mahler's is detestably bad music, that others
who think as you do, for example, have an equal right to their
conclusions. I think this is the very essence of <u>fair critical</u> [responsi-
bility] practice. I do not consider myself a high priest of art, I do
not pretend that my values of any music are conclusive. I do not
even claim that I can tell at a single glance at a score whether the
music is good or bad, whether it will perish quickly or last onward
into infinity.
        I must ask you a question. Do you really mean seriously to
claim to me that composers, even the greatest composers, are as a
rule fair or unbiased critics of other composers' works? Frankly,
I can hardly credit you with such an unhistoric statement. Do
you think, for example, that a composer who states that Beethoven's
Seventh Symphony makes him ripe for the madhouse, is in the least
intelligent or fair in this, his written judgement? The name of the
"critic" was Carl Maria von Weber. Do you take seriously what
Schumann wrote about Wagner's Tannheuser, or what Berlioz said
on the same subject, or what Debussy said of Beethoven, that he
was a bore? These instances could be multiplied indefinitely. I am
afraid that the greatest names in the history of musical composition

do not connote either balance or perspective of musical judgement. For a final illustration of this obvious fact, let me quote you what an editorial board of five of the greatest composers in Russia said when they were asked by Koussevitzky, as a publisher, whether he should publish Stravinsky's "Petroushka." The score was unanimously rejected by these high and mighty gentlemen as being "not music"!

And then, Mr. Schoenberg, you really hurt my feelings. Apparently you think that I do not read scores. I hope you don't infer also that I am incapable of this. I can even tell you that the score of Mahler's Seventh Symphony has been in my library for years, while as for piano arrangements of his music, I have gone through half of his Fifth Symphony on two pianos and gotten up from the instrument being really unable to stomach any farther such vulgar music. I don't even find the thematic examples that you quote from the Mahler Symphony, either particularly distinguished as melodies, or even as representing the best thematic elements of that unfortunate work.

Now as to inconsistencies. My dear master, I assure you that so far as I am concerned you are intensely wrong. Why do you assume that I have written "in an unfriendly manner about Mahler and am now afraid to depart from a primary judgement". Why? In the first place you are uninformed on the subject. I have found things to praise and to enjoy, for example, in Mahler's "Lied von der Erde," which I formerly liked a good deal more than I do now, because its self-pity and sentimentalism is rather unpleasant to me. I enjoy pages of his first Symphony. I have gone "completely overboard" upon the first half of his Eighth, etc., etc. You seem to think that because I wrote well of of your Five Pieces this season that I have done so because I wrote well of them years ago. I can tell you frankly that I do not try to remember what I have writen in the past about music that I listen to in the present. But I think I do remember that I cursed your "Five Pieces" to high heaven and expected that I would dislike them the other night.[18] To my surprise, I found that I liked them and realized on hearing them this time how much effect their principles had upon modern music.

I am afraid I must unhappily come to the conclusion that I think very badly of the Mahler Symphony and that you think very well of it and that this is merely another case of critics, and their readers, disagreeing; as, thank God, they will always disagree, and in the expression of their convictions greatly contribute to the development of an art.

> With best wishes, I am
> Sincerely yours, Olin Downes

VI.S-D.o.8

Arnold Schoenberg
116 North Rockingham Ave.
Los Angeles 24, California   December 10. 1948

Mr. Olin Downes
205 West, 57th Street
New York, N.Y.

Dear Mr. Downes:
        I assume Mr. Mitropolous has received a letter directed to me, so as I received the enclosed letter to him.
        I return this and would like to [e]receive the right one. Maybe there is an opportunity for more argument, for more fights.

> I am, most sincerely
> yours

VI.Mi-S.o.1

Dimitri Mitropoulos

December 9, 1948
Dear Master:
        Probably you received a letter addressed to me, because I received one addressed to you, and thinking you might be interested in what our mutual friend and critic answered to your letter, I send it on to you.

By the way, I am planning next season, 49-50, to revive your Variations Opus 31 with the Philharmonic.

I wish you always good health,
Devotedly, D. Mitropoulos[19]

VI.D-S.o.6

WESTERN UNION
DECEMBER 13, 1948

ARNOLD SCHOENBERG
116 ROCKINGHAM AVE LOSA

SORRY I DISDIRECTED LETTER[20] OF WHICH SHALL FORWARD A COPY MY MISTAKE THE MORE REGRETTED SINCE YOUR LETTER AND MY REPLY SEEMED TO ME INTERESTING FOR PUBLICATION ESPECIALLY AS YOU ADDRESSED ME FORMALLY AS MUSIC EDITOR OF THE TIMES. NEED HARDLY SAY I SHALL WELCOME CONTINUANCE OF "MORE ARGUMENT MORE FIGHTS" WITH SUCH A SINCERE AND DISTINGUISHED ARTIST IF YOU SO DESIRE

BEST REGARDS OLIN DOWNES

VI.S-D.o.9

Arnold Schoenberg
116 N. Rockingham Avenue
Los Angeles, 24, California

Mr. Olin Downes, Music Editor
New York Times
New York, N.Y.   December 21, 1948

Dear Mr. Downes:

Before responding to some of the points of your very interesting letter, I must mention that I did not expect that in its imperfect form of a private letter it would be published. I was in a fighting mood, caused by your criticism of Mahler. I felt this can be a fight for death and life, in which case one is not obliged to worry about the fairness and correctness of the blows one deals out. If they only hurt.

Nevertheless I should not have pretended that you do not study scores and that you are prejudiced by your own previous judgements. This, however, can not have hurt you as much, as I am hurt by your reproach of illogicality - there is nothing worse to me than that. Fortunately you can not prove Mahler's vulgarity and neither can I prove my attack on your musicianship. It seems to me that the scale goes down on your side and that a true equilibrium requires some additional weight in favor of my logic.

In your letter to Mr. Mitropoulos *) you say that music is to you like a religion and you reserve for yourself the right to be intolerant against a believer of a different faith. I would call this the claim of a fighter. But I will rather tell you a story:

Several years ago an announcer over a nationwide network broadcast attacks on my music to a crowd of two and a half million listeners. I thought this man is an . . . . Oh perhaps it is better even now not to tell you what I thought But at this time I was belligerantly desiring to tell all the audience what I was thinking.

You write? "Chacun a' son goût," and you are fortunate enough to tell hundred thousands of your readers, which is your taste. But how can I inform those two and a half million radio listeners that their announcer is . . . wrong. One who possesses such an unlimited power must have a sense of responsibility.

You claim the right of a fighter, the right to be intolerant. Is it logical to deny the opponent the same rights if he is infuriated to a degree which makes him refusing to see the forest as long as he has to conquer individual trees.

It is the word "taste" which excites me.

*) Only at the very end of this letter I discovered that it had been delivered to me by mistake only.

In my vocabulary it stands for "arrogance and superiority complex of the mediocrity"

And:

Taste is sterile - it can not produce.

And:

Taste is applicable only to the lower zones of human feelings, to the material-ones. It is no yardstick in spiritual matters.

And:

Taste functions mainly as a restricting factor, as a negation to every problem, as a minus to every number.

"Chacun a son gout" wants to make believe that there exists an enormous number of ways to be extremely personal - but there is not enough caviar, or gold or good luck in the world for everybody. And those "chacuns" must share the little "gout" which exists, which of course is a commonplace mass product, with very few marks of personal distinction.

You write that your preference to your taste means simply that you express your personal opinion and that everybody is entiteld to his own. "Entiteld" is the right word. Has he who disagrees with you a chance of telling this to the same audience as often as he disagrees?

Furthermore: you do notpretend "that your ideas of music are conclusive." Contrast this lightharted standpoint to the standpoint of an artist like Mahler, who would have preferred to die a thousand times, than to being forced to believe he was wrong.

I hope you will understand why your condemnation of a great man and composer on the basis of personal taste enraged me. Then I will gladly admit that another cause to this fury derived from the fact that between 1898 and 1908 I had spoken about Mahler in the same manner, as you do today. For that I made good subsequently by adoration.

And frankly, this is what I resent most: Why should you not also have expirienced such transformations in your mind, from Saulus to Paulus with many of the greats in the arts, including besides Brahms and Wagner, Strauss and Mahler, even Mozart and Beethoven?

Still, I am not a windbag of an unsolid fixation, who gamingly changes his position for no intelligible reason. All these changes corresponded to my progressive development in various phases of my life, before maturity was reached. A very characteristic expirience of mine may serve as an illustration: Between 1925 and 1935 I did not dare to read or listened to Mahler's music. I was afraid my aversion against it in a preceding period might return. Fortunately, when I heard in Los Angeles a moderately satisfactory performance of the Second, I was just enchanted as ever before: It had not lost of its persuasiveness.

Now finally to your question whether I believe composers are as a rule fair or unbiased critics of other composers: I think they are in first line fighters for their own musical ideas. The ideas of other composers are their enemies. You can not restrict a fighter. His blows are correct when they hit hard, and only then is he fair. Thus I do not resent what Schumann said about Wagner, or Hugo Wolf about Brahms. But I resent what Hanslick said against Wagner and Bruckner. Wagner, Wolf, Mahler and Strauss fought for life and death of there I ideas.

But you fight only for principles, or rather the application of principles.

At the end I can tell you that I agree with the last of your points: " . . . . that this is merely another case of critics and their readers, disagreeing as, thank God, they will always disagree, and in the expression of their convictions greatly contribute to the development of an art". - negatively or positively.

> With best wishes, also for Christmas and New Year,
> I am most sincerely yours
> Arnold Schoenberg

VI.D-S.o.7

> 205 West 57th Street
> New York 10, N.Y.

December 31, 1948

Dear Mr. Schoenberg:

Replying to your kind letter of December 21st, I must explain to you in the first place that I took your first letter to me to be intended for publication because it was addressed at the top of the page in strong capital letters "To Mr. Olin Downes, music editor of the New York Times", and because also there was nothing of a purely personal nature in it and there was no suggestion in the letter itself that it was intended only as a personal communication. The envelope, as I now recall, was marked "Confidential", but it is customary in mail addressed to me at the music department at The Times for that mail to be opened and turned over to whichever member of the department is concerned with its subject without submitting the matter to me at all. Such a stamp on the envelope as "personal," "confidential," or other direction of like nature is the means used by correspondents to see that the letter comes directly to my eyes. And since, moreover, various correspondents, often totally unknown to me, take such means of getting routine announcements or musical news which should go to other members of the department instead of to me, all letters are opened and the trusted secretary of the department sees that each one goes to one whom it concerns.

Therefore I deemed your letter discussing a subject upon which I had written in The Times, and one that had interested many of our correspondents, as eminently appropriate for publication.

On studying your last letter, I come to one conclusion which probably goes to the root of our different positions in its argument, and which in turn will perhaps explain to you my charges of "illogicality." I think the fundamental point has to do with this: that I consider criticism of an art an art in itself and not at all as a mere accessory of an art's creative development. It seems to me that you withhold the right to criticize from an authoritative standpoint from everybody except the leading composers. You speak of your fighting spirit, but apparently deny me mine. Perhaps I in my turn am now assuming too much in inferring this to be your position. I have to tell you that I consider the few really representative music critics that we have or have had in history, as men wholly qualified by knowledge and training, by intuition and taste for the art that they serve. In fact I think, as I pointed out in my previous letter, that the representative critic of an art is likely to be less rather than more prejudiced in his estimates than a representative composer. I do not think that Hanslick was any less of an idiot in his opposition to Wagner than I think that Weber, whom certainly we would have supposed to know better, was idiotic in his remarks about Beethoven. In fact, I am in the habit of allowing a composer much more leeway for prejudice and illiberalism toward other composers whose esthetic differs from his than I am to permit

music critics an equal degree of latitude. The critic being less subjective in his thinking is more likely to be just; the composer, wholly
subjective and of an unconditioned creative impulse, is not expected
to see eye to eye with those who differ artistically from him.

And as for your definitions of taste, I completely disagree
with them. I hold taste to be an inseparable attribute to any
manifestation of art, and perhaps my strongest objection of Mahler
is his incredible and appalling lack of taste!

> With best wishes for a Happy New Year, I am
> Sincerely yours,   Olin Downes

Mr. Arnold Schoenberg
116 N. Rockingham Avenue,
Los Angeles 24, California

New York Times[21]
November 12, 1948

Work by Poulenc Concert Feature

Composer Assists Mitropoulos and Philharmonic
in Doing Harpsichord 'Champetre'

By Olin Downes

Dimitri Mitropoulos was assisted at the concert of the
Philharmonic Symphony Orchestra last night in Carnegie Hall by
the composer-pianist Francis Poulenc in the performance of his
"Concert Champetre" for harpsichord (or piano). Mr Poulenc was
fortunate in the placing of his work (played for the first time by this
orchestra) between Mendelssohn's overture to "Ruy Blass" and
Mahler's Seventh Symphony. It was as though a picture that had
charm and sophistication were set between some awful paintings of
bad periods and ginger-bread styles. Everything on the program,
which Mr. Mitropoulos conducted with unflinching gusto, built up

to the concerto, which in turn was unfavorable for the Mahler symphony.

Under ordinary circumstances we might say that the Poulenc music was witty and ingenious but rather superficial; with, however, some delightful folk-tunes, or tunes in the folk-manner, strewn through it. But the context of the program emphasized its distinctions. And as the Mahler symphony went on and on from one dreary platitude and outworn euphemism to another, one regarded Poulenc with ever-increasing esteem. A composer who does not strut and roar and groan in moods of psychiatric conceit! A musician who sports wittily with an idea till he has used it for what it is worth, and then turns to other engaging matters, and who has precision and style, expresses what he desires to express with skill and without mannerism.

Mr. Poulenc added materially to the effect of his music by his finished performance as a virtuoso and the competence and modesty of his achievement. The audience welcomed him warmly.

There is little that this writer cares to say on the subject of Mahler's symphony. He does not like it at all. There are those who do like it. They have every right to enjoy the uncut hour and a quarter, more or less, that the symphony consumes in performance. It is to our mind bad art, bad esthetic, bad, presumptuous and blatantly vulgar music. There is no need to particularize. Nothing would be gained by it. After three-quarters of an hour of the worst and most pretentious of the Mahler symphonies we found we could not take it, and left the hall.

Chacun à son goût.

New York Times[22]
November 21, 1948

MAHLER AGAIN

Reactions of Disputatious Correspondents,
Their Views and Dissenting Opinions

By Olin Downes

CORRESPONDENTS take us to task, and correspondents praise us highly, according to the point of view, for our comment which appeared in THE TIMES on Mr. Mitropoulos' recent performance with the Philharmonic-Symphony Orchestra of Mahler's Seventh Symphony.

Let the prosecution first speak. The writer is Mr. Charles Cole of this city:

I am not in the habit of writing "letters to the editor," but my disappointment concerning your review of last Thursday's Philharmonic concert ("Ruy Blass," "Concert Champêtre" and Mahler's Seventh) is the basis for this note.

In the past I have generally agreed with your reviews. When I did not, I at least found them interesting and honest. To my mind the music critic fills the function of relating to the readers how the musicians in question interpreted and played the music. There is no need to discuss the music (if it has been heard before) except when the discussion is for the purpose of explaining the rights or wrongs of the musician's interpretations or tonal conceptions etc. In the case of new music it is correct and proper (to my sense of values) to have the critic give his readers some insight into the work as well as stating his ideas as regards the performance.

Review under Attack

Now to the review in question. Mendelssohn's "Ruy Blass" may well be dismissed for it is an overworked "warhorse." I am anxious to know, however, if the orchestra played it well or not. The Poulenc was intelligently discussed as to the first impression of the music.   Still I do not know how the orchestra played the music, even though the composer's fine playing was mentioned.

You said, "There is little this writer cares to say on the subject of Mahler's symphony," after you had used a quarter of your space berating it and one-half of the review before you finished. Had I agreed with you I, in all honesty, might not now be writing, but I do not agree with your dislike of Mahler. I still do not know why you dislike Mahler (I will assume that the work is rare enough to warrant a musical discussion) except that I now know you are able to write some fairly long and intellectually insulting words which fail to give reason for musical censure. I repeat that my question is not with your feeling towards Mahler.

From your review I gain the impression that the orchestra played badly, which I think you must admit it did not. In the past you have disliked other music--this season by Mr. Mitropoulos and the Philharmonic--and have still given us an idea of performance values. I only hope that when you left early you waited until the end of a movement and were not as rude as others at the concert. The sum total of your ideas of performance as to the entire program, was "Mr. Mitropoulos conducted with unflinching gusto." Even for only three cents I believe we deserve more.

For the Defense

And now a witness for the defense, writing us from Central Square, N.Y.--Mr. Sidney Eastwood Lane:

Monday mornings have compensations if one lives in the country 300 miles from New York with ample time to enjoy THE TIMES while watching a snowstorm out of the corner of one's eye.

I am enjoying hugely your comments on the Mahler symphony recently played in Carnegie Hall.

It is tough to strongly dislike something over the years and yet, with milquetoast diffidence be too inarticulate to voice resentments. How beautifully you have done that for me! I feel like the farmer who recognized that Emerson has some of his ideas.

May I contribute an analogous phrase lifted from an article in a recent issue of Punch in which the writer deplores a recently performed symphonic work in London. He closes thus: "It encourages one to hope that humanity has at last touched bottom in its insatiable pursuit of the tediously obvious."

Thus there are Mahlerites and anti-Mahlerites, the latter agreeing with us who dislike the greater part of Mahler's music as they do, and the former angry champions of the composer in whom they believe as much as we do in Jean Sibelius! This is the way it should be in an art which thrives best when there is the hottest dissension among its devotees. For music is no static thing, any more than human expression of any sort is static. But now, with a gratified bow to Mr. Lane for his orchids, how about Mr. Cole's conception of a critic's proper role in reviewing a concert?

It surprises us. He thinks, if we understand him, that the

principal function of a critic who reviews musical events is "relating to the readers how the musicians in question interpreted and played the music," and that there is no need to discuss the music if it is already known except when the discussion is for the purpose of explaining the rights or wrongs of the musician's interpretation.

Begging his pardon, we don't see the critic's primary function in that light at all. The estimation of the performance of a composition per se, is an accessory of artistic criticism and not at all its central object. It is the art that challenges us--not the interpreter. It is in the discussion of the music per se that the principal value of criticism lies. Nor does this function apply only to the first performance or early performances of a given work. First impressions of a new work have the freshness and impact--"the shock of recognition" born out of the sense of a new form of beauty (if so it proves to be).

But this is not all. Time passes and with its passage values change. Thus we are far more concerned with the light in which Debussy's "L'Après-midi d'un Faune" appears to us today half a century after its creation, to us of the post-impressionistic period, than we are with the incidental fact of its admirable interpretation of Mr. Stokovski.

But hold on! We did not wait to remark that we had little to say of the Mahler symphony after we had used a quarter of our space berating it. We said that prior to berating it to the modest length of about a half a stick, as the newspaper jargon puts it--no more. In this space we gave as briefly as possible our reasons for so disliking it, which seem to have escaped Mr. Cole.

The Seventh

We said, in substance, that we found the Mahler Seventh Symphony to be music which strutted and roared and groaned in moods of psychiatric conceit. We said that it was to our mind bad art, bad esthetic, bad, presumptuous and blatantly vulgar music. We felt that having said so much there was no need to go into further detail. We acknowledged that there were those who did like this music, who had every right to enjoy the hour and a quarter that it consumes in performance. No! We didn't stay till the end of a movement. We jumped from our seat right in the middle of the third part, as if we had been shot from a cannon. Nerves could

hold out no longer. We nearly bowled over an usher in our haste
to get to the door. Anyhow, we would never have caught the
edition, if we'd stayed a minute longer.

As for Mr. Mitropoulos' "unflinching gusto," we number
ourselves among the warmest admirers of his incandescent personality among the leading conductors of today, and absolutely deny
aspersion upon him or the orchestra.

Alas that we should be so misunderstood! We only thought
it terrible that such a conductor and orchestra should be spent on
such material. Gracious heavens! What is expected of us? Are we
to say that we liked the Mahler symphony?

VI.D-S.o.8
WESTERN UNION

MARCH 10, 1949

ARNOLD SCHOENBERG=
116 NORTH ROCKINGHAM AVE REDWOOD ROAD LOSA=

WILL YOU JOIN WITH OTHER OUTSTANDING AMERICAN
MUSICIANS IN SENDING THE FOLLOWING CABLE OF
GREETINGS TO DIMITRI SHOSTAKOVICH "WE ARE
DELIGHTED TO LEARN OF YOUR FORTHCOMING VISIT
TO THE UNITED STATES AND WELCOME YOU AS ONE OF
THE OUTSTANDING COMPOSERS OF THE WORLD. MUSIC
IS AN INTERNATIONAL LANGUAGE AND YOUR VISIT
WILL SERVE TO SYMBOLIZE THE BOND WHICH MUSIC
CAN CREATE AMONG ALL PEOPLES. WE WELCOME
YOUR VISIT ALSO IN THE HOPE THAT THIS KIND OF
CULTURAL INTERCHANGE CAN AID UNDERSTANDING
AMONG OUR PEOPLES AND THEREBY MAKE POSSIBLE
AN ENDURING PEACE." PLEASE WIRE ME AT SUITE 71 W
44 ST=
OLIN DOWNES=

VI.S-D.o.10

NIGHTLETTER TO OLIN DOWNES
March 11, 1949

Being Scapegoat of Russian restrictions on music I cannot sign. But I am ready to send the following: Disregarding problem of styles and politics I gladly greet a real composer.

Signed Arnold Schoenberg

New York Herald Tribune[23]
September 11, 1949

MUSIC IN REVIEW

Schoenberg Celebrates Seventy-fifth Birthday
With Attack on Conductors

By Virgil Thomson

ARNOLD SCHOENBERG will be seventy-five years old on September 13. Among the ceremonies planned to honor the great man are four broadcasts of his works over KFWB in Los Angeles on four successive Sundays beginning today. These will be produced and directed by Julius Todi, forming part of the Contemporary Chamber Music Series in a set of radio programs known as "Music of Today," all of which come under Mr. Todi's direction and some of which are broadcast nationally. Unfortunately, the Schoenberg programs will not be heard in the East.

"Music of Today," incidentally, also sells scores and recordings at reasonable prices to members (one becomes a member by buying $ 10 worth) and plans shortly to publish a magazine, as well as to offer clubs and colleges a modern-repertory service. Its radio activities have been sponsored by Local 47, American Federation of Musicians, and honored by the International-Broadcasting Divi-

sion of the State Department, which records all programs for
retransmission to foreign countries. The address is "Music of
Today," 5833 Fernwood Avenue, Hollywood 28, Calif.

The Text of Schoenberg's Complaint

TODAY'S program consists of Schoenberg's Five Pieces for
Orchestra, op. 16, and an address by the master. Next Sunday his
String Quartet No. 2 will be played and on the two following
Sundays, in two parts, his "Pierrot Lunaire." On these later
occasions Mr. Schoenberg will make a short announcement regarding a project to publish at his own expense certain works not at
present available to the public. Today he will make the following
remarks [Schoenberg's radio address]:

"Olin Downes in New York Times expresses astonishment
over a report that Twelve-Tone-Music is spreading out in all of
Western Europe while 'here one considered it to be a dying art.' Let
me correct this: one did not only 'consider' it a dying art; one
understood to 'corriger la fortune' by 'making' it a dying art.

"When in 1933 I came to America I was a very renowned
composer, even so that Mr. Goebbels himself in his 'Der Angriff'
reprimanded me for leaving Germany. Thanks to the attitude of
most American conductors and under the leadership of Toscanini,
Koussevitzky and Walter suppression of my works soon began with
the effect that a number of performances of my works sunk to an
extremely low point. A year ago I had counted in Europe alone
about a hundred performances of my works. There was also
opposition and violent propaganda against my music in Europe.
But musical education was high enough to meet the opposition of
the illiterate. Therefore there existed a satisfactory number of first-
class musicians who at once were able to recognize that logic, order
and organization will be greatly promoted by application of the
method of composing with twelve tones.

"Even under Hitler, twelve-tone music was not suppressed,
as I have learned. On the contrary it was compared to the idea of
'Der Fuehrer' by the German composer Paul von Klenau, who
composed operas in this style. In order to try to make this art a
dying art, some agitators had to use a method, which I will baptize
'the prefabricated history.' Namely, assuming that history repeats

itself, they compared our period to that of Bach, or rather of Teleman, Kayser and Mattheson. Even if this comparison is correct, I can be very happy. Because we see how Bach has died, and how "hale and hearty" Teleman's, Kayser's and Mattheson's music is alive.

"It should be discouraging to my suppressors to recognize the failure of their attempts. You cannot change the natural evolution of the arts by a command; you may make a New Year's resolution to write only what everybody likes; but you cannot force real artists to descend to the lowest possible standard to give up morals, character and sincerity, to avoid presentation of new ideas. Even Stalin cannot succeed and Aaron Copland even less.[24]

The Prosecution rests!

It is not the intention of your reviewer to argue with this extraordinary statement or to defend it very far. All the musicians mentioned in it are alive and present. They can defend themselves. I should like to offer my readers, however, the reminder that a world-famous composer and musical leader of seventy-five may quite justifiably feel bitter about a situation that keeps his works largely unplayed and partly unpublished.

His attack on Aaron Copland seems to me unjustified, since Mr. Copland has never, to my knowledge, acted to prevent the dissemination of Schoenberg's work, little as he may approve it. The attack on Olin Downes is weak, too; but so is Mr. Downes's position with regard to the twelve-tone school. Modernity, after all, has never been his forte; nor has he ever pretended that it was.

The case of the Big Three conductors is graver. They really should have played the twelve-tone master; they really should. Their position has sort of demanded that they cover the field; and they have failed to do so, for all their assiduity toward other regions of modern repertory. And it is not as if the all-powerful public were opposed to twelve-tone music. Reiner, Stokowski, Mitropoulos, Ormandy, Rodzinski and many others have looked at it without beeing turned into pillars of salt. (Actually, I believe, Koussevitzky did play a Schoenberg piece once long, long ago.) Well, I hope the Big Three will answer the twelve-tone master or get somebody to answer for them. Any other tactics toward him would be rude, or else an admission of guilt. Given the fame, position and opportuni-

ties of these leaders in musical taste, is so spectacular an omission
on their part fair play? Is it not, rather, a neglect of duty? That is
the question Schoenberg raises. That is the question I should like
to hear them answer.

New York Herald Tribune[25]
September 25, 1949

MUSIC IN REVIEW

Aaron Copland Replies to Schoenberg;
Conductors Silent Regarding Attack

By Virgil Thomson

ARNOLD SCHOENBERG'S birthday blast at the conductors who
have not played his music (and quite incidentally at Aaron Copland)
was printed in this column on Sept. 11. No defense has yet
appeared from Toscanini, Koussevitzky or Walter, the leaders
accused of attempting "suppression" of his works; and I imagine
none is likely to. It is not the custom of conductors so celebrated
to argue with a mere composer. Mr. Copland, however, has paid to
his elder colleague (and to this office) the compliment of a warmly
indignant reply. Here it is.

VI.Co-T.
Apology Demanded   Palisades, New York
                                                        September 11, 1949

> "DEAR VIRGIL:
> Imagine my astonishment on reading your column this
> morning to find Arnold Schoenberg coupling my name with that of
> Joseph Stalin[26] as one of the suppressors of his art. You were
> good to have called this attack 'unjustified;' but it is much too
> negative merely to say that 'Mr. Copland has never, to my knowl-
> edge, acted to prevent the dissemination of Schoenberg's work, little
> as he may approve of it.' I both approve of it and I have helped to

disseminate it. I approve of it in the sense that, for better or worse, Schoenberg's music has proved itself one of the major influences in the contemporary music world and therefore deserves adequate hearing. I have disseminated it in lectures and in arranging concerts for more than twenty years and was instrumental in seeing to it that the Columbia Recording Company issued 'Pierrot Lunaire' under the auspices of the League of Composers. True, I can't be listed as an apostle and propagandizer of the twelve-tone system; but since when is that a crime? Unless Mr. Schoenberg considers it such he clearly owes me an apology.

After considerable puzzling over the reason for this gratuitous slam I suddenly arrived at the obvious solution. Mr. Schoenberg must have seen my picture in the papers in company with Shostakowitch on the occasion of his brief visit here last spring. In America it is still possible (I hope) to share a forum platform with a man whose musical and political ideas are not one's own without being judged guilty by association. What Dimitri Shostakowitch said during that visit, condemning the music of Stravinsky, Hindemith and Schoenberg, may make some sense as the statement of a citizen of the Soviet Union; but it certainly makes no sense over here. I dissociate myself from such an attitude absolutely. If that is the seat of Mr. Schoenberg's misunderstanding of my position it is easy for me to reassure him. Unlike Stalin I have no desire to suppress his music!

Greetings, "Aaron."[27]

Conductor's Silence

MR. COPLAND'S rebuttal is complete in his first paragraph; Schoenberg is clearly wrong about the facts. The dean of modernism has no doubt been unaware of the activities on his music's behalf engaged in by a confrere not of his school. And it is characteristically generous of Copland to render apologies unnecessary by explaining in his second paragraph how such a misunderstanding may have arisen. Moreover, he has put himself on Schoenberg's side in the latter's indictment of the Big Three conductors. For if Copland, as a composer, has considered it his duty to help Schoenberg's music toward "adequate hearing," how much more has that been the duty of interpreters. A composer might be excused for neglecting to disseminate another's work, though Copland is guiltless here even of that. But for any major conductor to neglect consistently a major composer is a failure on that conductor's part in his main public function, which is the dissemination of good music. Abstention leaves him saying either "I do not recognize in Schoenberg a major composer" or "I do not pretend to catholicity in my programs." In the first case, he must defend himself to the musical world, in the second case before his suscribing public. In either, I think, he resigns from omniscience.

VI.S-T.o.1

Arnold   Schoenberg
116N.RockinghamAvenue
Los Angeles 24, California

December 23, 1949

Mr Virgil Thomson
New York Herald Tribune
Music Critic
New York City, N.Y.

Dear Mr. Thomson:
    I received the clipping of your Sunday 25. column only yesterday.
    I am sorry that so much time has elapsed without my fault.
    As I have now written this explanation, I assume that it should be printed, and I would be grateful if you could do it.
                    Sincerely yours,
Encl.

R.H.[28]

VI.S-T.o.2

IN ANSWER TO AARON COPLAND'S REPLY
(*New York Herald Tribune*, Sept. 25)[29]

I did not see a picture of Aaron Copland and Dimitry Shostakovitch and I did not know about their discussion. But some of Mr Copland's malicious remarks about my dwindling attractiveness to audiences has been reported to me. That, of course was mere propaganda and could be ignored.

But as a teacher who for about fifty years has worked hard to provide young people with the tools of our art, with the technical, esthetic and moral basis of true artistry, I could not stand it to learn that Mr. Copland had given young students who asked for it, the advice to use "simple" intervals[30] and to study the masters. Much damage had been done to an entire generation of highly talented American composers, when they in the same fashion were tought to write a certain style. It will certainly take a generation of sincere teaching until this damage can be repaired.

And only in this respect did I couple Mr. Copland with Stalin: they both do not consider musical composition as the art to present musical ideas in a dignified manner, but they want their followers to write a certain style, that is to create an external appearance, without asking about the inside.

This I must condemn.

But otherwise, if my words could be understood as an attempt to involve Mr. Copland in a political affair, I am ready to apologize - This was not my intention.

Arnold Schoenberg, December 23, 1949.[31]

New York Herald Tribune[32]
October 2, 1949

Schoenberg and the Conductors;
Record Bears Out His Position

By Francis D. Perkins

ARNOLD SCHOENBERG'S recent speech[33] in Los
Angeles in a broadcast honoring his seventy-fifth birthday has
aroused comment, but no one has yet publicly advocated the
suppression of his music. It seems unlikely that American conductors in general, or Messrs. Toscanini, Koussevitzky and Walter in
particular have ever joined in an anti-Schoenberg campaign. But
not to play a composer's works, for whatever reason, is more
harmful to his interests than any active opposition which at least
calls the public's attention to him.

That Mr. Schoenberg has reason for bitterness over the
infrequency of the performance of his music in this country is
suggested, so far as the New York orchestral field is concerned, by
a look at a list which this department has maintained for twenty-five
years. During that time, large orchestras have given thirty-seven
performances of eleven Schoenberg works in Manhattan concerts
for paying audiences. "Verklärte Nacht" received seventeen of these
performances; it has been played by the Philharmonic-Symphony,
Philadelphia Orchestra, National Orchestral Association and Boston
Symphony--Dr. Koussevitzky presented it in Carnegie Hall on Feb.
3, 1934.

Orchestral Performances

THE NOTEWORTHY merits of "Verklärte Nacht" need no
restatement here, but this is an early and retrospective work, readily
assimilable by any one who does not find Wagner too advanced, and
a conductor can hardly claim that he had done his duty by Mr.
Schoenberg by offering this tone poem and letting it go at that.
The other ten works figuring in this list have had the following
performances by large orchestras in public Manhattan concerts:

Ode to Napoleon: Philharmonic-Symphony under Artur
Rodzinski, Nov. 23, 24, 1944.

Kammersymphonie No. 2: New York City Symphony under
Leopold Stokowski, Nov. 19, 20, 1944. (This was first
played by the New York Friends of Music chamber orchestra
under Fritz Stiedry, Dec. 15, 1940).

Five Pieces for Orchestra: Symphony Society under Walter
Damrosch (three pieces only): Nov. 29, 1925; Philharmonic-
Symphony under Dimitri Mitropoulos, Oct. 21, 22, 1948.

Gurrelieder: League of Composers concert under Stokowski,
April 20, 1932.

Pelléas and Mélisande: New York City Symphony under
Stokowski, Nov. 4, 1941.

Suite for strings: Philharmonic-Symphony under Otto
Klemperer, Oct. 17, 18, 19, 20, 1935.

Variations for Orchestra: Philadelphia Orchestra under
Stokowski, Oct. 22, 1929.

Theme and Variations in G minor, Op.43b: Philharmonic-
Symphony under George Szell, Nov. 1, 2, 3, 1945.
Philadelphia Orchestra under Eugene Ormandy, Feb. 22,
1949.

Concerto for String Quartet (after Handel): Philharmonic-
Symphony under Werner Janssen, March 21, 22, 1935.

Cello Concerto (after Georg Matthias Monn): Emanuel
Feuermann and National Orchestral Association under
Leon Barzin, Feb. 19, 1938.

The piano concerto, Op. 42, was broadcast by Eduard Steuermann
and the NBC Symphony under Mr. Stokowski on Feb, 6, 1944, but
has not yet reached Carnegie Hall. Thirty-seven performances in
twenty-five years is an average of one and a half performances a

season, a record which does not correspond with Mr. Schoenberg's high standing in the international world of contemporary music. A truly catholic list of programs should give due and periodic representation to all significant composers of the present, both the conservatives and the innovators.

But there is a point of conflict between the need for catholiclicity in an orchestra's repertory and the fact that many conductors, like other interpretive musicians, have their preferences and aversions, and are not equally at home in all kinds, styles and periods of music. Some conductors may have overlooked Mr. Schoenberg's music, seeing no reason for a wide digression from the standard list; others may frankly dislike it. Still others, while admitting Schoenberg's importance, may have views corresponding to those expressed by Ignace Jan Paderewski in a press conference some twenty years ago. The great pianist said that he seldom played contemporary music, not because he had a poor opinion of it, but because it did not appeal to him. A musician can claim with some justification that he respects a particular composer's works, but since they seem alien to him, he avoids them because he doubts his ability to do them interpretative justice.

The Conductor's Mission

A RECITALIST, however, is concerned mainly with his own interest and artistic aims. The conductor's responsibility extends further, especially if he is at the head of a large metropolitan orchestra which, apart from the radio and phonograph, provides all or most of the community's musical supply in this field. He cannot, as a recitalist might, ignore an important phase of contemporary music in the belief that there are others who can attend to it. If he is faced with music which, while significant, seems baffling and vexatious at first acquaintance, he should make an earnest and persevering attempt to understand it and convey it to his hearers.

If a conductor is to accomplish his artistic mission, he must be prepared to give persuasive performances of certain works which do not particularly appeal to him. Suppose, however, that a conductor should strive nobly to come to terms with a significant, but disaffecting score and still find that his aversion is complete and invincible, or conscientiously feel that he cannot interpret it adequately? In that case, it is not necessary to force him to present this music. Most of our major orchestras have one or more guest conductors assisting the regular incumbent; others have a multiple conductorship.

It is then up to the orchestra's musical director or, in the case of a multiple conductorship, to its management or board of directors to see that its list of leaders represents a comprehensive diversity of tastes. But have all the conductors who have given little or no attention to Mr. Schoenberg's music made an extensive and wholehearted attempt to become acquainted with it?

VI.Co-S.o.1

Aaron Copland River Road Palisades,
New York, Feb. 13, 1950

My dear Mr. Schoenberg:
Virgil Thomson allowed me to read the letter (see p. 265) you sent him in answer to my communication (see p. 263) in this column in the Herald-Tribune of several months ago. My sincere wish to clear up, if possible, any cause for misunderstanding between us prompts me to address you directly. My appreciation and understanding of the work you have done for music in the past fifty years, and my respect and reverence for the ideals you have upheld for so many years are such that I find it painful to discover that you think of us so far apart. That is not as I see it, and I take this opportunity to try to clarify my own position for you.

It is clear to me that whoever is reporting my ideas or remarks to you has been doing us both a grave disservice. It is quite untrue, for example, that I have advised students to compose in a "certain style" or that I have recommended "simple intervals". These impressions must have been gained from isolated sentences taken out of context by persons who do not know me well. I do not dictate stylistic choice by my students. In my mind their style should fit their temperament--there is no other way to write honest music. I myself have never followed any for[m]ula for composition. I have composed in both a complex and a simple style. Insofar as my compositions exemplify a certain aesthetic other composers may be able to extract useable principles from them, but that is their own affair. It is the teacher's role, as I see it, to make evident the expressive and intellectual content of music written in all styles, old and new,--beyond that point the student must work out his own salvation. Can these principles be so very different from your own?

When I was in Hollywood over a year ago I attended an evening of your compositions at the Institute of Modern Art when you were scheduled to speak. That evening I heard you were unwell, which discouraged me from making any attempt to renew our slight acquaintanceship. I still recall our conversation at your 69th birthday celebration,--it is a memory, my dear Master, that I shall always cherish.

> Most sincerely,
> Aaron Copland[34]

VI.S-Co.o.2

Arnold Schoenberg
116 N. Rockingham Avenue
Los Angeles
49 California

Mr. Aaron Copland
River Road Palisades
New York. N.Y.   February 21 1950

Dear Mr. Copland:
Your letter from February 13 pleases me very much. True, I am a fighter, but not an attacker. I "backfire" only, when I have been attacked. But otherwise it is very easy to live in peace with me. I am always inclined to do justice to every merit and to sincerity. And I am sure that the Hungarian pianist who played your music (and Bartok's) for me a year ago in my home (I cannot remember his name) will have told you that I appreciated your

music without any restriction.

But there is at least one man here in Los Angeles who goes around forbidding people to "make propaganda" for Schoenberg, when they only speak about facts. And CBS has evidently intended to hit <u>me</u>, when they ordered "no controversial music" to be broadcast - while they broadcast quite a number of controversial music from other composers. And you might know also about the attitude of "MY" publisher G. Schirmer, who if possible tries to counteract performances of my music . . . . . . and many other similar facts.

You will perhaps understand then that I become inclined to believe people, who told me that you uttered surprise about the difference of attention paid to me here by audiences - in contrast to New York. How am I to know that this might be only gossip to sow discord? I believe that there are people who aim for production of enimity between public figures, but, considering facts I know, I have no way of discrimination.

When I said at the beginning of this letter that your letter pleases me very much, I can repeat this now, adding that I am always ready to live in peace, because I strongly believe that at least my sincerity deserves recognition and respect, so I am in the position to consider merits of other composers with kindness.

I don't want to conclude this letter without mentioning the great danger which the American nationalism might provoke. Will it not finally degenerate into antisemitism? We have seen such things.

> I am with best greetings,
> Yours,   Arnold Schoenberg

[written across this signed letter in crayon: changed for publication. For this version see p. 272].

VI.S-Co.o.3

February 21, 1950

Mr Aaron Copland
River Road Palisades
New York, N.Y.

Dear Mr. Copland:
Your letter from February 13 pleases me very much. True, I am a fighter; but not an attacker. I "backfire" only when I have been attacked. Otherwise it is very easy to live in peace with me. I am always inclined to do justice to every merit and to sincerity. I am sure that the Hungarian pianist Andor Foldes [the name given in hand writing] who played your music, (and Bartok's) for me, about a year ago in my home, will have told you that I appreciated your music without restriction.[35]

On the other hand, there is at least one man here in Los Angeles who goes around forbidding people to "make propaganda" for Schoenberg, when they only speak about facts which should interest a musicologist. CBS has evidently intended to hit at me when they ordered "no controversial music" to be broadcast - while they broadcast quite a number of controversial music from other composers. You might know also about the attitude of publishers, who, if possible, try to counteract performances of my music. There are many other similar cases.

You will perhaps understand then, that I considered it as malice, when you uttered surprise about my large audience in Los Angeles, in contrast to New York. How am I to know that this might be only gossip to sow discord? I believe that there are people who aim for production of enimity between public figures. Considering the abovementioned facts, I have no way of discrimination.

When I said at the beginning of this, that your letter pleases me very much, I can repeat this now, adding that I am always ready to live in peace. I strongly believe that at least my sincerity deserves recognition and respect. So, I am in the position to consider the merits of other composers with kindness.

I am most sincerely,

VI.T-S.o.1

New York Herald Tribune

European Edition	230 West 41st Street, New York 18
Published Daily in Paris	PEnnsylvania 6-4000

February 22, 1950

Dear Mr. Schoenberg:

I thank you for the charming letter and the answer to Aaron Copland. Convinced that your controversy with Mr. Copland was based on some kind of misunderstanding, I sent him your reply and asked him if he would agree to answer you directly. He now writes me that he has done so, including a copy of his reply.[36] I sincerely hope that this correspondence can take the place of a public dispute. Two musicians who have enjoyed the confidence of their students can accomplish no useful purpose, it seems to me, by questioning publicly each other's good faith. I do not wish to close my column to any musical matter which you take deeply to heart. If you continue to believe that Aaron Copland has spoken disrespectfully of your music and acted disloyally as a colleague, I shall always keep it open for whatever evidence you may have to offer.

With cordial greetings,

Ever respectfully yours, Virgil Thomson

VI.S-T.o.3

Mr Virgil Thomson
Music Critic
Herald Tribune
23o West 41st Street
New York, 18, N.Y.

Dear Mr. Thomson: February 25, 1950

I find Mr Copland's letter reconciliatory, thus finishing one part of the dispute. My answer to him of which I enclose a copy, takes note of that, but states a number of reasons, justifying my suspicions.

It seems to me, that some of my complaints about actions, almost tantamount to persecution, should be presented to the public. Their effect was suppression of my music, hindering both laymen and musicians to build their own judgement about my case.

I am far from resenting negative criticism, because I am capable of fighting that, but against suppression, I am powerless. I, personally, find boycott one of the most cowardly weapons.

I leave it to you to decide whether this correspondence should be publicized.

Thank you for generously offering me so much space of your column.

I am most cordially yours,   R.H.

Notes

1. Erwin Stein, *Arnold Schoenberg Letters*. London: Faber and Faber, 1964, pp. 206 and 260-265 (in this book p. 232, pp. 241-244, 248-251).

2. Irene Downes, ed. *Olin Downes on Music*. New York: Simon and Schuster, 1957, pp. 368-372.

3. See pp. 217, 230, 233.

4. Erwin Stein, *Arnold Schoenberg Letters*. London: Faber and Faber, 1964, pp. 260-265.

5. Paul von Klenau (1883-1946) was a Danish composer and conductor who was educated in Denmark and Germany. He was active as a conductor in Denmark from 1920 to 1926 and after 1940 in Germany. During his earlier career he was influenced by Schoenberg.

6. Facsimile from Schoenberg's draft.

7. Copyright (c) 1935 / 38 / 48 by The New York Times Company. Reprinted by permission.

8. Olin Downes' preview of the first New York performance of Schoenberg's Suite is taken from Schoenberg's personal copy, in which the composer's reactions are reflected by his underlined passages (given in this reprint). Schoenberg's additional German words (in square brackets) are simply the translations he needed to look up in a dictionary.

9. Copyright (c) 1935 / 38 / 48 by The New York Times Company. Reprinted by permission.

10. I. H. T. Corporation. Reprinted by permission.

11. For a translation see p. 216.

12. See pp. 224 ff.

13. *Modern Music*. A Quarterly Review. Published by the League of Composers. Vol. XXII, 1944, #1, pp. 3-5. Schoenberg's contribution printed above is the first of several short articles. The other essays are by Milhaud, Křenek, Rieti and Martinu (pp. 5-11).

14. Schoenberg's "letter to the editor" (p. 241) and Downes' reply (p. 245) were printed in the *New York Times* on December 12, 1948 under the following heading:

EXCHANGE OF VIEWS
Distinguished Composer Discusses Mahler, Himself and
Criticism--The Reply
By Olin Downes
A CERTAIN Mahler controversy, which the writer seems to have started, has instigated, among other correspondents, the comment of one of the most distinguished masters of modern composition--Arnold Schoenberg. Here is Mr. Schoenberg's comment (p. 241).

15. *New York Times*, November 12, 1948, see p 253. A rebuttal of other correspondents can be found in the *New York Times* of November 21, 1948 (see p. 254).

16. This letter [the musical examples in the original are in Richard Hoffmann's hand] and Downes' response of 3.XII.1948 have been reprinted in *Olin Downes on Music*, ed. Irene Downes. New York: Simon & Schuster, pp. 370-372. See also note 1.

17. The underlines as well as the added words (given in square brackets) are by Schoenberg.

18. For the earlier review of the "Five Pieces," see *Olin Downes on Music*, ed. Irene Downes. New York: Simon & Schuster, 1957, pp. 46-48.

19. This is the cover letter with which Mitropoulos forwarded the "disdirected" letter of December 3, 1948 to Arnold Schoenberg (see p. 245).

20. In this cable Downes refers to his letter dated December 3, 1948 (see p. 245). Similarly, Schoenberg referred to the "disdirected" letter in his letter to Downes dated December 10, 1948 (p. 247). For further comments see p. 216.

21. Copyright (c) 1935 / 38 / 48 by The New York Times Company. Reprinted by permission.

22. Copyright (c) 1935 / 38 / 48 by The New York Times Company. Reprinted by permission.

23. I. H. T. Corporation. Reprinted by permission.

24. Schoenberg's handwritten version dated August 22, 1949 (preserved at the Arnold Schoenberg Institute, Los Angeles) is identical to the printed version except for occasional differences in spelling.

25. I. H. T. Corporation. Reprinted by permission.

26. See Schoenberg's radio address (reprinted on September 11, 1949 in the *New York Herald Tribune*), p. 260 above.

27. Quoted by permission.

28. Richard Hoffmann, born in 1925 in Vienna, is a cousin of Gertrud Schoenberg. A noted composer, Hoffmann studied with Schoenberg from 1947 to 1951, and also served as Schoenberg's secretary from 1948 until Schoenberg's death. Hoffmann's academic appointments include positions at UCLA and Oberlin College. At present Hoffmann divides his teaching between Oberlin College and the University of Vienna.

29. This date here is merely Schoenberg's reference to the article of September 25, 1949 (p. 262). Schoenberg gave his date (December 23, 1949) at the end of this hand-written rebuttal (p. 265).

30. See Copland's letter of February 13, 1950 on p. 269 below.

31. Schoenberg's carbon copy of this letter and his cover letter (p. 264) are in the Library of Congress.

32. I. H. T. Corporation. Reprinted by permission.

33. See p. 260 above.

34. Quoted by permission.

35. In a letter to Roy Harris of May 17, 1945 (see Stein, *Schoenberg Letters*, pp. 233-234), Schoenberg listed Copland as the first among the ten foremost American composers.

36. See Schoenberg's reply to Copland (February 21, 1950) on pp. 270 and 272.

CHAPTER VII

Schoenberg's Basso Continuo Realizations

Schoenberg contributed basso-continuo realizations for three compositions by Georg Matthias Monn (1717-1750) and for one by his younger brother, Johann Christoph Monn (or Mann, 1726-1782), published in the *Denkmäler der Tonkunst in Österreich*, vol. 39, Vienna, 1912 (see also Chapter II, pp. 51 ff.). The only other extant realizations by Schoenberg are found in the so-called "Tuma Manuscripts" where Schoenberg realized in pencil four of the seven compositions by Frantisek Tuma (1703-1774).

The correspondence between Schoenberg and Adler includes several references to Schoenberg's work for the *Denkmäler der Tonkunst in Österreich* and his continued interest in additional commissions for basso-continuo realizations. Adler's mention of a Divertimento[1] in a letter to Schoenberg of January 11, 1912 (see p. 85), clearly refers to the four Monn realizations published in the *Denkmäler* (vol. 39, II, 1912).

Another letter by Schoenberg of January 13, 1912, (see p. 85) could be connected--at least in part--with his Tuma realizations, because he informed Adler then that he did at least six realizations, and that he remembered clearly an Andante in E-flat Major in 4/4. Indeed, one of Schoenberg's Tuma realizations, the Partita a tre in c-minor, includes such an Andante in E-flat Major in 4/4 called Aria; there are no movements in that key in any of Schoenberg's Monn realizations for the *Denkmäler der Tonkunst in Österreich*.

The very fact that Schoenberg turned the Tuma realizations over to Adler in pencil even though he preferred to submit his manuscripts in ink (February 9, 1910; see p. 75) may support further the possibility that Schoenberg's Tuma realizations predate those of the four works by Monn.

Additional evidence suggests the possibility that Schoenberg may have realized several more figured basses, for in a rather early letter to Adler (February 9, 1910, p. 75) he makes a reference to a packet of several compositions, from which he was allowed to select the ones that he would do. Schoenberg informed Adler here that he had chosen some, that he would like to keep the packet longer for further consideration, and that he would return the pieces which he was certain not to do through a servant. In the same letter he went on to tell Adler about the realizations which he had actually completed, offering to ready them for print.

Late in 1911 and in early 1912, it became necessary for Adler to press Schoenberg concerning the proofreading of the Monn compositions to be published during that year in the *Denkmäler der Tonkunst in Österreich*.[2] Eventually the matter came to a conclusion when Schoenberg returned the Monn proofs to Adler on February 7th as indicated by Schoenberg in his letter of February 6, 1912 (p. 89).

It therefore seems unlikely that Schoenberg's references to three pieces already completed in early 1910 (February 9, 1910, p. 75), or to the four and a half completed pieces turned over to Adler through Mr. Fischer (January 16, 1911; p. 77) can be connected with the Monn realizations for which Adler had to wait so long in early 1912.

Adler's letter of January 15, 1912 (p. 87) gives a summary of Schoenberg's basso-continuo realizations extant at the time, stating that Schoenberg contributed four and Labor also four for the *Denkmäler* vol. 39, and that Schoenberg's other realizations (possibly the four Tuma compositions?) had been deferred from publication at this time.

Concerning the history of the "Tuma Manuscripts," Dr. Paul A. Pisk sent me the following communication:

> The history of the manuscripts by Frantisek Tuma (1704-1774) needs comment. After extensive studies of piano, harmony and orchestration, I, being scholarly inclined, enrolled in the University of Vienna as a candidate for a Ph.D in musicology. The leader of the Music Historical Institute was Professor Guido Adler, one of the founders of modern musical scholarship. Professor Adler was also the editor-in-chief of the *Denkmäler der Tonkunst in Österreich*, a series still ongoing today. The advanced students took part in this work, deciphering medieval manuscripts, scoring renais-

sance music from parts, and filling out the figured
bass of baroque and early classical music. Some of
this work was assigned to outsiders. Professor
Adler, who was also a philanthropist, knew about
Schoenberg's financial difficulties. Hence, several
works were edited by Schoenberg for the *Denkmäler*. The Partitas by Tuma were some of the works
which Schoenberg did not finish, leaving the manuscript with Adler. At that time I was about to
emigrate to the United States, and I informed him
of my intent. Professor Adler gave me the "Tuma
Manuscripts" for possible future publication.
However, I donated this Schoenberg manuscript
to the Library of Congress on October 1, 1938. In
1968 the *Tuma Partitas* were published in Germany
the Musik Verlag Hans Gerig, Köln (M.C.A. for
U.S.A.), edited by Rudolf Lück. In his introduction several errors have to be corrected.[3]

First: This manuscript was never in the Schoenberg estate but in Professor Adler's possession for
the *Denkmäler*.

Second: Schoenberg never kept the manuscript
and neither did he take it with him when he
emigrated to the United States (as quoted in
Lück's introduction).

Third: On the first page of the manuscript my
own signature and the Library of Congress com-
ment--Gift Dr. Paul A. Pisk--are proof of the
actual provenance of this manuscript.

                            Paul A. Pisk
                            September 22, 1987

General standards for the realization of basso-continuo
parts in modern scholarly or practical editions were established by
Max Seiffert (1868-1948), among others. Seiffert was one of the
Baroque experts of the early 20th century, and he contributed, for
example, realizations for Buxtehude cantatas to the *Denkmäler der*

Tonkunst in Österreich (vol. 14, 1903). From this perspective it appears that Schoenberg's basso-continuo realizations of 1912 may be counted among the earlier of such modern realizations. At that time there were no new research publications on the techniques and styles of basso-continuo, and, for that matter, Schoenberg would probably not have consulted such studies anyway because he was not inclined to read musicological treatises or books on music history. This he made quite clear in his *Harmonielehre* of 1911 when he declared, "I have never read a history of music."[4]

The reaction to Schoenberg's figured bass realizations was mixed. Even Adler himself, who found something good to say about them in his letter of January 11, 1912 (p. 85), may not really have been completely satisfied as can be gathered from a letter of Carl Prohaska (p. 56). The greatest rejection, however, came from Dr. Max Graf, the influential Viennese music critic. Graf's attack and Schoenberg's defense are printed below, followed by a discussion of Graf's criticisms.

II.Sig.o

Signale
No. 14.   Berlin, 2. April 1913
Professor Dr. Max Graf

ARNOLD SCHOENBERG'S BASSO CONTINUO

Der neueste Band der "Denkmäler der Tonkunst in Österreich"
(Wiener Instrumentalmusik im 18. Jahrhundert II) weist eine
besondere Kuriosität auf: bei vier der in diesem Bande veröf-
fentlichten Musikstücken hat Arnold Schönberg den Basso Continuo ausgesetzt. Man sieht, die Musikwissenschaft modernisiert sich
und trägt die radikalsten Krawatten. Noch kein Museumsdirektor
hat vernünftigerweise daran gedacht, ein altes Bild von einem
futuristischen Maler konservieren zu lassen, weil eine solche
Aufgabe Stilgefühl, historische Bildung, Erfahrung und Takt
voraussetzt und Eigenschaften dieser Art bei den Vertretern
futuristischer Malerei nicht vorausgesetzt werden können. Aber der
Leiter der österreichischen Denkmälerausgabe hat sich von solchen
Bedenken nicht zurückschrecken lassen, als er Arnold Schönberg die Ausarbeitung des Basso Continuo übertragen hat, obzwar
Arnold Schönberg in seiner "Harmonielehre" von sich rühmt, keine
theoretischen Schriften zu lesen, und die so viel diskutierte
Ausarbeitung eines basso continuo gewiss auch einiges theoretische
Wissen voraussetzt. "Das Gehör ist eines Musikers ganzer Verstand", sagt Arnold Schönberg in seiner Harmonielehre, und es ist
vielleicht nicht ganz uninteressant, zu sehen, ob das Schönberg'sche
Gehör für die Aufgabe die ihm gestellt wurde, genug Verstand
aufgebracht habe. Dazu sei die Symphonie a quattro von Matthias
Georg Monn gewählt (Seite 32). Ich sage eine Banalität, wenn ich
darauf hinweise, dass es eine Aufgabe der Basso Continuobearbei-
tung sei, den Gang der Harmonien eines Werkes zu verdeutlichen,
zu unterstützen, zu kräftigen.   Das richtige Verständnis der
Harmoniefolge ist eine Voraussetzung der Arbeit, aber Schönberg's
an moderne Harmonien gewöhntes Ohr kann sich solchen einfachen
Klängen wie der Monn'schen Harmonik nicht mehr anpassen. Seite
32, System 2, Takt 2 und 4 ist der halbtaktige Harmoniewechsel in
der Monn'schen Musik deutlich ausgesprochen. Aber Schönberg
wechselt im Continualbass am ersten, dritten und vierten Viertel der

II.Sig.t

                                        Signale
No.14.   Berlin, April 2, 1913
                                        Professor Dr. Max Graf

ARNOLD SCHOENBERG'S BASSO CONTINUO

The most recent volume of the *Denkmäler der Tonkunst in Öster-reich* (Viennese Instrumental Music in the 18th Century, II) exhibits a particular curiosity: Arnold Schoenberg has realized the basso-continuo of four of the compositions published in this volume. Here we see musicology modernizing itself and decked out in the most radical neckties. As yet no museum director has considered it sensible to have an old picture restored by a futuristic painter, since such a task presupposes a feeling for style, a historic orientation, and experience and sensitivity; qualities of this kind cannot be taken for granted in representatives of futuristic painting. But the director of the edition of Austrian Monuments was not deterred by such considerations when he entrusted Arnold Schoenberg with the realization of the basso-continuo, even though Arnold Schoenberg boasts in his *Harmonielehre* that he has read no theoretical treatises; yet the much discussed realization of a figured bass certainly presupposes some theoretical knowledge. "A musician's understanding depends totally on the ear," says Schoenberg in his *Harmonielehre*, and perhaps it is not altogether uninteresting to see if Schoenberg's ear has generated enough understanding for the task that was assigned to him. The Symphonia a quattro by Matthias Georg Monn (p. 32) may be singled out for consideration. I am stating a truism when I point out the purpose of a basso-continuo realization is to clarify, support, and strengthen the harmonic progressions of a composition. The true understanding of harmonic progressions is a prerequisite for this kind of work, but Schoenberg's ear, accustomed to modern harmony, can no longer adapt itself to such simple sounds as those of Monn's harmony. On page 32, system 2, measures 2 and 4 [p. 297, II, 1 and 2], the harmonic change by the half-measure is clearly indicated in Monn's music. Schoenberg, however, changes the harmonies in the continuo on the first, third and fourth quarter notes [Graf must have meant eighth notes because this movement is in 2/4]. Page 33, system 2 in

Harmonien [Graf muss Achtel Noten gemeint haben da dieser Satz
im 2/4 Takt ist]. Seite 33, System 2 wechselt in den Takten 8 bis 10
die Harmonie im 10. Takte; Schönberg nimmt in sinnloser Weise
die Modulation schon im 9. Takt voraus. Die gleiche falsche
Modulation ist Seite 33, System 3, Takt 2 zu konstatieren. Den
Modulationsgang am Schlusse hat Arnold Schönberg ebenfalls nicht
verstanden: Seite 38, System 2, Takt 9 bis System 3, Takt 5, obzwar
er ganz einfach ist: fortgesetzter Quintenfall von h bis a, bei dem
meist Sekund und Sextakkorde miteinander wechseln:

f#				d		
d	e	e	d	h	c#	e
h	h	c#	a	g#	g# etc. up to	a
a	g#	a	f#	f#	e	c#

Allein nicht nur beim Harmoniengang staunt man darüber, was
Schönberg alles nicht gehört hat, auch bei der Motivarbeit. Seite
33, System 2, Takt 8 beginnt in einer Fuge ein Zwischensatz, der
den rhythmisch charakteristischen Teil des Fugenthemas acht Takte
lang mit Absicht nicht verwendet.   Schönberg, welcher diese
künstlerische Absicht nicht bemerkt hat, lässt das vom Künstler
nicht benutzte Motiv in den Bass fortwährend hineinklappern und
bringt damit den neuen Einsatz des Motivs (Seite 33, System 3, Takt
[?]) um jede Wirkung. Dasselbe geschieht Seite 34, System 3, Takt
6, wo Schönberg den Eintritt des Motivs dadurch schädigt, dass er
es ohne jede Logik einen Takt vorher in seinem Bass anbringt, und
sogar mit dem gleichen Ton eintreten lässt. . Zu den unbegreifli-
chen Sinnlosigkeiten gehören jene Stellen, wo Schönberg ohne jede
Motivierung im Basso-continuo willkürlich Pausen anbringt (so
Seite 35, System 2, Takt 5 und 6, Seite 40, System 2, Takt 4) oder
ebensowenig motiviert eine Pause der Musik mit Tönen anfüllt
(Seite 39, System 1, Takt 3, das plötzlich in den Bass hinein-
stampfende cis) oder plötzlich gar den Violinen (!) die Bassstimme
entnimmt (Seite 40, System 3, Takt 2), weil er nicht an die Contra-
bassverstärkung der Cellostimme gedacht oder nichts davon gewusst
hat.   Von stilwidrigen Akkorden, die in einer Musik des 18.
Jahrhunderts unmöglich sind, will ich nicht erst sprechen, aber die
vielen harmonischen Unsauberkeiten dürfen nicht übergangen
werden.   Wir bewundern da z[um] B[eispiel[Seite 32, System 1,
Takt 7 eine Verdopplung der Septime, Seite 39, System 2, Takt 2

measures 8 to 10 [p. 298,II, 8-10] changes the harmony in the 10th measure [II, 10], and Schoenberg rather senselessly anticipates the modulation in measure 9. The same incorrect modulation can be observed on page 33, system 3, measure 2 [p. 298, III, 2]. Likewise, Schoenberg has not understood the modulation at the end: page 38, system 2, measure 9 through system 3, measure 5 [p. 303, II, 9 through III, 5], even though it is very simple: a continuous fall of fifths from b to a, alternating mostly between four-two and sixth-chords:

f#				d		
d	e	e	d	b	c#	e
b	b	c#	a	g#	g# etc. up to	a
a	g#	a	f#	f#	e	c#

One is not only astonished at Schoenberg's total lack of ear for harmonic progression, but also for motivic play. On page 33 an episode within a fugue begins on system 2, measure 8 [p. 298, II, 8] which purposely omits the rhythmically characteristic portion of the fugue theme for eight measures. Schoenberg, who did not notice this artistic intent, lets the motive, which was not yet utilized by the composer, go clattering along in the bass, thus taking any effectiveness away from the new entrance of the motive (page 33, system 3, measure [?]) [p. 298, m. ?]. The same happens on page 34, system 3, measure 6 [p. 299, III, 6], where Schoenberg ruins the entrance of the motive because he brings it in without any logic a measure earlier in his bass, and does so even on the same pitch. . . . Among the other incomprehensible absurdities must be counted those passages where, without any motivation, Schoenberg arbitrarily introduces rests in the basso-continuo (as on page 35, system 2, measure 5 and 6, page 40, system 2, measure 4) [p. 300, II, 5 and 6; p. 305, II, 4], or--also without motivation--fills a rest in the music with notes (page 39, system 1, measure 3, the c-sharp which abruptly intrudes in the bass) [p. 304, I, 3], or where he suddenly derives the bass voice from the violins (!) (page 40, system 3, measure 2) [p. 305, III, 2] because he did not think about the enforcement of the cellos by the double bass or knew nothing about it. I would prefer not to say anything about the chords that are stylistically inappropriate in an 18th century composition, but the many harmonic flaws cannot be passed by. On page 32, system I, measure 7 [p. 297, I,7],

eine horrible Verdopplung des Leittons in der tieferen Oktave, auf Seite 33, System 3, Takt 8 Quinten, noch viel hässlicher klingende auf Seite 34, System 1, Takt 5 (zwischen der Oberstimme des Cembalos und der Viola), auf Seite 36, System 3, Takt 1 und 2 und Seite 37, System 2, Takt 12, 13 und System 3, Takt 1, 2 Oktaven ... Kurz, die harmonische Toilette, in der Schönberg am Cembalo erscheint, ist nichts weniger als rein geputzt.

Über Schönberg als Komponisten lässt sich streiten. Dass er als Bearbeiter des Basso-Continuo, noch dazu in einer wissenschaftlichen Publikation, nicht am Platze war, darüber geben die Stichproben, die einem einzigen der von Arnold Schönberg bearbeiteten Werke entnommen wurden, Aufschluss. Verwunderlich ist, dass der Herausgeber dieses Bandes der österreichischen Denkmäler, Herr Wilhelm Fischer, alle die harmonischen und stilistischen Fehler des Schönberg'schen Basso Continuo nicht bemerkt, und noch verwunderlicher, dass der Leiter der Publikationen, Prof. Guido Adler, den historischen und musikalischen Widersinn nicht nachgeprüft hat, weil der Name Arnold Schönberg ihn geblendet hat. Aber der kritische Sinn der strengen Wissenschaft sollte sich durch einen Modenamen nicht so leicht aus der Fassung bringen lassen.

Prof. Dr. Max Graf.

II.[VII].A-S.o.9

Denkmäler der Tonkunst in Österreich
Leiter der Publikationen: Universitätsprofessor Dr. Guido Adler
in Wien XIX/1, Cottage, Lannerstrasse 9

18. 4. 13

Sehr geehrter Herr!
Ich habe nunmehr die Anzeige in den "Signalen" gelesen u[nd] kann Ihnen beistimmen, eine Erwiderung zu geben: kurz, da sie sonst nicht aufgenommen wird, sachlich, beiläufig im Umfang wie die

for example, we wonder at the doubling of a seventh; on page 39, system 2 measure 2 [p. 304, II, 2], a horrible doubling of the leading tone in the lower octave; on page 33, system 3, measure 8 [p. 298, III, 8], fifths; and much uglier sounding ones on page 34, system 1, measure 5 [p. 299, III, 5] (between the upper voice of the harpsichord and the viola); on page 36, system 3, measures 1-2 [p. 301, III, 1-2] and page 37, system 2, measures 12-13, [p. 302, II,12-13] and system 3, measures 1-2, [III, 1-2] octaves . . . In short, the harmonic garb in which Schoenberg appears at the harpsichord is anything but clear-cut.

    Schoenberg's qualities as a composer are debatable. That he was out of place for the realization of a basso-continuo, and at that in a scholarly publication, is proven by the examples which have been extracted from a single one of the compositions worked on by Schoenberg. It is astonishing that the editor of this volume of the Austrian Monuments, Mr. Wilhelm Fischer, did not notice all the harmonic and stylistic mistakes of Schoenberg's basso-continuo, and even more surprising that the director of these publications, Prof. Guido Adler, was so dazzled by the name of Arnold Schoenberg that he did not check out the historic and musical contradictions.   The critical acumen appropriate to strict scholarship, however, should not be so easily thrown off balance by a fashionable name.

Prof. Dr. Max Graf[5]

II.[VII].A-S.t.9

Denkmäler der Tonkunst in Österreich
Leiter der Publikationen: Universitätsprofessor Dr. Guido Adler
in Wien XIX/1, Cottage, Lannerstrasse 9

April 18, 1913

Esteemed Sir:
I have now read the account in the *Signale* and I agree with you concerning a reply: it should be brief because it would not be accepted otherwise, relevant, comparable in scope to the notice

Anzeige selbst, eher kürzer. Wenn Sie wollen richten sie sie in Form eines Briefes an mich. Nur muss ich mir vorbehalten, eventuell Ihnen Änderungsvorschläge zu machen oder selbst Änderungen vorzunehmen die aber Ihnen zum Nutzen gehalten sein sollen. Der Druckfehler cis (39 I 3) soll ohne weiteres als Solcher gekennzeichnet sein. Ich würde einige Zeilen voranstellen oder beifügen, vielleicht auch nicht. Wenn Sie die Absicht haben, dann bald. Das Weltenheil auch das Denkmälerheil hängt davon nicht ab!

Fr[eun]dliche Grüsse von Ihrem ergebenen

Guido Adler

Keine Musikbeispiele, alles in Buchstaben und Zahlen!

Denk 188.o.

<u>Dr. Graf</u> - Monn Bearbeitungen

Nicht um diesen Mann hier zu züchtigen, notiere ich das Folgende. Sondern auch, weil es einer Klarstellung bedarf.

Als ich nähmlich in Breslau mit Dr. Max Graf zusammentraf (sein Sohn - es war mir unbekannt, dass er der war - veranstaltete die deutsche Erstaufführung der "Glückl[iche] Hand") hatte ich ganz die Vorgeschichte unserer Beziehungen vergessen. Vergessen, wie Dr. Graf sich gegen Mahler und später gegen mich benommen hatte. Allerdings muss gesagt werden, dass er sich seit einigen Jahren emsig bestrebt zeigt, seine früheren Sünden zu büssen und ich könnte es nicht über mich bringen, ihm den Weg zur Besserung zu versperren; insbesondere, wo er es mit viel schriftstellerischer Begabung tut und mit grosser Wärme, die wirklich glaubwürdig erscheint. - Es geschieht also hier nicht, um zu rächen, sondern, wegen einer anderen Sache: meiner <u>Monn</u> Bearbeitungen und anderer d[er]gl[eicher] in den Denkmälern d[er] Tonkunst. Endlich nämlich wurden solche Bearbeitungen wieder einmal (seit Mozart und Brahms) von einem gemacht, der Formsinn, Phantasie und Klangsinn besitzt und Kontrapunkt kann: Grund genug, dass das Unglaubliche und Nie-Dagewesene geschieht, dass in einer <u>Tageszei-tung</u> (!) diese Sache besprochen wird, eingehender, als das jemals in Fachzeitschriften der Fall war und tadelnder und beschimpfender,

itself, and preferably shorter. If you wish, you can direct it to me in the form of a letter. I must, however, reserve to myself the right to recommend to you possible modifications or to make changes myself--changes which would be in your favor. The misprint c-sharp (39 I 3) [p. 304, I, 3] will naturally be characterized as such. I might precede this by a few lines or add some, but perhaps not. If you intend to do this, then do it soon. But, the salvation of the world or of the *Denkmäler* does not depend on it!
Cordial regards, yours faithfully
Guido Adler

No musical examples, everything in letters and numbers!

Denk 188.t.

Dr. Graf - Monn arrangements [i.e. basso-continuo realizations].
I state the following here not just in order to chastise this man, but also because clarification is needed. When I met Dr. Max Graf in Breslau (not knowing that it was his son who brought out the first German performance of the "Glückl[iche] Hand") I had completely forgotten the early history of our relations--forgotten how Dr. Graf had behaved towards Mahler and later toward me. It must be said, however, that for several years he has diligently striven to make amends for his earlier offenses, and I could not bring myself to stand in the way of self-improvement, especially since he does it with much literary skill and a great quality of warmth that seems entirely convincing. Thus, what I do here is not in order to take revenge, but because of another matter: my *Monn* arrangements [i.e. figured bass realizations] and others of the same sort in the *Denkmäler der Tonkunst*. Once again (after Mozart and Brahms) it happens that such arrangements have been made by somebody who has a sense of form, imagination, sense of sound, and facility in counterpoint--reason enough that the unbelievable and unprece- dented occurs, and that this subject matter is discussed in a *daily newspaper* (!) in more detail than ever was the case in professional journals, and in a more censorious and abusive fashion than that in which a young, blundering Ph.D. candidate would have been treated

290 Arnold Schoenberg Correspondence

als jemals irgend ein junger stümpernder Musik-Doktorand behandelt wurde, der da seine Harmonielehre-Übungen veröffentlichen liess. Immerhin hatte ich vorher die Händel-Bearbeitungen von Mozart und Brahms genau studiert und mich auch sonst mit der Frage befasst. Immerhin hatte ich auch sonst aus J.S. Bach und Ph.Em. Bach sowie aus Quantz (was Jalowetz bezeugen wird; und auch Stein) zu erfahren getrachtet, wie derlei gemacht worden ist. Immerhin zeigte meine Bearbeitung zwei dankenswerte Züge: 1.) das Bestreben die alten Werke durch Werkbehandlung näher zu bringen; 2.) dass ich mirs hätte leichter machen können. All das Grund genug, mich auch in solcher Eigenschaft, vor der Öffentlichkeit herabzusetzen: was vor mir gewiss noch niemandem passiert war. - Naturgemäss, denn es ist nicht mein angeborener Stil, sondern mein angelernter--zeigt meine Bearbeitung oft mehr Übereifer, mehr guten Willen, als Geschmack. In dem Bestreben Liebe zu erweisen, geht es mir, wie dem Bären mit dem Einsiedler: ich decke oft die nicht immer bedeutenden Themen mit der Überfülle meiner Begleitstimmen und mit meinem Kontrapunkt zu. Es fällt mir nicht ein das heute zu leugnen. Ja ich stehe nicht an zu erklären: es ist möglich, dass ich es hie und da schon damals gefühlt habe, ohne es jedoch ändern zu können. Denn gewisse Dinge kann man nicht ändern, wie ein Schneider: sie sind richtig in allen Massen, aber falsch. Andererseits aber weiss ich, dass ich - und ich finde das noch heute durchaus berechtigt - von vielen wirklich gelungenen Partien grosse Freude hatte; und wenn ich auch manches modernisiert hatte, so war ich so weit kaum jemals gegangen, als Mozart in seiner Bearbeitung des "Messias" von Händel, wo Mozart z.B. (in Peters Edition No. 8287; Seite 106 No. 24 Coro) eine Illustration des Textes hineinkomponiert hat, die allerdings schon fast zu kühn ist (nur nicht!): er bringt nämlich im 1.- 4, 6.- 9 Takt und einigen anderen Stellen in den Bläsern ein Motiv an, von welchem sich bei Händel auch nicht eine Spur findet, welches offenbar die Heerde charakterisieren soll. Hierfür findet sich bei Händel höchstens ein "Anhaltspunkt" in Takt 4-7 nach Buchstaben E auf Seite 112 (also 2 1/2 Takte vor und 1 nach F). Wie gesagt: niemals war ich annähernd so weit gegangen. Auch hatte ich nicht, wie Mozart, einige Bündel Sequenzen herausgeschnitten. Und ähnliches mehr. Woher aber kam der Groll: der kam von Schenker. Denn der Artikel war zweifellos von diesem inspiriert. Es war seine Ausdrucksweise, seine Gesichtspunkte und

who had had his harmony exercises published. After all, I had studied the Handel arrangements by Mozart and Brahms very carefully beforehand, and I had concerned myself with the question in other ways as well. Furthermore, I also was eager to learn from J.S. Bach and Ph.E. Bach as well as Quantz (which can be attested by Jalowetz and also Stein) how such work has been done. After all, my arrangements demonstrated two commendable features: 1. the effort to bring older works closer to us through treatment of this kind; 2. the fact that I could have taken much less trouble with them than I did. All this also seems reason enough to degrade me, which certainly has not happened to anybody else before me in public in connection with such efforts. Since this is not my inborn style but an acquired one, it is only natural that my arrangements often show more zeal, more good intentions than taste. In striving to show love, I act like the bear with the hermit: I often cover up themes, which are not always significant, with an overabundance of my accompanying parts and with my counterpoint. I have no intention of denying this today. Indeed, I do not hesitate to point out that it is possible that here and there I already felt it at the time, but without being able to remedy it. For there are certain things that one cannot change like a tailor: they are correct in all measurements, but still all wrong. On the other hand I do know that I--and I do find this still quite justifiable today--had great satisfaction with many truly successful passages; and even if I modernized some things, I hardly ever went *as far* as Mozart in his arrangement of the *Messiah* by Handel, in which Mozart, for example (Peters Edition # 8287, page 106, # 24 Coro), added a compositional illustration of the text which, to be sure is almost too audacious (oh no!): that is, in measures 1-4, 6-9, and some other places in the winds, he brings in a motif which obviously is supposed to characterize the flock, and of which in Handel there cannot even be found a trace: At best only a "point of reference" can be found in Handel in measure 4-7 after letter E on page 112 (that is 2 1/2 measures before and 1 after F). As stated before: I never went even approximately that far. Neither did I, like Mozart, cut out a series of sequences. And there are other things. But where did the animosity come from? It came from Schenker. Because the article certainly was inspired by him. It showed his manner of expression, his point of view and also his knowledge.

auch sein Wissen: bei aller Achtung vor Dr. Graf, (den ich heute für einen anständigen Menschen halte) aber diese musikalisch-technischen Dinge, die er mir hier vorgeworfen hat, sind nicht auf seinem Mist gewachsen. Ich kann natürlicherweise hierfür keinen Beweis erbringen. Vielleicht stellt sich die Wahrheit meiner Behauptung noch einmal heraus. Ich glaube für den Kenner kann kein Zweifel existieren.

Mit Dr. Graf stand ich damals ziemlich schlecht. Ich erinnere mich nicht, warum? Wahrscheinlich war er bös auf mich, weil er sich an mir vergangen hat; weil er schlecht über mich geschrieben hat. Das ist ja immer so, dass die Leute einem das Unrecht, das sie einem getan hat, nicht verzeihen können.

11. V. 1928 Arnold Schoenberg

With all respect to Dr. Graf (whom I consider today to be a decent human being), these musical-technical matters of which he accused me of here did not grow on his own compost pile. Of course, I cannot produce proof of this. Perhaps in time the truth of my assumption will come to light. I do believe that there cannot be any doubt for those who are well-informed.

At that time my relationship with Dr. Graf was quite poor. I do not remember why. It is likely he was angry with me because he had done me an injustice, for he he had written derogatorily about me. It is always true that people cannot forgive the injured for the injury which they have inflicted upon them.

May 11, 1928   Arnold Schoenberg[6]

Graf's criticism deals specifically with Schoenberg's interpretation of Monn's harmony, his quotations of Monn's melodic materials in the continuo realizations, and what he considered "violations" of the concept of voice leading such as the doubling of leading tones or sevenths, and parallels.

Monn did leave behind a brief summary of figured bass progressions without comments, and he may have used this compendium for teaching.[7] Among Monn's works, however, only the sacred compositions actually have figures. Thus, in Monn's chamber music, chordal interpretations of the bass line had to depend entirely on the harmonic implications of the upper parts. At times, however, such harmonic realizations of Baroque bass lines, even taking the upper parts into consideration, allow for variances in harmonic interpretation. This is where the misunderstanding between Schoenberg and Graf comes in.

The *Symphonia a Quattro in A Major* was singled out by Graf for detailed critical comments. The entire work has been reprinted here [pp. 297-305] from Adler's personal copy of this Denkmäler volume as an example of Schoenberg's figured bass style.[8]

Graf's first objection concerns a harmonic interpretation
in the opening movement. Graf felt that there should be only two
harmonies in both m. 2 and m. 4 of bracket 2 on p. 32 (297, II, 2
and 4), and that Schoenberg's differentiation between the chords of
the third and fourth eighth note respectively (not quarters as stated
by Graf; see his article p. 283) would be wrong. In response it can
be suggested that while Schoenberg's solution is quite correct, the
most appropriate harmony in these places would be be a vii of V
over a pedal point on e for the third and fourth eighth-notes in m.
11 and 13 (297, II, 2 and 4).

The second movement of Monn's *Symphonia a Quattro in
A Major* (pp. 298-303) is a double fugue based on these
materials:

Example 1, mm. 1-4

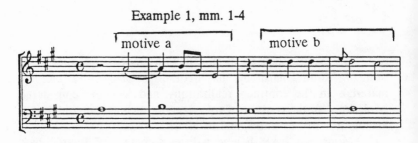

Graf's objections here concerning page 33, bracket 2, mm. 8-10
(298, II, 8-10) are debatable and Schoenberg's introduction of
Monn's motive b (example above) in the right hand of the accompaniment (298, II,10 to III,1) is actually rather elegant. In keeping
with our understanding today, and also for the sake of clarifying the
imitative entrances on this page, it may be more appropriate to
eliminate keyboard accompaniment altogether as implied by the
rests of the bass part (298, II,8-9, III,2, and III, 4-5).

The half-measure chord changes spelled out by Graf in a
table (see p. 285) for the passage on p. 38, bracket 2, measure 9
through bracket 3, measure 5 (303, II,9 to III,5) are questionable
because they are too rich and would cover up the transparent
imitative structure of the other instruments. Specifically, the
harmonies that Graf recommended here for the first beats (303, II,
9 to III, 3 respectively) could even be considered inappropriate

because of the unprepared non-chord tone entrances [303, II, 9, first violin; III,1, cello; III,2, first violin etc.]. Clearly, Schoenberg's rendition of this passage is far superior because of the light texture of his accompaniment, the avoidance of chords during the rests of the bass [303, III, 1 and III, 3] and the much simpler harmonies.

Schoenberg's introduction of thematic materials from the upper parts into the figured bass accompaniment found even less favor with Graf, and Graf's arguments against Schoenberg's treatment is much less convincing. First of all, the introduction of thematic materials into basso-continuo realizations in imitative compositions is very desirable because it enriches the imitative texture. In the second movement (pp. 298-303), Schoenberg's artful imitative additions in the continuo part are even more welcome because they enliven this rather lengthy movement. As to Graf's particular complaints and his insulting accusation that Schoenberg did not notice the composer's artistic intent, there is no way to determine now what the "artistic intent" of Monn may have been. Concerning Schoenberg's simultaneous utilization of Monn's opening motives a and b (see Example 1 on p. 294) on p. 299, III, 3-5 (motive b), Graf overlooked that this motivic material had entered the continuo much earlier (298, I, 12-13). Graf also failed to notice how beautifully both motives fit together as a combination of theme and counterpoint, and this is extremely effective on p. 298, II, 4-5 between the right hand of the keyboard and the second violin. It almost seems as if Graf selected his passages at random.

Further objections by Graf concern the absence of some bass notes in the continuo part. Concerning p. 35, bracket 2, m. 5 (300, II, 5), it can be suggested that Schoenberg felt, for the sake of variation, that the full authentic cadence in f-sharp minor should end in a new piano beginning, and he used the initial bass motive of the very opening of this movement (297, 1-4) in the right hand of the continuo. Schoenberg may have come to this conclusion because Monn omitted the final bass note of this cadence (300, II, 5) and perhaps also for variety because of the repetitive entrance of the lowest string part with the same motive on the same pitch in the next two measures (p. 300, II, 5-8).

Concerning p. 40, bracket 2, measure 4 (305, II, 4) in the final Presto movement, Schoenberg's solution is the only acceptable one because the lowest string part has a full measure rest, and the big skip in the viola is imitated by the re-entering bass.

Finally, Graf's rejection of Schoenberg's decision to dupli-
cate the two unison upper string parts with the left hand of the
continuo realization in measure 2, bracket 3 of page 40 (305, III, 2)
and the quotation of the actual notes of the cello and viola parts in
the right hand of the harpsichord in the same measure, proves
beyond any doubt that Graf was ignorant of the concepts of balance
and form. These "unison" materials with ascending sixteenth notes
appear three times in this movement (305, I, 5-9; II, 8-10; III, 2-6),
and Schoenberg's solution for the final statement of this material
(305, III, 2-3) is a stroke of genius, bringing this movement and the
entire work to a most effective conclusion.

Symphonia a Quattro in A Major by Matthias Georg Monn

Nevertheless, it is unfortunate that Schoenberg did not follow the example of Max Seiffert's realizations of Buxtehude's cantatas, published in vol. 11 of the *Denkmäler der Tonkunst in Österreich* in 1903, which Schoenberg may or may not have known. Seiffert used great restraint in his realizations: there are no doublings of the left hand in the continuo, nor are there alterations, omissions or additions to the bass part. The harmonizations are much simpler than those by Schoenberg, but there is also no interaction between the imitative structure of the upper parts and the continuo.

When compared to the other four Monn realizations by Josef Labor in the same *Denkmäler* volume (# 39), it becomes quite obvious how far superior Schoenberg's realizations are to those by Labor, with whom, incidentally, Schoenberg never studied as maintained by Eric Blom in *The New Grove Dictionary of Music and Musicians* (vol. X, p. 342, Labor). As suggested by a relatively large correspondence, Adler held Labor in high esteem. Labor's realizations, even if less complex than those by Schoenberg, are very unimaginative and even boring, particularly because of his perpetual octave doublings in the left hand and very square chordal treatment.

Schoenberg's perception of himself was unfailingly honest. This is born out again when he himself took issue (Denk 188, p. 289 ff.) with his own basso continuo realizations of 1912, and Graf's reaction in *Signale* in 1913 (p. 283, ff.) after some 15 years had elapsed.

It can be concluded in all fairness that Schoenberg's vehement rejection of this insulting criticism was quite justified (Schoenberg to Adler on March 14, 1913, see p. 101).

As for Schoenberg's understanding of harmony, Graf's accusations were without any basis, because Schoenberg's comprehension of harmony in any style was beyond question. What is most significant, however, is the fact that these realizations, like anything he touched, bear the stamp of his own creativity.

Notes

1. *Divertimento in D Major* by Johann Christoph Mann (Monn). *Denkmäler der Tonkunst in Österreich*, vol. 39, II, Vienna: Artaria, 1912; Leipzig: Breitkopf & Härtel, 1912, pp. 107-115.

2. See the letters of November 6, 1911; January 11, 1912; January 13, 1912; January 15, 1912; January 22, 1912, February 6, 1912 in Chapter II, pp. 83 ff.

3. Franz Tuma, *Sinfonia a quattro in e minor*, for strings and basso-continuo, realized by Arnold Schoenberg and edited by Rudolf Lück. Cologne: Hans Gerig, 1968.

   Franz Tuma *Partita a tre in c minor*, for 2 violins, violino obligato and basso-continuo, realized by Arnold Schoenberg and edited by Rudolf Lück. Cologne: Hans Gerig, 1968.

   Franz Tuma, *Partita a tre in A Major*, for 2 violins and basso-continuo, realized by Arnold Schoenberg and edited by Rudolf Lück. Cologne: Hans Gerig, 1968.

   Franz Tuma, *Partita a tre in G Major*, for 2 violins and basso-continuo, realized by Arnold Schoenberg and edited by Rudolf Lück. Cologne: Hans Gerig, 1968.

   Lück's introductions are identical in these four editions.

4. Arnold Schoenberg, *Harmonielehre*. Vienna: Universal Edition, 1911.

5. *Signale für die Musikalische Welt*, ed. August Spanuth/Berlin, and Ferdinand Scherber, Vienna, vol. 71, No. 14, April 2, 1913, pp. 505-507. This weekly journal was widely read in Germany and Austria. In the translation editorial additions are given in square brackets because Adler used parentheses in the original.

6. This is   Schoenberg's statement of May 11, 1928 concerning his basso-continuo realizations of 1912. Preserved at the Schoenberg Institute in Los Angeles, siglum *Denk 188*.

7. Georg Matthias Monn, "Theorie des eneralbasses in Beispielen ohne Erklärung." Manuscript score, Vienna, Österreichische Staatsbibliothek, 19101.

8. *Denkmäler der Tonkunst in Österreich*, XIX Jahrgang, part II, vol. 39. Wiener Instrumentalmusik im XVIII Jahrhundert II, ed. Wilhelm Fischer. Vienna: Artaria; Leipzig: Breitkopf & Härtel, 1912, pp. 2-40. References to Monn's *Symphonia a Quattro in A Major* are identified by the original page numbers of the *Denkmäler* volume as given above, and by page numbers of the reprint in this book (pp. 297-305); bracket numbers start with I on each page (Roman numerals), and measure numbers with 1 in each bracket (Arabic numbers). Reprinted by per-permission.

INDEX OF LETTERS

The letters in this volume are identified by siglum and date, with the siglum consisting of:
- chapter number
- initials for the writer and recipient
- original language or   translation (o or t)
- ordinal numbers, beginning with the earliest letter.

Unsigned letters come from the estate of the writers.

A	=	Adler
C	=	Casals
Co	=	Copland
DTÖ	=	Denkmäler der Tonkunst in Österreich
D	=	Downes
F	=	Feuermann
M	=	Malkin
Mi	=	Mitropoulos
P	=	Pena
S	=	Arnold Schoenberg
GS	=	Gertrud Schoenberg
T	=	Virgil Thomson

Letters between Schoenberg and Adler

Siglum:	Date:	Page:	Location:*
II.S-A.o.1		60	UGA
II.S-A.t.1	11.16.1903	61	
II.S-A.o.2		60	UGA
II.S-A.t.2	2.17.1904	61	
II.S-A.o.3		62	UGA
II.S-A.t.3	5.26.1904	63	
II.S-A.o.4		62	UGA
II.S-A.t.4	6.1.1904	63	
II.S-A.o.5		64	UGA
II.S-A.t.5	6.9.1904	65	
II.S-A.o.6		66	UGA
II.S-A.t.6	10.27.1904	67	
II.S-A.o.7		68	UGA
II.S-A.t.7	11.11.1904	69	
II.S-A.o.8		70	UGA
II.S-a.t.8	1.7.1905	71	
II.S-A.o.9		70	UGA
II.S-A.t.9	[1903-1905]	71	
II.S-A.o.10		72	UGA
II.S-A.t.10	no date	73	

* UGA =	University of Georgia
LC =	Library of Congress
SchI =	Schoenberg Institute, Los Angeles
NYT =	New York Times
NHT =	New York Herald Tribune

II.A-S.o.4		92	LC
II.A-S.t.4	9.3.1912	93	
II.S-A.o.21		92	UGA
II.S-A.t.21	9.7.1912	93	
II.S-A.o.22		96	UGA
II.S-A.t.22	3.5.1913	97	
II.A-S.o.5		96	LC
II.A-S.t.5	3.9.1913	97	
II.S-A.o.23		98	UGA
II.S-A.t.23	3.13.1913	99	
II.S-A.o.24		100	UGA
II.S-A.t.24	3.14.1913	101	
II.A-S.o.6		106	LC
II.A-S.t.6	3.18.1913	107	

[the letter is in another hand but signed by Adler]

II.S-A.o.25		108	UGA
II.S-A.t.25	4.10.1913	109	
II.A-S.o.7		110	LC
II.A-S.t.7	4.12.1913	111	
II.A-S.o.8		110	LC
II.A-S.t.8	4.16.1913	111	
II.A-S.o.9		286	LC
II.A-S.t.9	4.18.1913	287[1]	
II.S-A.o.26		112	UGA
II.S-A.t.26	5.9.1913	113	

---

1. This letter appears in Chapter VII where it is more relevant in the context of the discussion.

Letters between Adler and Casals

Letters between Schoenberg and Casals

Letters between Schoenberg and Feuermann

V.F-S.o.1		202	LC
V.F-S.t.1	1.1.1939	203	
V.S-M.o.1		204	LC
V.S-M.t.1	10.10.1933	205	

Letters between Schoenberg and Downes, Copland and Schoenberg, Copland and Virgil Thomson

VI.S-D.o.1	undated draft [before 10.13.1935]	217	SchI
VI.S-D.o.2	11.8.1938 [not sent]	230	LC
VI.S-D.o.3	11.8.1938	231	UGA
VI.D-S.o.1	11.14.1938	232	LC
VI.S-D.o.4	8.27.1944 [not sent]	233	SchI
VI.S-D.o.5	3.31.1946	236	LC
VI.D-S.o.2	4.15.1946	237	LC
VI.D-S.o.3	5.13.1947	237	LC
VI.S-D.o.6	5.14.1947	238	UGA
VI.D-S.o.4	5.21.1947	239	LC
VI.S-D.o.7	undated [before 12.12.1948]	241	UGA
VI.D-S.o.5	12.3.1948	245	LC
VI.S-D.o.8	12.10.1948	247	UGA

SELECTED BIBLIOGRAPHY

Included here are only those materials directly pertinent to the letters and other documents presented in this book.

Bach, Johann Sebastian. *Bach-Gesamtausgabe.* Edited by the Bachgesellschaft Zu Leipzig. Leipzig: Breitkopf & Härtel, 1851-99.

Blom, Eric. "Josef Labor." In *The New Grove Dictionary of Music and Musicians,* ed. Stanley Sadie. London: Macmillan Publishers Ltd., 1980.

Corredor, J. Ma. *Conversations with Casals.* Translated by André Mangeot. New York: E. P. Dutton & Co., Inc., 1957.

Downes, Irene, ed. *Olin Downes on Music.* New York: Simon and Schuster,1957.

Fischer, Wilhelm, ed. *Wiener Instrumentalmusik im XVIII Jahrhundert, II.* Denkmäler der Tonkunst in Österreich, ed. Guido Adler, XIX Jahrgang, part II, vol. 39. Vienna: Artaria, 1912; Leipzig: Breitkopf & Härtel, 1912.

Graf, Max. "Arnold Schoenberg's Basso Continuo." *Signale für die Musikalische Welt,* 71, no. 14 (2 April 1913): 505-507.

Itzkoff, Seymor W. *Emanuel Feuermann, Virtuoso.* Tuscaloosa, Alabama: University of Alabama Press, 1979.

Kahn, Albert E. *Joys and Sorrows: Reflections by Pablo Casals.* New York: Simon and Schuster, 1970.

Littlehales, Lillian. *Pablo Casals.* London: J. M. Dent, 1949.

Lück, Rudolf. "Die Generalbass-Aussetzungen Arnold Schoenbergs." In *Deutsches Jahrbuch der Musikwissenschaft für 1963*, ed. Walter Vetter, 26-35. Leipzig: Peters, 1968.

Means, Mary Gail. "A Catalogue of Printed Books and Music in the Guido Adler Collection." M.A. thesis, University of Georgia, 1968.

Monn, Georg Matthias. "Theorie des Generalbasses in Beispielen ohne Erklärung." Manucript score. Österreichische Staatsbibliothek, Vienna.

Neumann, Frederick. *Ornamentation in Baroque and Post-Baroque Music, with Special Emphasis on J. S. Bach.* Princeton, N.J.: Princeton University Press, 1978.

Quoika, Rudolf. "Josef Labor." In *Die Musik in Geschichte und Gegenwart.* Kassel: Bärenreiter, 1949-68.

Reilly, Edward. R. *Gustav Mahler and Guido Adler: Records of a Friendship.* Cambridge: Cambridge University Press, 1982.

_____. *Gustav Mahler and Guido Adler: Geschichte einer Freundschaft.* Translated by Herta Singer-Blaukopf. Vienna: Bibliothek der Internationalen Gustav Mahler Gesellschaft, Universal Edition, 1978.

_____. "The Papers of Guido Adler at the University of Georgia: A Provisional Index." Type-written manuscript. Hargrett Rarebook Library, University of Georgia, 1975.

Rufer, Josef. "Hommage à Schoenberg." *Arnold Schoenberg: Berliner Tagebuch*, ed. Josef Rufer, 47-92. Frankfurt am Main: Propyläen Verlag, 1974.

Schoenberg, Arnold. *Harmonielehre*. Vienna: Universal Edition, 1911.

_____. *Instrumentalkonzerte nach Werken alter Meister*. In Sämtliche Werke, Abteilung VII, Series B, vol. 27, Part 2, edited by Nikos Kokkinis. Mainz: B. Schott & Sons; Vienna: Universal Edition AG., 1987.

_____. "A Dangerous Game." In "On Artists and Collaboration: A Symposium." *Modern Music* 22 (1944): 3-5.

Stein, Erwin. *Arnold Schoenberg Letters*. London: Faber & Faber, 1964.

Stein, Leonard, ed. *Style and Idea: Selected Writings of Arnold Schoenberg*. Berkeley and Los Angeles: University of California Press, 1984.

Tuma, Frantisek. *Partita a tre in A Major for Two Violins, Violoncello and Basso-Continuo*. Basso-continuo realized by Arnold Schoenberg. Edited by Rudolf Lück. Cologne: H. Gerig, 1968.

_____. *Partita a tre in c Minor for Two Violins, Violoncello and Basso-Continuo*. Basso-continuo realized by Arnold Schoenberg. Edited by Rudolf Lück. Cologne: H. Gerig, 1968.

_____. *Partita a tre in G Major for Two Violins and Basso-Continuo*. Basso-continuo realized by Arnold Schoenberg. Edited by Rudolf Lück. Cologne: H. Gerig, 1968.

_____. *Sinfonia a Quattro in E Minor for Strings and Basso-Continuo*. Basso-continuo realized by Arnold Schoenberg. Edited by Rudolf Lück. Cologne: H. Gerig, 1968.